extreme answers to extreme questions

Katie E. Gieser
Paige Drygas
Christopher D. Hudson
Ashley Taylor
Carol Smith
C.J. Watson
Linda Washington

Extreme Answers to Extreme Questions

Copyright © 2001 by Thomas Nelson Publishers.

Contributors:
Project Manager: Katie E. Gieser
Q & A's: Carol Smith, Julia Novatsyk, C.J. Watson, Linda Washington
Profiles: Paige Drygas, Ashley Taylor
Editors: Kate Etue and Gillian Taaffe
Brand Manager: Hayley Morgan

Scripture quotations are from the New King James Version, copyright © 1982 by Thomas Nelson Publishers.

Developed and produced with the assistance of The Livingstone Corporation. Project staff includes:
Katie E. Gieser, Paige Drygas, Christopher D. Hudson, and Ashley Taylor.

Designed by Mozdren and Associates, St. Charles, Illinois.

Typesetting by Carol Barnstable.

Published in Nashville, Tennessee, by Thomas Nelson, Inc.

Library of Congress Cataloging-in-Publication Data
Extreme answers to extreme questions.
     p. cm.
  ISBN 0-7852-4594-4
  1. Christian teenagers–Religious life–Miscellanea. I. Thomas Nelson Publishers.
  BV4531.3 .E98 2001
  248.8'3–dc21

                                                      00-066211

Printed in the United States of America
4 5 6 – 04 03 02

Table of Contents

Introduction

What are your toughest questions? The ugly ones that everyone tries to avoid? The personal ones that you're too embarrassed to ask? The hardest questions that no one seems to know the answer to? Extreme Answers to Extreme Questions tackles hundreds of the most challenging questions ever with straight-up answers for you, for where you are now. These answers aren't forged out of thin air; they're based on the solid Word of God. Sometimes it seems like the Bible doesn't talk about real-life issues, but believe it or not, God has a lot to say about them. The Bible has every answer we need for this life—it's up to us to read and understand what He is saying. So, dig in to Extreme Answers. Throw out your best questions. And hold on for the ride of your life. The Truth can never be shaken.

ABUSE

Is there hope for someone who has been sexually abused?

"Heal me, O LORD, and I shall be healed; save me, and I shall be saved, for You are my praise."
Jer. 17:14

Sexual abuse is a tragedy. The victims who are left behind may suffer for years with the hurt and pain they've endured. One's most powerful healing comes when God is invited to be a part of the process. First, He can help you forgive the person who violated you. He can restore feelings that had become numb and replace anger with love. And second, He can turn even something this horrible into an opportunity to share his forgiveness and grace. Lots of times we have struggles so that we can better relate with others who need Christ. "The Father of Mercies and God of all Comfort...comforts us in all our tribulation, that we may be able to comfort those who are in any trouble" (2 Cor. 1:3-4).

SEE FOR YOURSELF: Pss. 40:1-3; 116:5-7; Is. 41:13; 57:18, 19; Hos. 14:4

There's a kid in my class that comes in with bruises. Why do some parents beat their own kids?

That's a tough question. The way life is supposed to work is that parents look out for kids and take care of them. But that doesn't always happen, does it? In the Old Testament there were parents who failed to take care of their kids. There was one king, named Manasseh, who offered his son in an occult worship ritual involving fire. God was beyond furious with Manasseh. Our world is so different from the world that God desired. He wanted us to have a world where kids are loved and safe, but sometimes it's not. Parents don't always grow up like they should. They don't learn to control their own emotions. They take their anger and frustration out on their kids. They get so caught up in their own needs that they forget that their kids need them to be adults and good parents.

SEE FOR YOURSELF: 2 Kings 21:6

1

AGE

Why did people live so long in the Old Testament?

> Methuselah lived one hundred and eighty-seven years, and begot Lamech. After he begot Lamech, Methuselah lived seven hundred and eighty-two years, and had sons and daughters.
>
> Genesis 5:25-26

It's amazing, isn't it? Adam's age was listed as 930 years. Abraham was supposed to have lived 175 years. Methuselah's age was listed as 969 years old when he died. Whew! Talk about having a long history. Now, we know that the Bible is true. People certainly could have lived that long. After all, the world was very new. Adam was going to live forever if sin hadn't entered the scene. When you think about it, 930 years isn't very long compared with forever. There weren't the impurities in the environment. It was a cleaner, newer place to live. But it also might be that they counted time differently back then. They were in the process of figuring out the calendar and the clock and how everyone could keep track the same way. So we don't really know if 930 years meant the same thing in Adam's day as it does now. That doesn't make it not true. Until we get some more information, we won't know for sure.

Why do we get old?

According to the story of creation in Genesis, when God created the world, He created it with the intention of nothing dying. It was perpetual health. Then sin entered the world—people chose their way over God's way—and decay began. Everything started slowly falling apart. God told Adam, after the forbidden fruit event, that part of the curse was that he would return to the dust that God had made him from. That really is what happens to our bodies. They are new, then they grow old, then they stop working, then our spirit leaves them, and they go right back to dust. That process is called "getting old."

SEE FOR YOURSELF: Genesis 3:19

ALCOHOL

Alcohol: A refreshing beverage or potential poison?

Do not look on the wine when it is red, when it sparkles in the cup, when it swirls around smoothly; at the last it bites like a serpent, and stings like a viper.
Prov. 23:29-35

The problem with drinking is that it's so easily abused. Some people don't stop with a glass of wine or a beer at dinner; they continue to drink until they are either lightheaded and confused, or drunk and totally disoriented. Either way, their judgment is impaired. They can harm themselves or anyone else in their path. A lot of believers have decided to just stay clear of alcohol. Proverbs says it seems attractive, but eventually it is as devastating and as painful as a snakebite. Drinking may cause you to make decisions that seem fun at the time, but stupid the next morning. In fact, it's entirely possible that you could do something that you have to pay for for the rest of your life. People tell you not to drink because they care that you make wise decisions and that you live a long and healthy life. You'd be smart to take their advice. Don't let a chemical control you.

However, many Christians embrace drinking in moderation as a great way to relax and enjoy the company of friends. The Bible speaks clearly against drunkeness, but not against drink. But, either way, it's illegal if you're underage—so don't do it until you're old enough.

SEE FOR YOURSELF: Prov. 13:15; 14:18; 20:1; 31:4 5

How come I can drink wine in church, but I can't have any at a party?

Some churches do serve wine for communion. Real wine. The fermented kind. None of that Welch's stuff. But you've got to admit that that little cup or sip is a far cry from a glass, or two, or three. Now, I don't know how old you are, but a big part of your not having wine at a party must come from either your parents, your state's legal age, or your denomination's stand on drinking in general. The Bible doesn't say that drinking wine is bad under every circumstance. What the Bible says is that drinking too much, letting wine control you, is wrong. Many people feel that it's safer to stay away from wine altogether. They explain that in Bible times people had to drink wine because the water was so impure. Today we can drink the water (and it can cost almost as much as wine). So these people, some call them teetotalers, say one sure way to not get drunk is don't take the first drink. There's some wisdom in that. But God doesn't let us off that easily. He expects us to be moderate in everything. He expects us to have control and keep everything within the right limits. When you drink wine at church, there are plenty of limits to it. How is it at the parties you go to?

My dad drinks like three or four beers every night, but not more. If drinking a little is OK, but drinking a lot is wrong, how much can you drink before it's a sin?

And do not be drunk with wine, in which is dissipation; but be filled with the Spirit. Eph. 5:18

There are a lot of things that are black and white, right or wrong. Lying is a sin. Killing is a sin. Cursing God is a sin (and stupid, too). There are other things in life that aren't black and white. They require something called "discretion" or "wisdom." It's because of these things that we have to work to stay tight with God, to know what He thinks. The truth is that some people can drink some alcohol and not be affected by it as much as someone else. The real truth is that some people can't drink at all, or they will be addicted and overdo their drinking and destroy themselves. Because alcohol can be so destructive, some people will tell you it's wrong to even take one drink. What the Bible says is that it's wrong to get drunk, in other words to let alcohol control you. The Bible talks a lot about this because in those days everyone drank wine, so they needed to know how to control its power in their lives. You will have to sit before God and decide with Him what amount of alcohol is too much for you. When you know that, then you'll know where it becomes sinful for you.

ALIENS

Are there aliens on other planets? Can they become Christians?

> And He said to them, "Go into all the world and preach the gospel to every creature."
> Mark 16:15

The most honest answer to that question is "We don't know." God makes us responsible for our world. He doesn't say anything in the Bible that means He made other worlds. There is no evidence in Scripture to make us think that. But we sure hear a lot about other worlds these days, don't we? Some of us really like the idea of aliens and other species that we can get to know. If God did make other planets and other kinds of planet-dwellers, there's no reason to think He wouldn't offer them the same grace He offers to us. But that's not information He chose to share with us. All He told us is "Go into your world and let them know about Me."

> In most places in the ancient world, a for-eigner("stranger") had no legal rights. The land of Israel, however, was different. God's people were expected to treat foreigners just as they would treat each other. They were to show that God's law applied to everyone.
> Deuteronomy 1:16

ANGELS

So Jacob went
on his way,
and the angels of
God met him.
Gen. 32:1

Do angels actually interact with people?

OO. OO. 29   OO. OO. _O

They certainly did during Bible days. Take Jacob,
for instance. The Bible says that after he left
his father-in-law's house he came to a place
where the angels met him. We don't know exactly
what that meant, but we know that Jacob saw something
that he perceived to be angels, and he acted on that. Angels are among
us today. We don't have any way to prove that we've interacted with one, but that
doesn't mean we haven't.

OO. OB. B2   OO. OB. B3   OO. OB. B4   OO. OB. B5   OO. OB. BB

Are angels just dead people who were good? If they are, then are the bad ones ghosts?

Angels are beings God created for His service. Since Satan was once an angel,
they do have a sense of choice, but as far as what the Bible tells us they aren't
humans or ex-humans. They are different. They do God's bidding, like delivering
messages and looking out for us. They can travel through time and dimensions.
They are spirits. The bad ones are called demons, evil spirits. As far as we know,
they are angels who fell from God's service. Movies and books and stuff give the
impression that ghosts are people who have died, but their spirits are still hanging around. That's not a given. There are evil spirits hanging around, though. In
church you'll hear a phrase "spiritual warfare." It means that there are angels and
demons fighting all the time even though we are unaware of it. From what we
know, those soldiers don't include dead people.

SEE FOR YOURSELF: Matt. 4:6; Luke 4:10, 11; Pss. 34:7; 91:11-12

Do angels die, like people do?

Evidently not. Jesus didn't talk about this directly but we can learn something about it indirectly from a question He was asked. Someone asked Him if a woman was married to several men during her life, whose wife would she be in heaven? Jesus answered that in heaven no one will be married or unmarried. He also said no one would die because everyone would be equal to the angels. Sounds like He didn't expect any funerals with halos, doesn't it?

> Nor can they die anymore, for they are equal to the angels and are sons of God, being sons of the resurrection.
>
> **Luke 20:36**

What happened to the angels who sinned with Satan?

Those angels were thrown out of God's presence. Peter says plainly that they were cast into hell. There are a lot of things we don't know about hell (and a lot more we don't want to know) but we know one thing, it is hell because God is not there. It is to be apart from God's presence. That's an easy thing for us to take lightly because we don't really know what it would be like to be in a place completely devoid of God. It is surely much worse than we can imagine. It is that kind of place that those demons call home base.

SEE FOR YOURSELF: 2 Peter 2:4

Do angels get married?

No, they don't. Jesus answered a question once about how marriage and remarriage works once people get to heaven. Jesus said that in heaven there will be no recognition of marriage, but that people will be like the angels. That means neither people nor angels are coupled up in heaven.

SEE FOR YOURSELF: Matthew 22:30

Do I have a guardian angel?

A lot of people seem to be confused about angels. They like the idea of angels, their protection and presence, but they haven't paid much attention to the Commander of angels. We wear angel pins, read angel books, and hang little angels on everything. Maybe it's just easier to believe in them than in God. They don't ask you for a commitment. They don't convict you of sin. But here's the kicker—angels can't save you either. Angels belong to God. And God uses angels to protect His believers. He can deploy them at any time to defend His followers. They do as they are commanded by Him. So rest secure, knowing that angels hover around those who love God—but loving God is the key.

> For He shall give His angels charge over you, to keep you in all your ways. In their hands they shall bear you up, lest you dash your foot against a stone.
> Ps. 91:11-12

Do God and the angels have body parts like people?

No. Angels are spirits. Now, when they appear to humans sometimes they take on human form. But when some of the prophets, like Ezekiel, saw visions of angels, they were beings very different from people. They had several faces and wheels spinning around them. It would have taken all the special effects teams of Hollywood to describe the angel scene that Ezekiel saw, and even if a movie recreated it, probably no one would believe it.

SEE FOR YOURSELF: Ezekiel 10:14

So do I honor my parents, even when they're wrong?

Meet Evan.

Everything in Evan's life seemed pretty cool. His summer was such a breeze, working mornings at a golf course, mowing the greens, and then he had afternoons off to train for football or to go out on the boat with his friends. Summertime—no worries. He thought he would never want school to start again.

His mom left for a women's church retreat. She needed the time away, since her life consisted of taking his little sisters to sports, camps, and the mall. His older sister Katie had planned to be at home that weekend, but at the last minute, she took off for Colorado to visit her college roommate. That's when it happened. His dad had struggled with alcohol in the past but really had seemed to be doing fine lately. Maybe it was subconscious, like as soon as any sense of "authority" left town he just couldn't resist it any longer. At any rate, Evan was the one there to deal with the situation.

His dad had said he was going to visit friends on the other side of the lake, but he didn't come back and didn't come back. Evan started to worry but wasn't sure what to think. As much as he tried to trust his dad, Dad seemed to blow it an awful lot. When the phone rang, he had a sinking feeling in his stomach. The voice on the other end confirmed his fears.

A kind stranger from Bellevue Hospital broke the news to Evan. His dad had been in a drunk driving accident almost four hours ago. On his way home from their friends' house, his reflexes were so dulled by alcohol that he couldn't handle the sharp turn in the road. His motorcycle slid out from under him, throwing him roughly into a ditch along the road. He had lain there for hours before being found.

He was lucky, very lucky. With only a badly broken arm, the surgeons were able to set the bones and sent him home within days. His sisters blew up in anger at first but then longed for their dad to come home. As hard as it was, his mom was trying to forgive him (again), praying the whole time for grace to get her through. But Evan was a bit harder. He kept his emotions to himself, closed off from everyone, and he had little to offer his dad but a cold shoulder.

Even after a few weeks, Evan was still boiling inside. He hated his dad now, and he knew his bitterness was so very wrong. Yes, his dad had wronged the whole family, but would the bitterness ever end? Evan didn't know what else to do, so he started praying.

And as he prayed, the Lord eased his anger. He began to look his dad in the eye again. Their conversations resumed. Slowly but surely, Evan found ways to forgive his dad and even to respect him again. Finally, a few months later, they started laughing together, and their friendship picked up again. Evan could never forget what his dad had done, but he chose to forgive him and to give him a second chance—not because he wanted to but out of respect for his father.

ANGER

Does being a Christian mean never getting mad?

"Be angry, and do not sin": do not let the sun go down on your wrath.
Eph. 4:26

No. We feel angry when we are mistreated or we see someone else mistreated. Anger is a natural emotion just like all of our other emotions. It's a warning sign that something is happening that we need to respond to. Now, the responding thing, THAT'S where you have to think about the Christian thing to do. Paul wrote to the Ephesians: "Be angry, and do not sin." The anger wasn't the sin he was referring to (duh!), but the response could be. Sometimes it's like God commands us to live one way, but when we become angry we throw all that out the window. We say things we normally wouldn't say, and we treat people in ways that we know we shouldn't. Christians should treat other people with respect. Our anger doesn't give us a reason to throw out God's commands to love others. We have to stay in control of our anger and not let it run our lives. It's not our anger that gets us into trouble as much as our lack of control over our anger.

ANIMALS

You number my
wanderings;
Put my tears into
Your bottle;
Are they not
in Your book?
Ps. 56:8

My dog died. I keep
crying, but I don't let
anybody know because I
feel dumb about it. Why
does it hurt so bad if he
was just a dog?

Because you loved him. You lost a friend. Any way you look at it, that hurts. You might
find that more people understand than you think. Once you can at least mention it
you might find that most people have a story about an animal that they've lost along
the way. I can understand when you say you feel dumb, but what you are going
through is not dumb. And it matters to God. David (who was later King David of
Israel) wrote Psalm 56 when he was miserable. He had been captured by his country's
worst enemies. You might want to read the whole Psalm if you don't believe he was
miserable, but he really was. He said something really great though. He said that God
put his tears in a bottle and recorded them. Do you get that? David knew his tears
mattered to God. Your tears matter, too. Your dog must have been a good friend. It's
good that God gave you that friend. It's OK to be sad.

Do animals have souls?

There is no evidence from the Bible that God put souls in animals. In fact in the
story of creation, there is a distinct difference between the way God created people and the way he created everything else. Only with people did God breathe
into man to make him a living being. A lot of people think that is what set people
apart from the animals. Now when you look into your dog or cat's eyes, you might
say, there's got to be a soul in there! They definitely do have personalities. They
are family members. Sometimes they feel more like friends than any people we
know. When they die, we want to believe that they'll make it to heaven and be
waiting there for us. The Bible doesn't say specifically that they won't. But it does-
n't give us the information that you're looking for either.

SEE FOR YOURSELF: Genesis 2:7

My dad kicks my dog when he's mad. Is it a sin to be mean to an animal?

He has shown you, O man, what is good; and what does the LORD require of you but to do justly, to love mercy, and to walk humbly with your God?
Micah 6:8

It's a sin to be mean. It feels even worse to us when someone is mean to an innocent thing like an animal. There's a great Bible verse in the little book of Micah in the Old Testament. It tells us what God requires of us:

1. To act justly
2. To love mercy
3. To walk humbly with God

Kicking the dog doesn't really fit into any of those categories, does it? So it can't be a good thing. Your dad isn't making a good choice. That happens some-times. Dads, like kids, mess up. In every situation like this it really comes down to, are we being the people like God wants us to be? There's not a rule for each and every action. But if we answer that question, we usually know what is a sin and what is not. So, yes, I think it's a sin to kick an animal just because you are mad and want to take it out on something.

APPEARANCE

Do I have to wear Christian paraphernalia to be a "good Christian" or to please God?

First impressions. Yuck. You look. They look. You shake hands; fake a smile. Yep, you've got this one figured out, wrapped up in a box, and slapped into category A, B, or C. He's either "hip," "drip," or "wanna-be." However you do it, you still label people. Everybody does, and we all do it based on the superficial. Looks determine the label—straight teeth, good haircut, right jeans—all the right stuff. Guess what? God doesn't give a rip about jeans or haircuts. People's looks aren't even an issue for Him. His radar locks onto the heart and makes an inspection there. He wants to know who you are way down deep inside. How do you really feel? Are you really mean as a yard dog, or do you cut other people down because your heart's been broken and really hurting? God knows the truth about people—good and bad. He always looks past all your stuff and sees your heart.

SEE FOR YOURSELF: 1 Chr. 28:9; . 2 Chr 6:30; Jer. 20:12; Acts 15:8, 9

You can tell what kind of person somebody is by how they dress, right? So why should I hang out with people who look freaky or bummy?

You can tell SOME things about people by the way they dress. And SOMETIMES you can get an idea about whether or not a person is like you by the way they dress. There's a problem though with deciding if someone is worth your time by the way they dress. James wrote about this in his book in the New Testament. He said if you pay attention to a finely dressed person, but ignore the poor man in dirty clothes you're showing partiality. James was talking specifically about treating poor people well, but it has something to do with a lot of different kinds of people. You might not want to hang out with people who look like they make different lifestyle choices than you, but that doesn't mean you can't treat them with respect and value their presence as people.

SEE FOR YOURSELF: James 2:2-9

Is it OK if I dye my hair really wild colors?

What God really cares about is WHY you want to color your hair in really wild colors. That's an important thing to know. Do you just have an inner desire for orange hair? Are you trying to be accepted by a certain crowd who values nonconformity? Are you trying to show someone that you have the guts to do it? Are you proving that you don't care what someone thinks? Trying to shock someone? Trying to stand out in a crowd? The Bible gives us overall guidelines that might help. One of them is this: whatever you do, do it in Jesus' name as an act of gratitude to God. How does the reason for your dye job fit within that test? Remember that God is much more concerned with your heart than with the hair on your head (which, by the way, he has numbered, Matt. 10:30). The choices you make reflect something about your heart, though. A big part of life is figuring out that connection.

> And whatever you do in word or deed, do all in the name of the Lord Jesus, giving thanks to God the Father through Him.
> Col. 3:17

Why do people who have curly hair want straight hair and people who have straight hair want curly hair?

It's just human nature to want what we don't have. It's not just a hair thing. People want different noses, different figures, different kinds of skin, different proportions to their bodies. Are we ever satisfied? There's just something that makes us think what we have isn't good enough. If that wasn't a part of human nature no one would have ever made up the phrase, "The grass is always greener on the other side of the fence." The truth, though, is that God had a hand in making us the way we are. He delights in us. He doesn't compare us. Psalm 139 says that God was with us when we were being formed in our mom's womb. It also says we are fearfully and wonderfully made, whether our hair is straight or curly and no matter what kind of nose we have.

SEE FOR YOURSELF: Psalm 139:13-15

Why do some people think wearing makeup is wrong?

The Bible has a lot to say about our outside versus our inside. Peter wrote that we should not worry as much about how we "adorn" our body as we do about how we "adorn" our spirit. When some people interpret those kinds of verses in the Bible, they come to the conclusion that the stuff we do to the outside of ourselves is unnecessary. Some may think it's even wrong. Other people believe that makeup and jewelry aren't wrong, but we have to remember that making ourselves look good on the outside is not enough. Who we are inside is just as important. How different do you think any of us would be if we spent as much time working on our heart as we do doing our hair, picking out our clothes and accessories, washing, making up and looking cool? What kind of shape would our heart be in? That's the kind of question that leads people to spend less time on the whole makeup thing. That doesn't mean that wearing makeup (or making yourself look good) is wrong for you. It just means that it's not all that matters.

> Do not let your adornment be merely outward . . . rather let it be the hidden person of the heart, with the incorruptible beauty of a gentle and quiet spirit, which is very precious in the sight of God.
> **1 Peter 3:3-4**

My school has a really strict dress code. How short can a skirt be before God says it's wrong?

God says, "Be modest." God says, "Spend as much energy drawing people to your inner qualities as to your external assets." What you'll find about God is that He is less into measuring your skirt length than He is into measuring your heart, your devotion toward Him and your devotion toward people. With each generation in our culture the ideas about modesty change. Most likely your ideas about what is decent and modest are different from what your parents think. That's the nature of parents and their teenagers. God did put you in your home though and give you the parents you have. So, at least try to meet them in the middle. If your skirt is so short that people think, "Now THAT'S a short skirt," maybe you should think about it a bit. Your clothes should represent you, and you should represent God's presence in your life. Make sure all that is in place, and you probably won't need a tape measure.

SEE FOR YOURSELF: 1 Tim. 2:9

My dad says I can't have long hair because it's just for girls and sissies. Didn't Jesus have long hair?

00. 00. 29

If anyone seems to be contentious, we have no such custom, nor do the churches of God.
1 Cor. 11:13-16

Hairstyles are a cultural thing. There is not a moral right and wrong to them. There was an oath people took in the Bible (like Samson) that required them to not cut their hair, so it grew very long. Some of the Jewish men had the custom of not cutting the sides of their beards so they had long, long sideburns. Jesus probably did have longer hair (barber techniques were not so sophisticated then), but other cultures at the same time had short hairstyles. Paul, who lived around the time that Jesus lived, wrote that it was important for men and women to look different and so men should have short hair, but women should have long hair. Because Paul wrote that, a lot of people not only dislike long haircuts on men, but short haircuts on women as well. If that was the custom of the day, then Jesus' hair probably wasn't down His back or anything. Most people take on the ideas of their generation about hairstyles. In the 1960s, long hair was a sign of revolution; in the 1970s, it was stylish. These days people have all different styles of hair. Your dad has ideas based on the way he was raised, just like you will one day. Your hair doesn't make you who you are, so don't ruin your relationship with him over it. It will always be true that God is more concerned with your heart attitude than the length of your hair.

My mom says I can't get a tattoo because it's wrong. Where is that in the Bible?

The Bible does in fact have something to say about tattoos. One verse that speaks very directly to the topic is Leviticus 19:28, which says, "You shall not . . . tattoo any marks on you: I am the LORD." This doesn't leave a whole lot of room for debate. God clearly rules out tattoos. Now back to your mom. There's another reason why you shouldn't get a tattoo, and this one's pretty powerful. "Come on," you might argue, "That's such an old rule. There's other stuff we ignore in the Old Testament." Maybe. But here's one you can't ignore. One of God's top ten rules (a.k.a. the Ten Commandments) says straight up, "Honor your father and your mother" (Exodus 20:12). So if your mom doesn't want you to have a tattoo, then suck it up, no tattoo for you. It's all about respect. Sometimes in these conflicts with our parents, the issue shifts entirely from the original topic (wanting a tattoo) to a new one (winning the argument, getting our way). Your mom may have any number of reasons why she doesn't want you to have a tattoo. She might see it as a sign of rebellion. She might think it's too permanent a choice. Regardless, at this point, we have to step back and keep things in perspective. For now, show some respect. You've got the rest of your life to do your own thing.

If all Adam and Eve wore were fig leaves, why do we wear clothes?

Actually fig leaves weren't all Adam and Eve wore. That's what they covered themselves with when they realized they were naked. But then God made them clothes out of skins, probably animal skins. These animals were the first fatalities because of sin. So your question should be "If Adam and Eve wore animal skins, why do we wear clothes?" or maybe just "Why do we have to wear clothes at all?" It was a strange twist when Adam and Eve first chose their own way over God's way. The serpent talked them into disbelieving that God was really serious about the whole death thing. Once they chose their own way, though, and ate that forbidden fruit, they saw life all differently. They saw each other differently. If we still lived in an innocent world where evil had not entered, we could probably all walk around in our birthday suits. We don't live in that world though. We live in a world where we need to protect ourselves from the elements and from other people. That means clothes.

SEE FOR YOURSELF: Genesis 3:21

17

ASTROLOGY

What's the big deal about astrology?

"You will be lucky in love toward the end of the month." "Be careful when you choose new friends." "What's your sign?" Sound familiar? You can find phrases like these in almost every popular fashion magazine and daily newspaper. There are people who trust astrology so much that they actually make decisions based on their horoscopes. Whoa. If you're a Christian, you can use the astrology pages to line your garbage can. Zechariah calls astrology lies, delusion, false dreams, and vain comfort (10:2). Pretty harsh words, huh? He goes on to say that if you trust in astrology, you're as lost as a dumb wandering sheep. You've got something so much greater—and someone you can totally depend on—the Holy Spirit. His job is to guide you, to help you make good decisions, and to give you insight about your future (see John 16:13). Always put your trust in God, who knows everything. Never put your trust in a psychic or an astrologer. God says, "They shall not deliver themselves from the power of the flame." In other words, they can't save themselves, so they certainly can't save you. Only He can.

SEE FOR YOURSELF: 2 Kin. 21:6; Jer. 33:3

> Behold, they shall be as stubble, the fire shall burn them; they shall not deliver themselves from the power of the flame; it shall not be a coal to be warmed by, nor a fire to sit before!
>
> Is. 47:13-14

Where's my heart?
Meet Kendall.

As the sermon droned on, Kendall's mind started to wander. She couldn't help it. This interim pastor was terrible. As much as she tried to listen, it was a lost cause. So she just gave up. She looked a few rows in front of her and saw Jaci, looking gorgeous as always for church. That girl had more money than she knew what to do with, so she definitely invested in herself. At seventeen, Jaci had acrylic nails, Mac make-up, all Banana Republic and J. Crew clothes, and a sweet new car. Kendall couldn't help but envy her.

Jaci's new leather jacket caught her eye. She had seen one just like it at the mall the other day. Black, with sleek lines, it was that fine leather that feels so soft and expensive. And expensive it was. The price flashed across Kendall's mind, and she started to wonder.

Could she possibly afford one? If not that black one, then she had seen another black one that was a little longer that she really liked. Why not? If Jaci could have one, then why not Kendall? Now that she was working Saturdays, she was starting to bring in a little money, but with Christmas right around the corner, she knew it would be tight. She wouldn't be able to buy presents for anyone else. But what if she could save enough for that coat . . .

Her mind tuned in and out on the pastor's dull words. "And what the Lord meant when He said, 'Where your treasure is, there will your heart be also,' He meant that we shouldn't be consumed with material things. They're just things. If you obsess over them, you've put your treasure in the wrong place. Nice stuff offers no long-term happiness, and as soon as we get the one thing we want, then we still want more. The more we feed this addiction, the less satisfied we'll ever be. You know it's true," he finished. The words hit home (even from the awkward pastor). Where she had felt torn and distraught, she now felt peace.

So as the choir director started the special music, Kendall wondered what her brother might want for Christmas. Her eye caught on the angel tree, and she thought of giving presents to a child whose dad is in prison.

ATTITUDES

What should my attitude be about my life?

> But if a man lives many years and rejoices in them all, yet let him remember the days of darkness, for they will be many. All that is coming is vanity.
> **Eccl. 11:8**

The past is long gone. Tomorrow is a dream, and right now is the only moment you have to enjoy. Are you wishing your life away, hoping that the next thing will make you happy? When I get my driver's license. When I graduate. When I get to college. When I get married. The wish list could go on forever. One day you'll be old and realize you missed the whole thing. God has given you every moment of your life as a gift. How are you living this gift? Are you hoping someone will come into your life and give it meaning? Are you wanting your teenage years to be over so you can be an adult? Are you wishing it would just all go away? Are you just numb to the passage of time? If so, ask the Lord to restore your joy, to give you eyes to see your purpose, and to help you make the most of these once-in-a-life time days.

SEE FOR YOURSELF: Prov. 27:1; Eccl. 3:11-13; . 27:1; 1 Pet. 4:7

After making his sacrifice, the unclean person received a dab of blood on his ear, his thumb, and his toe. These three places symbolized the three main activities of life: thinking, working, and walking.
Leviticus 14:14

AUTHORITY

Do I have to listen to people just because they're older than me?

For we were born yesterday, and know nothing, because our days on earth are a shadow.

Job 8:9

Ever had anyone say, "You think you know everything"? They were being sarcastic, taking a jab at you. They were reminding you that your knowledge is limited. The Book of Job says the same thing—that you are only on this earth a short time, and you know very little. Job says that you would be wise to learn from your parents and grandparents, and all the years they have already lived. Because of their age, we sometimes assume they couldn't possibly contribute anything to our generation. Not so. You'd be foolish to believe they haven't felt the emotions you deal with or struggled to make hard decisions. So lay down your stereotypes, listen to your ancestors, and learn from their understanding. The more you listen, the more you learn.

SEE FOR YOURSELF: Prov. 4:1-5

BECOMING LIKE JESUS

> But the path of the just is like the shining sun, that shines ever brighter unto the perfect day.
> Prov. 4:18

The number one goal: how do I become like Christ?

A match is struck inside the heart of each believer at the very moment he or she decides to trust in Jesus Christ as the One who delivers him or her from sin. For some, the flame burns dimly for a while. And for others, it's the match that sets the forest on fire. As you begin to learn more about the Lord—His forgiveness and grace—the flame begins to burn brighter. At some point you decide to begin living what you believe—giving forgiveness and grace to others. The flame burns brighter still. You grow in knowledge and in truth.

You begin to understand why they call grace amazing. Then one day you realize that you look more like Jesus today than you did this time last year. You decide that that's a great goal—each year looking more like Jesus than you ever have before. The fire has become a blaze, and your lifestyle keeps getting brighter and brighter.

SEE FOR YOURSELF: Judg. 5:31; Dan. 12:3; Luke 11:36

BEING A CHRISTIAN

Why does it seem like being a Christian and having fun don't go together?

One reason is because a lot of Christians feel so passionately about their beliefs that they can go a little extreme on the serious side. Another reason is that sometimes people get so caught up in the do's and don'ts of following God that they forget the relationship. Jesus did a lot of fun things. The Bible doesn't come right out and say it, but it gives us some clues. His first miracle that we know about was to make wine out of water to keep the host at a wedding from being embarrassed. And listen to this... Jesus said one time that John the Baptist came living an extreme lifestyle that set him apart and people called him weird. On the other hand, Jesus said, He (Jesus) hung out with all kinds of people and the religious leaders accused Him of being a drunk and a glutton. Do you get that? Jesus must have laughed and talked for people to accuse Him of being a partyer (even though He never sinned). So being a Christian doesn't mean NOT having fun. Jesus had fun, and He loved sinners enough to hang with them.

BIBLE

Does it matter which version of the Bible I read?

> Be diligent to present yourself approved to God, a worker who does not need to be ashamed, rightly dividing the word of truth.
> 2 Tim. 2:15

Yes, it does matter. You need to read a version of the Bible that you can understand. You need to read a version of the Bible that is easy for you to read consistently. There are a lot of versions out there. Some of them use very formal language. These usually interpret the Bible word for word. Others translate the thoughts of the Bible instead of each word. These translations usually sound more informal. They sound like a regular person talking. As the Bible gets translated more and more, you'll see notes about how one word can be interpreted several ways or how one manuscript said one thing while another manuscript said something else. Don't worry. The Bible is still a powerful book. It is still God's Word. We just know more now about how different scrolls were translated. The Bible is still God's truth, and it's still our responsibility to study it and understand it.

If the preacher at my church says one thing and the one on TV says another and they both are talking out of the Bible but they don't agree, how do I know who's right?

OO. OO. 29   OO. OO   o

Knowing this first, that no prophecy of Scripture is of any private interpretation, for prophecy never came by the will of man, but holy men of God spoke as they were moved by the Holy Spirit.

2 Peter 1:20-21

It's tough to face the fact that even with all of their studying and training, even preachers don't agree exactly on what different parts of the Bible mean. There are two things that are important for you to know about that. First, the Bible does say that there is one right interpretation. Some people will tell you things like "whatever a verse means for each person is OK." Well, that's not what Peter thought. He said that no prophecy was of any private interpretation. If men had made up the Bible that might be true, but God had a hand in there. There is one right way to interpret it. The second thing is this: the only thing you can do is search out those parts of the Bible and make the best call you can. Read some books, look up some words. Pray for guidance. At some point we all have to say, "I think this means THIS," and trust God to teach us along the way if we're wrong. We're all just trying to figure it out with God's help: the preachers, the teachers, the students and people who write the answers to hard questions like this one.

BLESSINGS

Do I have to do anything to get God's blessing?

> I will bless those who bless you, and I will curse him who curses you; and in you all the families of the earth shall be blessed.
> Gen. 12:2, 3

God had a plan for a man named Abram. God knew that Abram would believe Him, and that Abram would live out his faith by his actions. Because God knew that, He promised Abram that the world would be blessed because of him.

God blessed the world through Abram in two ways. First, Abraham (the name God gave Abram later) became the prime example for everyone who would ever put their faith in God. His descendants were honored and proud to be called the "children of Abraham." Paul said that anyone who has the same kind of faith that Abraham did is a child of Abraham. But the greatest blessing that God gave through Abraham—the thing God was specifically talking about here—is Jesus. Jesus was born on earth as a part of God's chosen nation—the children of Abraham. God redeemed all of the sin in your life through Jesus, a descendant of the man whose greatest claim to fame was the simple fact that "he believed in the LORD" (Gen. 15:6).

SEE FOR YOURSELF: Gen. 15:4, 5; 17:4-8; Luke 1:54-55; Gal. 3:14, 29

Blessings were taken very seriously in Old Testament times. To bless someone was to call for God's favor and goodness in his life. What's more, the act of blessing someone somehow carried with it the power to make the blessing a reality. Once a blessing was spoken, it couldn't be taken back or changed.
Genesis 27:4

26

CARE OF SELF

Let your garments always be white, and let your head lack no oil.
Eccl. 9:8

Why should I take care of myself?

Why not? Solomon says that life is too short to not enjoy it. He says, "Let your garments always be white, and let your head lack no oil." In other words, always be clean and look your best. Too soon you'll be at the end of your life, and you won't want to have looked like a bum all the way through it. God has given you a gift in your body. Even if you're not the most handsome or most beautiful, everybody appreciates your efforts to do the best with what you've got. Neat and clean doesn't mean "most hip and most expensive." It means clean clothes, combed hair, brushed teeth. All of those things will show the world that you have dignity and self-respect. Think of it as a "thank you" to God for making you as you are. After all, if you look like you care about yourself and take yourself seriously, other people will, too.

SEE FOR YOURSELF:Num. 8:6; Zech. 3; Rev. 19:7-8

Is it EVER OK to get drunk?

No. It's as simple as that. When you're drunk, you've lost control of your body to a chemical, a substance—a thing of the world. Being drunk limits our ability to serve and glorify God—just like any other sin. Now, if you've gotten drunk in the past, there is forgiveness for you. But you cannot allow a pattern of losing control to mark your life. "Do not be drunk...but be filled with the Holy Spirit" (Eph. 5:18).

> Likewise exhort the young men to be sober-minded, in all things showing yourself to be a pattern of good works . . . that one who is an opponent many be ashamed, having nothing evil to say of you.
>
> Titus 2:6-8

Truth in the small stuff?

Meet Joel.

It started small. Each time he thought to himself, *It's no big deal. Who cares?* He blew it off so easily.

But it had started to catch up with him. Those little white lies all piled up on each other, and it quickly became a habit. So what if he "softens the truth a little," just "leaving out a few details here and there." So what? *Why make a big deal out of it? It doesn't hurt anyone,* he thought.

The lies seemed to come easier and easier over time. When his mom asked what time he got home, he said 12:30 (yeah, right). "Why pick a fight that just doesn't matter?" he justified. When she asked if the party was supervised, he assured her that it was (sure, Joel). After all, it would only make her worry. To the question about where else they went, he left a few details out—after all, who cares? Somewhere along the way, he lost sight of the truth.

He and his sister were close, and they decided to go to a movie together the next Friday. But when his friends planned a guys' night, he decided to shade out with his sister. No big deal. He told her that his coach had asked them to stay late to do a team fundraiser, and sorry, he just couldn't get out of it. She was disappointed but naturally thought that coaches are just that way.

It wasn't until his friend Ryan called that night that she found out. Since Ryan was supposed to be at the "fundraiser" too, she knew something was up. It didn't take long to find out who the liar was.

When he saw the pain in her eyes, he knew she felt betrayed. He knew he was wrong, and he knew what he had to do to change it. He started paying attention to everything that slipped out of his mouth, and he weighed each word. Slowly he won her trust back, and slowly he got back into the truth. Lying had been a habit (and a hard one to break), but it was much easier to live with himself this way. Even when his mom asked the questions he wanted to avoid, he didn't. He faced up to the truth and accepted whatever it brought. It really worked out much better than lying.

CARING

Does God care about me?

Jacob got off to a bad start in his spiritual life. First, he talked his older brother, Esau, out of the inheritance he was supposed to get as the firstborn. Later, he tricked his father, Isaac, into thinking he was Esau so that he could get the special blessing that Isaac wanted to give Esau. It didn't look like Jacob had much of a chance to do anything great for God. In fact, we might think his belief in God was kind of flimsy. But God had chosen Jacob. In spite of the sneaky things he'd done, the Lord appeared to Jacob in a dream and said, "I will not leave you until I have done what I have spoken to you." There may be times when God's promises seem way out there—beyond the realm of possibility—especially when you know you haven't kept up your end of the deal. Even when your faith is a lot stronger than Jacob's was, there may be days when you want to say, "No way. God isn't going to do that—not for me." Don't give in. Instead, listen with all your heart, with every ounce of your faith to hear God say, "I will not leave you until I have done what I have spoken to you."

SEE FOR YOURSELF: 2 Sam. 23:5; 1 Kin. 8:56; 2 Kin. 20:9

> Behold, I am with you and will keep you wherever you go, and will bring you back to this land; for I will not leave you until I have done what I have spoken to you.
> Gen. 28:13-15

Does God always take care of Christians?

Having one of those blacker than black days? Just make the world stop—you want to get off? No one is making sense. Nothing helps. You keep fighting back tears. You are overcome with sadness and pain. No one could possibly understand. Maybe no one can understand—no one but God. God promises to encourage you in your darkest hour. If you will seek Him with all of your heart, He will come to you. He will show you the path that leads out of your situation. He will conduct a holy pep rally just for you. He will wipe away your tears. He will carry your heavy load. He is much better at all this than you are, so let Him take it from here. Climb up into His strong arms. Lay your head down. And rest.

My soul melts from heaviness; strengthen me according to Your word (Ps. 119:28).

SEE FOR YOURSELF: Matt. 11:28-30; Rom. 15:4

30

CHANGE

> Then I will give them one heart, and I will put a new spirit within them, and take the stony heart out of their flesh, and give them a heart of flesh.
>
> **Ezekiel 11:19**

Can I really change my life?

Maybe not by yourself. It's hard to change habits and perspectives and old ways of thinking. But God can change you. That's exactly what he has been about for the history of the world. Even in the Old Testament he begged his people to come to obey him so that he could change them. The prophet Ezekiel said it like this: "I will put a new spirit within them." That's exactly what he does. He changes us from the inside out. Ezekiel describes the before and after as a heart of stone and a heart of flesh. That sounds like a pretty impossible change, huh? But that's what God's love in our lives is all about. Paul wrote in 2 Corinthians that we become a new creation when we are in Christ.

How do I handle change in my life?

One of the few things that you can count on in this lifetime is change. Just when you have everything kind of figured out, boom—it's time to go in a different direction. So many things happen that throw us off balance—new schools every few years, best friends move away, divorce, new teachers with new expectations, Dad gets transferred and the whole family has to move, new stepparents with stepsiblings, the death of someone you love. Life is continually changing. Isaiah says not to look back and long for what used to be, that God is creating something new—new roads in the wilderness and new rivers in the desert. You may be a creature of habit, and change may make you uncomfortable. But one measure of your success will be how easily you adapt to change—to the new things God is doing in your life. You will miss all the blessing He has for you in this day if you continue to long for the past. Set your eyes toward the future and welcome the new paths that God is making for you.

Pouring oil on a person's head was a common way of preparing someone for a new job or a promotion. This anointing ceremony, as it was also called, was performed by a person with God's authority.
Exodus 28:41

SEE FOR YOURSELF: Is. 42:16; Jer. 29:11; 2 Cor. 5:17, Is. 43:18, 19

CHARACTER

How do I "walk the walk"?

> I will set nothing wicked before my eyes; I hate the work of those who fall away; it shall not cling to me.
> Ps. 101:3

A club's initiation is like a test to see if you are worthy of the club. The greater test, in this case, is the test of your character. At many times in your walk as a believer, you will be tested, most of the time in your weakest places. A character test puts all your talk on the line. You may have been talking "Jesus talk" for a long time, but it's time to walk the talk. If your club asks you to do something illegal, or immoral, or offensive—don't. Don't even try to rationalize it. Just walk away. If they won't allow you to join—their loss. Why associate yourself with people who look cool on the outside but encourage evil on the inside? Doing the right thing may cost you. It may cost you the club, or some friends, or some status thing. But God promises to honor your right decisions. He will bless you for choosing well.

SEE FOR YOURSELF: Ps. 1:1; Rom.12:9; 1 Cor. 15:33-34; Phil. 4:8

CHARACTER OF GOD

OO. OO. 29   OO. OO. 30

Will the world ever really see God's greatness?

Yes, but not until the very end. Ezekiel quotes God as saying, "Then they shall know that I am the Lord." Now, God doesn't sit in heaven like a little person saying, "I'll show 'em one day. You just wait." He doesn't need the recognition of the world. He's God, after all. But there will come a time when He will say, "enough" and will step to front stage and reveal himself. Whether people respect Him or reject Him, they will know He exists and that He is Lord of all.

If Adam and Eve only had to wear clothes because they sinned, do God and the Angels wear clothes?

First, let's review. God is a spirit. The angels are spirits. They don't have bodies like us that can be tempted to sin and that get cuts and bruises to exposed skin. Clothes wouldn't function for them the same that they do for us. When angels are described in the Bible they are not described as naked men. I'd think that if they appeared as naked men, some one would have mentioned that fact. Sometimes they aren't even described as being in human form. Ezekiel saw some angels in a visions and described them as a combination of all kind of different things: wheels, animals, wings, hands. What a sight! We don't know all the reasons that Adam and Eve had to wear clothes after their eyes were opened. It was a good way of showing that a time of innocence was over. Suddenly people needed to protect themselves from the elements and each other. Not only were Adam and Eve different, but the world they lived in was different.

In Old Testament times, God occasionally showed His "glory," a visible symbol of His presence, to human beings. The best way to describe this glory is as a burning fire or bright light. God's glory appeared in the tabernacle over the lid of the ark of the covenant.
Psalm 26:8

SEE FOR YOURSELF: Ezekiel 10:21

33

Why does God let murderers and rapists live?

God gives us all a chance. It would make more sense to our human mind if God would immediately punish the "bad" people and reward the "good" people. Now THAT would be a world we could understand. God doesn't do that, though. Even when Jesus was on earth, He didn't hang out with only the good people. He hung out with tax collectors (who were despised in that culture) and sinners. The religious leaders of Jesus' day couldn't understand it. We certainly don't understand it when it comes to cruel and violent people. But God gives us all the same chances to change.

> He said to them, "Those who are well have no need of a physician, but those who are sick."
> Matt. 9:11-13

It seems like computers can almost think for themselves. If they ever could, would God love them and let them into Heaven?

If thinking was what it takes to have faith and a relationship with God, then computers being able to think would make a difference here. But just acknowledging information with your mind really isn't what it takes to connect with God on earth or in eternity. The book of Romans says that with the heart people believe and then become righteous. The Bible also says that even demons believe in Christ. (They obey him too when they have to.) But that doesn't make them righteous. That doesn't give them a relationship with Him. It's more of a heart thing than a head thing. Computers being able to think doesn't give them souls, or the ability to choose right and wrong. Only people fit those categories.

SEE FOR YOURSELF: Romans 10:10

If God made us in his image, why do we all look so different?

Jesus did a very clever thing once. Some religious leaders were asking Him about taxes. They were trying to trip Him up actually and get Him in trouble with the government. He picked up a coin and said, "Whose picture is here?" (It was Caesar's picture engraved there.) Then He said, "OK, give to Caesar what has his image on it and give to God what is God's." So Jesus was saying, "What bears God's image? You do. Give yourself to God." But you are right, we don't bear God's image according to the color of our skin or the shape of our nose. We show God's image by our ability to love and be loved and our ability to choose between good and evil. It is our will and our soul that show that we are like God and that we belong to Him. That makes sense when you realize that God is a spirit, so He doesn't have a body. We are like Him in spirit, not body.

> "Show Me a denarius. Whose image and inscription does it have?" They answered and said, "Caesar"s." And He said to them, "Render therefore to Caesar the things that are Caesar's, and to God the things that are God's."
> Luke 20:24-25

Will God ever disappoint me?

That's a tricky question. Not because God is tricky, but because life is tricky. Life disappoints us often. If we expect God to make life go our way, then it might feel like He has disappointed us. That's not true though. God will never let us down in terms of what He has really promised to do: to never leave us and to capture our souls for eternity if we'll only put our faith in Him. Life will bring many disillusioning things our way, but God will keep His promises. The Bible says He's able to keep what is committed to Him: our souls.

SEE FOR YOURSELF: 2 Tim. 1:12

Does God test us?

There is a huge difference between a test and a temptation! God will never tempt you with evil (James 1:13). However, you will encounter testings from God. It works sort of like school. Just like a teacher, God will test you to help you see if you've truly learned what He's been teaching you. You are sitting in class, and you find out your former best friend is going through a tough time. His dad has run off with his secretary, leaving your friend and his mom to fend for themselves. Now, the reason he is your former best friend is because you found out he was spreading some false rumors about you. What are you going to do?

> But, O LORD of hosts, You who test the righteous, and see the mind and heart.
> Jer. 20:12a

(a) Rejoice under your breath, thinking he got what he deserved, while spreading the news about what his dad has done all around the school.

(b) Feel bad for him, but let him work through this all on his own.

(c) Look past your own hurts and see a friend who really needs somebody to encourage him through this situation with the Word of God, as well as with plenty of love and understanding.

If you answered *c*, you passed the test! If your answer was *a* or *b*, you are probably going to have to take the same test, or one just like it, over again before long. Pass the test the first time, and you won't have to keep taking it. There's a big difference between knowing what to do and doing what you know! The difference is between passing or failing. Get in God's Word, find out what to do, and do the right thing. Pass the test!

SEE FOR YOURSELF: Pss. 7:9; 26:2; Jer. 17:10; James 1:12-15

Will God forget my questions or my problems?

Your teacher gave you a final exam. One question—"What is the meaning of life?" You read it and feel sick. What does she want? An essay? A word? A drawing? You hate stuff like this. You look at the teacher for some kind of direction. She just gives you that "do your best" look. God is not like that teacher. Life is not a test on which you just hope you get the right answer. God gives you the answers Himself. He gives them over and over again. He even reminds you when you forget. Everybody wonders "What does He want? What does God require from me?" Read Deuteronomy 10:12, 13 for yourself. He gives you the answer.

And now, Israel, what does the LORD your God require of you, but to fear the LORD your God, to walk in all His ways and to love Him, to serve the LORD your God with all your heart and with all your soul, and to keep the commandments of the LORD and His statutes which I command you today for your good?.
Deut. 10:12, 13

SEE FOR YOURSELF: Mic. 6:8; John 13:34-35; Deut. 10:12-13.

CHOICES

Without counsel, plans go awry, but in the multitude of counselors they are established.
Prov. 15:22

How can I make right choices?

00.00.29

00.00

When it comes to making decisions, it doesn't matter how old you are. The smartest thing to do is to consult with wise people and think about their counsel when you make your plans. It's just that when you are younger, you live with your wise counsel—your parents. As long as you are in your parents' home, God has made them the guardians of your decisions. They are responsible to Him for the freedoms they give to you and for the decisions they let you make on your own. Little by little, as you get older, more things will be left up to you. As you choose wisely, you will be given even more freedom. Your day is coming—all the decisions will be yours. In all your independence, don't be surprised if you find yourself calling home just to ask, "What do you think about this?"

SEE FOR YOURSELF: Eph. 6:1-3; Col. 3:20; 1 Pet. 5:5

How do you feel about large families? In Old Testament times, the family unit included everyone from grandparent to multiple wives, from widowed daughters to servants. God used the family structure to spread His message from generation to generation: Abraham wanted Isaac's wife chosen from his family in order to keep his family unified.
Genesis 24:4

Respect and obedience—even when it hurts?

Meet Carmen.

Everything seemed perfect about him. He was older, really mature, and had his own place. Carmen was so sick of immature high school guys, and finally she had met someone who had really won her heart. The only problem? A thirteen-year difference in age. She was only seventeen, and he was thirty. In her mind, it wasn't a problem. You always hear about couples who are years apart in age, and when it just clicks, well why question it? She could tell that he was crazy about her too, and she knew she was falling in love.

Her parents did not approve. And not just, "Carmen, well maybe not." It was more like, "No way! I forbid you to see him." The three of them talked through it over and over again. She pleaded, they threatened, she begged, they denied, she screamed, they screamed back, she cried, they didn't budge. They went in circles, and feelings got stronger each day. It was a formula for disaster.

Clint kept calling, and even though her parents cringed, Carmen spent hours on the phone with him. Sometimes they talked late into the night, just talking through things and all about their frustration. She hadn't seen him since her parents had given "The Mandate." They hadn't left any room for confusion. Clearly, without exceptions, they forbade her to see him. She cried herself to sleep.

When Clint called at two in the morning, she picked the phone up quickly, hoping they couldn't hear it down the hall. She had turned the ringer on their phone off so they wouldn't wake up. Instantly she was wide awake, so eager to talk to the man she loved, but still feeling guilty because of her parents. "Carmen, I'm right outside your house. Just sneak out and come over now," Clint said softly.

Her mind moved fast. She knew what he was asking, and she knew what it would mean. She might be able to pull it off, she thought, without them ever knowing. She felt so torn. But she just couldn't do it. "Clint, I can't. It's not right. You know my situation, and you have to understand." But he didn't. He left that night, and she really didn't hear from him much again. An occasional call told her he was still alive, but within weeks he was dating someone else, and she knew it was over. The pain she felt was so sharp.

At first she thought she paid a price for obedience. In time she realized that she would have paid a higher price for disobedience. She risked breaking her parents' trust, losing a piece of herself, and making a serious mistake that night. Obedience protected her from the worst.

How do I choose a college?

Choosing a college is a big decision, but not too big for God. As you and your parents begin to narrow the field, make sure you are continually covering the whole process in prayer. If God directs your steps, Proverbs 16:3 says you'll succeed ("your thoughts will be established"). Your plans have no strength if they're not from God. Begin by choosing the schools that interest you and have a curriculum in your field of study. Then "commit your works to the LORD" by taking time to pray. Visit some campuses. Take time to pray. Apply for scholarships and grants. Take time to pray. Talk over finances with your parents. Take time to pray. Go through the acceptance letters and ask yourself, "Can I honor God and live a life that glorifies Him at any of these schools?" If the answer is yes, then pick the one you like. If the answer is no, then throw out the losers, and choose from the remainder. Between you and God and your parents, you are sure to make a wise decision and find a school you'll love.

SEE FOR YOURSELF:Ps. 37:5; Prov. 3:6; Matt. 6:33

> Commit your works to the LORD, and your thoughts will be established.
> Prov. 16:1-3

Next year I can vote. Should I vote for the guy who says he's a Christian or the guy who seems like the best politician?

He said to them, "Whose image and inscription is this?" They said to Him, "Caesar's." And Jesus answered and said to them, "Render to Caesar the things that are Caesar's, and to God the things that are God's."
Mark 12:16-17

Excellent question—and one with a lot of levels of answers. We sure consider it a plus if someone who is leading our country or our city is a person that cares about what God thinks. But, we have to remember that the responsibilities of a politician are not only spiritual ones.

Jesus recognized the difference between government leadership and spiritual leadership. Some people tried to trick Him once by asking if they should pay taxes. They thought He might say that we don't owe the government anything. (They were hoping anyway, so they could get Him in trouble.) Jesus looked at a coin that had Caesar's face on it (like our coins have faces on them). He told them to give to Caesar his due, but to also give God His due. We have a responsibility to do those things too.

I know people who are spiritual people, but they would make a mess as a senator or even a city councilmen. I wouldn't vote for them. I know some great Christians who are terrible plumbers. I wouldn't hire them to fix my sink. You have to think about what job needs to be done and pick the best person for that. But make sure that person has a political agenda that agrees with your values and desires for our country. Our vote is our voice—use it for good.

CHURCH

Do I really need to get up every Sunday to go to church?

> I was glad when they said to me, "Let us go into the house of the LORD."
> Ps. 122:1

Going to church is important for several reasons. First, the church is something God wanted and established on earth. It's the place He's made for His people to come together and learn about Him and serve Him and worship Him. Second, it's a place for you to find Christian friends and people you can look up to. Third, it's a place for you to get to know God and His Word and a place where you can be encouraged.

You may be thinking, *Yeah, but those things don't really happen. The church is full of hypocrites.* You're right. It is. It's full of humans—imperfect people who blow it, just like you. Jesus came to help imperfect people. What's important is that there are also some incredible people in church, people whose hearts are really longing to be like Jesus. These people can be awesome friends and role models for you.

You may be thinking, *Okay, but church is stuffy and boring.* Give me a break. There are so many kinds of churches today!—some with forms of music (even electric guitars and drums!) and worship that may really appeal to you. Or that are led by young, energetic pastors who really know how to relate to you. Give church a chance. Look around at different ones; just make sure you find one that confesses Jesus Christ as the only Lord and Savior. Pray about your decision and ask Him to help you find your place. Get involved and grow with other Christians. It'll change your life.

SEE FOR YOURSELF: Ps. 26:8; John 2:17; Acts 2:46-47; Heb. 10:25

Why won't some churches let women be priests or ministers?

> And I do not permit a woman to teach or to have authority over a man, but to be in silence.
> **1 Tim. 2:12**

Hmmm. Touchy subject. You probably know that at the time in history when the Bible was written women were not treated equally with men. That means legally they didn't have full rights as people. The rights women had only came in their relationships with their husbands or fathers. This is why the Bible talks so much about the church taking care of widows. They had no rights. It's like women were considered possessions of the men in their lives. It was up to those men to make all their decisions and care for them. Now, Jesus really broke the rules on this one. He treated women with respect in a way that was unusual for his time. There are several places in Paul's letters where he talks about women. He says that men should lead the church. He says women should be quiet. Some churches believe Paul's instructions were cultural things that were true for that culture, but not true for today. Other churches think that they were guidelines that should still be followed today. Either way, it doesn't affect how God views women. Look to Jesus' example for that. It just affects the customs of who makes decisions and how. We'll all have to keep struggling with this one because there are a lot of disagreements about it.

My friend says he's a Christian, but his church is on Saturdays. My aunt's church meets on Sundays and Wednesdays too. Does God care what day of the week you go to church?

Remember the Sabbath day, to keep it holy.
Exodus 20:8

Churches meet at all different times nowadays. Originally the Jews considered Saturday the worship day. One of the Ten Commandments says, "Remember the Sabbath, to keep it holy." The Sabbath is Saturday. Then after Jesus came, the day of worship was changed to Sunday, the day of His resurrection. Since then some denominations have gone back to Saturday, and others have added more services. Some churches even offer services on Saturday AND Sunday. I think it would be safe to say that God is more concerned with the fact that you set aside time to worship Him with other believers, than WHEN you do. I think God is also concerned that we honor the Sabbath as a day of rest. Some of us get so busy with church that it's more of a workday than any other day of the week. God RESTED after Creation. We are supposed to follow that pattern, and God will bless us if we do. Part of keeping Sabbath holy is taking time out for God to renew us. Part of it is just hanging out with Him.

My dad says he believes in God, but he doesn't like church. My mom says he's going to hell if he doesn't go to church. Is that true?

00. 00. 29   00. 00.

And let us consider one another in order to stir up love and good works, not forsaking the assembling of ourselves together, as is the manner of some, but exhorting one another, and so much the more as you see the Day approaching.
Hebrews 10:24-25

Not necessarily. Here's the deal: we're saved by grace through faith, not by works—not by going to church. So hang with me. Hell is the only place where God is not. If people choose to live their lives apart from God in this lifetime, then that is the place where they spend eternity apart from God. If people choose to connect with God in this lifetime, though, they connect with Him in eternity. Only your dad knows whether he is connecting with God. That's more than just believing in God's existence. It's also knowing God's love and claiming His sacrifice that made a way for us to believe in Him. Again, only your dad knows where he stands with that. Maybe if you ask him, he'll talk to you about it. One of the things we do when we connect with God is we also connect with other believers. We gather in groups and encourage each other. We worship God together. We call it church. Going to church doesn't automatically make us connected with our heavenly Father. Maybe what your mom's concern really is, is this: if your dad is connected with God, why doesn't he want to go to church? Maybe it's time for your whole family to sit down together and talk about that.

COMFORT

Can God comfort me better than people can?

Let, I pray, Your merciful kindness be for my comfort, according to Your word to Your servant.
Ps. 119:76

You studied your brains out for the chemistry exam. The teacher handed it back to you with a big fat D on it. All your friends and their parents went camping last weekend, but your family wasn't invited. You were laughed out of the locker room for refusing to take some pills that were supposed to help you train better. The coolest guy in school asked you out and then only wanted you to write his research paper.

Disappointment. Rejection. Failure. Sometimes it seems unbearable. You need someone to hear your story and say they understand. You need someone to let you cry and give you a big hug. You need someone to comfort you. Where do you go?

There are lots of places to run to, but most of them will leave you empty. God promises to be there and to really comfort you. His love brings faith for the moment and hope for the future. He gives you strength when you don't have any. He looks into your heart and sees how you're feeling and what you need. Then He pours out comfort by His Holy Spirit. No wonder they call Him the Comforter.

SEE FOR YOURSELF: Is. 49:13; John 14:15-18; 2 Cor 1:3

COMMAND- MENTS OF GOD

What is the most important command for me to follow?

A religious leader asked Jesus that very same question. Jesus answered him by quoting a verse from Deuteronomy. The verse said to love God with all your heart, soul, mind, and strength. Does that surprise you? Maybe you thought Jesus would give a list of do's and don'ts. When you think about it, though, if you love God with every part of you, then you are going to have the best chance at obeying him in every other way. That's why it's the most important command. Some people have said, "Love God and do what you want." As long as you're doing the first part, then you're free to do the second.

God's laws: Annoying rules or serious conditions?

God told Moses to give lots of laws to the people of Israel. He did that because He wanted to bless the people. You're thinking *What? Why would He make them do all that stuff if all He wanted was to bless them? Why didn't He just bless them anyway?* Think about it. God is holy. He has rules for living. He will not bless sin. He could not have a bunch of people running around doing whatever they wanted and then bless them in spite of it. The laws don't exist so that God can play "boss" and bark orders to people. They were necessary conditions for the blessing that comes from holy living. Jewish law had 613 points, or rules, that had to be obeyed before a person could approach God. Imagine that. It would be impossible for anybody to meet all those demands. When Jesus came, He fulfilled the law—all 613 points. When Jesus lives in you, every rule is obeyed. The law is satisfied and you can approach God. You are free from having to live up to all those rules. Jesus has done it for you.

> The Ten Commandments are God's laws for living. They apply to us today every bit as much as they applied to the Israelites in the wilderness. God's morals do not change. As if the Israelites needed a reminder, God began the commandments with an announcement of who He is an what He had done for them.
>
> Exodus 20:2-17

SEE FOR YOURSELF: Ex. 20; Deut. 5:1-22; 1 Chr. 22::13; Gal. 3—5

CONFES-SION

> "Come now, and let us reason together," says the LORD, "Though your sins are like scarlet, they shall be as white as snow."
>
> Is. 1:18

Does God care if I confess my sins to Him?

You've got a personal invitation to a private dinner with a king. What? Sure you do. It's right here in Isaiah 1:18. God invites you to come and reason things out. He's letting you know that He really wants you to talk over your life with Him. It's not that He doesn't already know exactly what's going on—He just wants the pleasure of knowing you care enough about Him to share it. Specifically, this verse is referring to sin. The Lord invites people to confess their sin to Him and turn their lives around. With God, it's that simple. All you've got to do to get your life headed in the right direction is talk it over with Him. He'll take it from there.

SEE FOR YOURSELF: Pss. 51:9; 62:8; Is. 43:25

Setting a standard?
Meet Ben.

Every summer the fam packs up the van and off we go to Michigan to Family Camp week at Camp of the Hills. I guess it's a fun time. When I was a kid, I invited friends up, and we'd do the camp games all day. I still like the sports, but some of the group games are getting old. At least we can spend the whole day skiing on the lake or whatever. Yeah, I guess it's still fun.

A lot has changed since we started coming (then again, I was six at the time). Every year the counselors change, and you never know what kind of a group they will be. Over the years, my relationship with the counselors has gone from "that little kid" to someone who is actually old enough to hang out with them after hours. A couple of the guys are really cool, and believe me, these girls have been working on their tans all summer (especially Jamie!). So as I was saying, it's nice to be included now.

At night, the families go off to their own cabins, and the counselors are left with some free time to themselves. This guy Jake usually stops by and grabs me before all of us get together. Our standard ritual is to grab some stuff from the meal hall and take off for the woods. About a half mile in, there's a perfect campfire spot, and no one would ever find it.

Yeah, some of the guys light up right away. It wasn't bad at first, when just a couple of them did it. But as the week progressed, they were all smoking pot, and soon even Jake was smoking. The girls kept looking at me, waiting to see what I would do. I knew I was being tempted, but I didn't want to look like a loser in front of them all. I definitely felt the pressure.

But I stood my ground, and I did it for a couple of reasons. One, it would really disappoint my parents. They don't always know everything, but my mom especially is pretty sharp about knowing what I'm into. Two, I'd be a fool to start that habit before soccer season in the fall. If I wanted to be a starter this year (which trust me, I did), then there's no way I could afford to permanently dull my reflexes with pot. And three, and most important, I did it for God. I knew that He wanted me to live a pure life, set apart for Him, and that does not include pot. I knew I had an opportunity to honor Him and to make a statement to my friends. So I did.

Eventually, I stopped going to the campfires. They became all about pot, and no one was really having fun. After I left, so did a few of the other guys and a couple of the hot girls. And remember Jamie? Well let's just say the rest is history . . .

CONFI-DENCE

> "In returning
> and rest you
> shall be saved;
> In quietness and
> confidence
> shall be your
> strength."
> Isaiah 30:15

How can I get more confidence?

You know, confidence is really courage in many ways. It's having the courage to face life and to know that between you and God, it'll be OK. When you know that, not many things will chase you. You might be surprised to hear where the Bible says you can get confidence? Where do you think? At self-help classes? On the karate team? In a makeover or new haircut. Nope. Confidence comes in getting quiet before God. Isaiah said that it comes in returning to God and resting in him. When you sit before God and know who He is and let Him love you, then you walk out into the world with a different air about you, because you know you are loved and protected. Try it and see.

CREATION

How did God create me?

Remember when you were in kindergarten and you made plaster imprints of your hands or a sculpture out of pipe cleaners? Remember how excited you were? When you made something you were proud of, you couldn't wait to show it off. You were so careful until you got it home and put it in a safe place. And every once in a while you'd take a look at it and grin. You loved it. God made you and that's why He loves you. You were His idea.

Even though you may not always act like your Father, the truth is that you are His child and His love for you will never end. Just as you carefully created your kindergarten masterpiece, God crafted each part of your being just exactly the way He wanted it. He made you a certain way so that you could be everything wonderful that He wants you to be. You're a part of His heart because He thought of you and then gave those thoughts life and created you. He's in love with you. He thinks you're awesome. And you are, because you're His.

SEE FOR YOURSELF: Gen. 1:27; Is. 43:7; 44:2; 1 John 3:1

> The LORD has called Me from the womb; from the matrix of My mother He has made mention of My name. And He has made My mouth like a sharp sword; in the shadow of His hand He has hidden Me, and made Me a polished shaft; in His quiver He has hidden Me.
>
> Is. 49:1, 2

CULTS

Are cults really dangerous?

00. 00. 29

Yes. Why? The Bible says it is because they
cause you to believe something that is
not true. Truth doesn't get a really big slap on
the back in our world. We say, "Oh, everybody can believe
what they want. What does it matter?" But it does matter. It matters whether we
believe in God. It matters whether we know how to connect with Him. It matters
whether we understand how to secure our souls in His love. The nature of a cult is
that it follows a belief other than God's work in the world through Jesus Christ.
That's a dangerous thing to mess with.

> "Because you
> have spoken
> nonsense and
> envisioned lies,
> therefore I am
> indeed against
> you," says the
> Lord God.
> Ezekiel 13:6-8

DATING

What's the harm in a little fling?

> Therefore, putting away lying, "Let each one of you speak truth with his neighbor," for we are members of one another.
>
> Eph. 4:25

That depends on what type of relationship you are involved in and what kind of little fling you're talking about. First, the fling. God's rule is no sex outside of marriage. So that's the harm if the fling involves sex. But if it doesn't, let's talk about what kind of relationship you're in. Let's say you're in a relationship in which you and the other person have committed to only date each other. You've made a commitment of some kind. Your little fling (seeing someone else) means that you care more about yourself than that other person. It says you're willing to lie. It says that you enjoy the other person's attention, but it's not enough for you. It says something about how much you value and respect the other person and how much they can trust you. That trust is what a little fling can harm.

Why do guys always break my heart?

Do guys really ALWAYS break your heart? Romantic relationships are tough. There are so many expectations. We all want to be loved so much, but men and women love in such different ways. On top of that we see so much romantic love on TV that we end up wanting really passionate, mature love before we are able to be passionate and mature at the same time (if there is a time we can ever do that). Maybe your heart is looking for something that guys can't give you. Have you ever thought of that? Sometimes we think that if someone will love us we will feel so safe that we won't need anybody or anything else. But that's not ever true. At the bottom of it there are things we need that can only come from God. No guy can give it to us no matter how good a guy he is. That's hard lesson that can take a whole lifetime (sometimes) to learn. You can be sure of this though. God is with you in your broken heart. The Bible says that in Psalm 34. You aren't alone. Don't give up. Just keep figuring out who can give you what you really need.

SEE FOR YOURSELF: Psalm 34:18

How will I know when I am in love?

Tough question. Knowing when you're in love can be a little confusing. In our culture we think infatuation is the same as love. Do you know what infatuation is? It's the attraction that most often comes before love. We get a crush on someone that develops into infatuation. Infatuation is really fun. It makes you feel lighter than air. It gives butterflies in your stomach. On TV and in the movies being in love is almost ALWAYS portrayed as infatuation. But being in love is deeper than that, though. You fall in and out of infatuation. People get married all the time who are just infatuated with each other. Then the infatuation wears off. After a while life gets hard and the butterflies of a serious crush will NOT last in the midst of the hard parts of life. Love will though. If you are in love you are willing to stick with someone even when they don't look good, even when they are at their worst, even when you don't enjoy it. When you are in love, you have not just fallen into it. You have chosen to be there. You have passed some real life tests. You are willing to put the other person ahead of yourself. You're willing to do what's best for the relationship even if it's not what is the most fun for you. You'll know you're in love when you get past the butterflies to the yucky parts, but you still would not Want to be there with anyone else.

> Love suffers long and is kind; love does not envy; love does not parade itself, is not puffed up; does not behave rudely, does not seek its own, is not provoked, thinks no evil; does not rejoice in iniquity, but rejoices in the truth.
> 1 Cor. 13:4-7

Asking Rebekah's opinion about marriage plans was an unusual courtesy. Marriages were generally arranged by young people's families. Very few women (and few men, for that matter) had the authority to go against their family's wishes.
Genesis 24:57

I'm 18, can I date a 30-year-old?

Legally, if you're eighteen, in most states, I guess you CAN date a 30-year-old. If you're seriously asking the question though, you or someone who cares about you must have some hesitations about it. You CAN date a 30-year-old, and it CAN end up being a really good thing. But you've got to keep in mind: Is this the best thing for both of us? Ask yourself some questions: Why do I want to date this person? Because he's older and exciting, or because he's your friend and you share the same passions? Are you dating with the same goals in mind? The older you are, the more you begin to think about marriage (generally)—is this just a fling for either of you? And most importantly, do you share a love and passion for Christ? If you think you've got the right answers for these questions, great! But I would still suggest you find someone who you both trust to give you advice and encouragement in your walks with Christ and your relationship with each other.

> Without counsel, plans go awry. But in the multitude of counselors they are established.
> Prov. 15:22

Why is it so fun to hold hands with my boyfriend?

For a LOT of reasons! Touching and being touched is a powerful way of loving and being loved. Add to that being touched by someone that you have a crush on and there are fireworks galore! Did you know there is a whole book of the Bible about stuff like that? It's called Song of Solomon. It's a love poem. It's as mushy as can be, filled with sweet talk between a king and his wife. At one point the wife says, "Let him kiss me because his love is better than wine." Wine was their main drink back then. Everyone knew what really fine wine tasted like, so they knew exactly what she was talking about. How do you think she felt when the king held her hand? God made human bodies to enjoy being touched—it's His gift to us! As babies we want to be held. As children we want to be hugged. No matter how old we are we like it when people touch us, whether it's holding hands or sitting close. All the better if it's someone we think is really groovy.

SEE FOR YOURSELF: Song 1:2

I'm sorta scared of my boyfriend, but I love him so much. My friends say I should leave him before I get hurt, but doesn't the Bible say that loves sticks around?

There is no fear in love; but perfect love casts out fear, because fear involves torment. But he who fears has not been made perfect in love.
1 John 4:18

The Bible does say love sticks around, but I'd like you to think about what you are calling love. The Bible also says that there is no fear in love. Love means being accepted and cared for. And when you are talking a romantic, ongoing relationship, love means it goes both ways. You can't love your boyfriend enough for both of you. From what you are saying, I'm not sure he loves you back in the same way. He might say he does, but if his actions scare you and your friends, there's something wrong with this picture. It's also important to recognize what "sticking around" can mean. You don't have to stay in a romantic relationship that is abusive in order to "never give up." You can back off romantically, but remain his friend. And, most importantly, you can pray for him. Sounds like he needs a little more of God's peace and love in his life before he can be a good partner for you. Love him—just make sure that you're not trying to be God's love in his life. It's probably time for you to step back and let God work.

Does God care if I date someone from another race or religion?

Does God care? Do you mean, does God consider it wrong? Race—No. Religion—Yes. In the Old Testament God warned the people not to intermarry with different cultures. This was a religion issue. The nations surrounding the Israelites (whom they would intermarry with) worshiped idols; they did not worship God. God wanted the people's faith to be pure. In the New Testament God says not to yoke yourself together with an unbeliever. This can apply to marriage or other close relationships. So, if you're dating someone of another religion, who worships another god—or someone who doesn't worship any god at all—that's a problem.

> Do not be unequally yoked together with unbelievers. For what fellowship has righteousness with lawlessness? And what communion has light with darkness?
> 2 Cor. 6:14

By the time the New Testament rolled around, there was only a small nation of Jews who hadn't intermarried. So, as far as race is concerned, there really isn't any statement against it in the New Testament. In heaven, people from every tribe and nation will stand before God's throne and worship him together. God honored the interracial marriage of Ruth and Boaz (who both worshiped God) by including them in Jesus' human ancestry. In the early church, in Acts, people from across the world worshiped together. God does not care about the color of a person's skin, but the condition of his or her heart. That's what to think about when choosing whether or not to date someone.

DEATH

When I die, if I was good, do I go straight to heaven?

> And Jesus said to him, "Assuredly, I say to you, today you will be with Me in Paradise."
> Luke 23:43

This is the thing: It's not about being good. Yes, choosing to do the right thing is important to God. It's how we show Him our love. He calls it obedience. But going to heaven is about faith. It's about knowing that we can't be perfect and that God has to fix that for us. It's about believing that Jesus died specifically so we don't have to die spiritually. What does it mean to die spiritually? It means to be lost to God, to live eternity without Him. God chose not to let that happen. So He came to earth as a man and took on the responsibility for our imperfection. When you die you'll go straight to heaven if you are trusting God's sacrifice to get you there. When Jesus was on the cross dying, the thief hanging next to him said, "Remember me when you get to heaven." By saying that, Jesus knew that thief really believed in who Jesus was. Jesus said back to him, "Today, you'll be with me there." Jesus didn't say, "after you pass admissions and the entry level exam and then wait for a while in a holding cell." No, he said, "TODAY we'll be there together." So when you die, if you have trusted Christ's goodness, you'll go straight to heaven.

I'm afraid of dying. Is that a problem? Is it wrong?

We can take any fears we have to God and ask Him to comfort us in them. So you can take your fear of dying to God and let Him comfort you. You should understand, though, what the Bible teaches about death. Psalm 116 says that the death of God's saints (us) is precious to Him. That means He welcomes it. It's a transition for us into a place where we can know God more fully and where we can experience life the way He wanted us to. It's scary from this side because anything unknown is scary. Death is one big unknown. But from God's perspective it's like coming home. So take your fears to God and trust Him with your life. Let Him worry about the other stuff.

Setting my boundaries?
Meet Dalia.

I thought I loved him, I really did. Felix was everything I had always hoped for in a boyfriend—and more. He really was the tall, dark, and handsome guy I'd always dreamed of. At six feet four, the captain of the basketball team, a total gentleman, he treated me unbelievably well. Let's just say I was spoiled (a serious understatement). At least once a week, flowers showed up, at school, at home, even at work. This guy had amazing taste. One day he showed up on his motorcycle to pick me up after practice. It was a Thursday, nothing special, right? When he handed me the diamond necklace I knew this was too good to be true. He really treated me like he loved me. And he said he did.

We talked marriage. We knew it was a couple years off (at least), but this was no half-hearted relationship. Everything seemed so right, and I wanted so much for it to be true. At eighteen, I was old enough to be really in love but still too young to know whether or not he was right for me. So I kept praying that he was.

When his parents left town, it seemed ideal. We rarely had any space just to ourselves, without a parent or someone barging through, and sometimes it got old just going out all the time. So we definitely took advantage of the freedom and spent some quality time together at his house.

It seemed so natural, how much we loved each other and how much we wanted to express that to each other. Sometimes words just aren't enough, and every time I kissed him and he touched me, my heart soared. This time, though, things just kept going . . .

He was whispering how much he loved me in my ear and as his hands moved over my body, I knew I wanted him. Ever the gentleman, he hinted and then asked, would I let him sleep with me?

The moment of truth: What was I made of? I wanted him so badly, and I felt like everything was so right, but I felt my conscience stab me sharply. I gently pushed his hands off me, putting them down around my waist, and I pulled back so I could look him directly in the eye. Softly but firmly I told him no. He could read the "no" in my eyes and heard it from my lips. Though he still felt the desire, he knew where I stood. I had drawn a clear line, and at that moment, I vowed never to cross it.

What do I have to do to be with God when I die?

You have to believe in what God did for you through Jesus Christ. God is more concerned with our faith in Him than anything else. To have faith in God is a lot more than just saying, "Oh yeah, I think there's a God." It's believing that God exists and that what He says is true. If we believe what He says is true, then we know that to know God is to have a relationship with Him, to talk with Him, to listen to Him, to trust Him. It's not just knowing Him with our head; it's knowing Him with our heart. As we make that relationship a priority, then He guides us and keeps us safe. Another way of saying it is this: to be with God when you die, you need to live with Him while you are alive. It all starts with faith.

> For God so loved the world that He gave His only begotten Son, that whoever believes in Him should not perish but have everlasting life.
> John 3:15-16

If a baby dies, what happens to his soul? Is it like recycled or something?

Not recycled. If babies were recycled, then we'd be talking reincarnation. The Bible gives us no information that makes us think that reincarnation is a reality.

So what does happen when a baby dies? This is a really controversial topic. Everyone has really strong opinions, based in Scripture—and they tend to differ. So, I'll say right off—talk with your parents or youth pastor if you are concerned about this question. Part of our journey to knowing God is struggling with issues just like this one.

So, again, what happens when a baby dies? The Bible says nothing definite about this. Part of us has to look to God's justice and know that not all people will enter the kingdom of God. Babies, just like the rest of us, are saved by Jesus' work on the cross.

There's also the "age of accountability"—it doesn't seem fair that a baby, who hasn't had the opportunity to understand salvation, wouldn't go to heaven. So we look at and study God's mercy, goodness, and love for His creation.

The one thing we can be sure of is that God is "good to all and His tender mercies are over all His works" (Ps. 145:8).

SEE FOR YOURSELF: 2 Samuel 12:22-23

Would it be better to die young so you could be young in heaven, or can you be whatever age you want to once you're there?

OO. OO. 29

OO. OO. O

But, beloved, do not forget this one thing, that with the Lord one day is as a thousand years, and a thousand years as one day.

2 Peter 3:8

I know in the movies that show heaven people always look the same as they did on the earth when they died. I'm not sure heaven will really be like that, though. There is a story in the Bible where a poor beggar and the rich man he begged from, both died. They somehow caught sight of each other in eternity (this was just a story Jesus told, I don't know that we'll be able to do that). When they saw each other, they recognized each other. So maybe that means we will have enough of the same appearance to be recognized, or maybe we'll be able to recognize people's spirits. But time happens differently in heaven's dimension. Age isn't relevant. The Bible says a day is like a thousand years to God. It's all the same. No sun is rising and setting, no earth is rotating. So whether it's better to die young or old, it has nothing to do with what age you'll be in heaven.

Can God rescue me from death?

For the person who doesn't believe in Jesus, death has a lot of power. Death for them is the end of life on earth and the beginning of hell—forever. But Jesus promises to rescue His believers "from the power of the grave." He is the One who drove death into the ground. He is more powerful than death. He has beaten death for you. All He asks is that you believe that He died just for you and that you let Him redeem you. Then follow Him. What that means is that you have to give up trying to save yourself. You will never be good enough, do enough good deeds, or accomplish enough great things to overcome death. You don't even have to try anymore. Right now, right where you are, tell Jesus that you can't do it yourself; you are drowning in your own sin. Ask Him to reach in and rescue you. Hold on tightly as He pulls you to shore and breathes new life into you. Then stand up and follow the One who has rescued you for eternity.

SEE FOR YOURSELF: Is. 25:8; 1 Cor. 15:55; Rev. 21:4 ; Ps. 49:15

Will everyone die?

Justin was sixteen years old and a really awesome kid—the kind of guy everyone wanted to be around. He had such a great attitude—he even made work fun. One Tuesday night after supper, he hopped in his car to go to a Bible study. His mom kissed him and reminded him to buckle up and drive safely. Two miles from his house, Justin crossed the yellow line and hit another car. Justin died and so did the lady in the other car. No one could believe that Justin was gone. He had so much life ahead of him—he was really going to make a difference. A part of God's design is that we all die sometime. And even when we don't understand, we cling to the truth that God's timing is perfect. The coolest thing about Justin is that he really loved God and lived a life that proved it. When Justin left this earth and entered the presence of his Lord, the angels sang and the Savior surely said, "Well done, My son. I am so pleased with you."

SEE FOR YOURSELF: Eccl. 2:15-16; 3:19-20; Matt. 25:23; 1 Cor. 15:21-22

> Nevertheless man, though in honor, does not remain; he is like the beasts that perish.
> Ps. 49:12

How come dying has to hurt so much for some people?

When you think about it, death really is a horrible thing. We talk about how great it is to go to heaven. We are glad when really sick people are relieved of their misery. But you know, when God designed the world, death wasn't a part of it. People weren't supposed to die. Death came because sin entered the world. So even though death means going to eternity, it is hard to take. It's even harder to take when someone you care about is suffering and hurting while they face death. Sickness and death are a product of sin in our world. Nobody said it any clearer than Paul. He said that by Adam sin entered the world and by sin death entered the world. It was only through Jesus' resurrection that death lost some of its power over us. Why does it hurt one person more than others? I don't think anyone can answer that.

SEE FOR YOURSELF: Romans 5:12

DEMONS

Are demons strong enough to hurt Jesus?

00. 00. 29   00. 00. .o

It would be safe to say that, no, demons are
not stronger than Jesus. Neither could they
get anywhere near Him if He didn't allow it.
When Jesus was on earth He healed people who
were sick and He cast out demons. In Mark's Gospel demons
can't speak without His permission, they can't hurt Him without
His permission. Demons are not like God. They are not all powerful or all-knowing.
They can't read our thoughts or force us to do anything. They are only scary
because they live in a dimension that we can't see.

> Then He healed many
> who were sick with
> various diseases,
> and cast out many
> demons; and He did
> not allow the demons
> to speak, because
> they knew Him.
>
> **Mark 1:34**

What do demons do to people?

Once a person lets a demon have control over them, that demon can do a lot of
things. He can control what they say and even the way they act. Demons have
even been known to control the way people look at times. The bottom line,
though, is that demons want to destroy people. You might remember the guy
Mark talked about who had a legion of demons (a lot) in him. Mark says he went
around "crying out and cutting himself." Demons will do whatever they can to
destroy people.

SEE FOR YOURSELF: Mark 5:5

Are demons powerful?

Yes, they are. If demons are not held back by the power of God, they can be very
strong. People who are possessed or oppressed by demons have been known to do
things that require much more strength than that person would have shown by
themselves. In Acts some Jewish exorcists were trying to cast demons out of a
man and instead the man jumped on them and ran them out of the house. The
only thing that restrains demons is the name and power of Jesus Christ, because
they know better than we do just how powerful He is.

SEE FOR YOURSELF: Acts 19:16

63

DEPRES-SION

Anxiety in the heart of man causes depression, But a good word makes it glad.
Proverbs 12:25

My friend always seems sad and wears black most of the time. I'm so worried about her. What should I do about it?

The first thing is realize that there's only so much you can do for your friend. If she's been sad for a long time, then she might be depressed. The Bible talks about that. It says that anxiety can lead to depression. The Bible also says that a "good word" can make an anxious heart feel better. Whether your friend is depressed, or just quiet and into black, you can be there for her by being nice and letting her know that you care about her. You can also listen to her if she needs to talk. Remember that each person has to decide what to do with their problems and YOU can't decide for them. You can walk beside your friend and give her a smile, but you can't fix what's wrong.

DISCIPLINE

Will God's discipline hurt?

The LORD will perfect that which concerns me; Your mercy, O LORD, endures forever; do not forsake the works of Your hands.
Ps. 138:8

Some people have this idea of God as the "Big Guy" sitting up in heaven with a giant paddle just waiting for someone to step out of line so He can use it. Well, it's obvious that God isn't pleased when you do something you know you shouldn't. But He's not the guy with the paddle.

His discipline comes out of His love. Everything He does, even if it's not so pleasant to you at the time, has your best interest at heart. Look at how Jesus talked to Martha when she complained to Him about her sister: "Martha, Martha, you are worried and troubled about many things. But one thing is needed, and Mary has chosen that good part, which will not be taken away from her" (Luke 10:41, 42). He didn't scream at her; He just gently pointed her in the right way. He treated Thomas the same way. When Thomas wouldn't believe that Jesus had risen from the dead until he saw and touched Jesus' wounded hands, Jesus didn't refuse to show him what he needed to see. He did say, "Thomas, because you have seen Me, you have believed. Blessed are those who have not seen and yet have believed" (John 20:29).

You can count on God to treat you gently and mercifully, even when He's letting you know you're out of line.

SEE FOR YOURSELF: 2 Chr. 30:9; Lam. 3:22

DISCOUR-AGEMENT

> Anxiety in the heart of man causes depression, But a good word makes it glad.
> Prov. 12:25

How do you help your friends when they are discouraged?

Proverbs says that when someone gets worried, it can lead to depression, but a "good word" makes things better. So, the question is, what's a good word? Sometimes a good word can be, "It'll get better eventually," or "I'm here for you." It's a wonderful gift that you give a friend when you will sit with them when they are down. They don't want to hear you say they should feel differently, or that their feelings don't matter. But you can tell them that they aren't alone and that things won't stay so bad. Sometimes just hearing a voice that is happy makes someone feel better.

DIVORCE

"For the Lord God of Israel says that He hates divorce, for it covers one's garment with violence," says the LORD of hosts. "Therefore take heed to your spirit, that you do not deal treacherously."
Malachi 2:16

My parents just got divorced. Does this mean they aren't Christians?

The prophet Malachi said that God hates divorce. That's not pulling any punches, is it? Divorce is not the ideal that God wants for our lives. That doesn't mean that God hates divorced people. It also doesn't mean that God punishes people for a lifetime for being divorced. There is nothing that God can't forgive. But God did not choose for us to marry someone until we get tired of them and then ditch them. God meant for us to commit to one person and love them the way He loves us.

Your parents will probably need to spend some time grieving and refocusing on God. They may have struggled with some sins, but they can certainly still be Christians.

What does God think about my parents' divorce? Sometimes I hate it and sometimes I'm just relieved.

The Bible says that God hates divorce. That doesn't mean you shouldn't be relieved that your home is more peaceful. Your feelings are natural. It just means that God would like for us to live in a world where people didn't hurt each other. He wanted a world where families could get along. Marriage is supposed to be a kind of real life picture of God's relationship to people, unconditional love, sacrificing for each other. When two people give up on that marriage, it's sad to God. It's not the way He wishes our lives could be. He doesn't give up on us, though.

SEE FOR YOURSELF: Malachi 2:16

DREAMS

Can God fulfill my dreams?

OO. OO. 29

Lord, all my desire is before You; and my sighing is not hidden from You.
Ps. 38:9

OO. OO. 10

What do you secretly want to do with your life? Want to be an undertaker, but think all your friends would laugh? Want to be a chemist, but can't imagine how it could possibly happen? What does your heart long to do? God knows every one of your deepest desires. He put them there. He knows what makes you feel like time just flew by. He knows what fills you up and gives you a purpose. He knows what makes you so angry that you just have to do something. So trust Him with your dreams and passions. He will not laugh. He is not surprised. He knows exactly how to make it all happen. His timing will be perfect.

SEE FOR YOURSELF: Is. 66:18; Heb. 4:12

In biblical times, God often spoke to people through dreams. Rarely, were His messages obvious. Most of His dreams involved odd creatures and strange symbols, things that could only be explained by someone who knew God's plans.
Genesis 40:8

Taking a stand for my values?
Meet Alex.

Junior year was definitely the worst year ever. If I were the swearing type, I would throw in a few words here to emphasize just what I mean by that statement. All in one year, my dad lost his job, got a new one, moved us halfway across the country, and started me in a new school—a *private* school, Catholic, where the kids were rich and snotty. What a great start to the year.

So there I was, normal old me, not too rich, not too talented, not too anything, just plain old me. You can imagine that went over real well. When everyone else pulled into the parking lot with daddy's last year model Mercedes, I pulled in driving this old boat, my dad's idea of a character builder. "You shouldn't care what anyone says about you," Dad always says. Easy for him to say.

How can I phrase it best? Well, I started the year off "relationally challenged" (meaning almost no one talked to me ever). As I slowly started to meet people and tried to fit in, their acceptance was "a bit delayed" (meaning they thought I was poor and boring). The pressure was clearly on me to fit in at this sophisticated new school. As a Christian, I found that even more difficult, since the easiest way to fit in was through drinking, smoking, and partying (plus buying a little nicer clothes). I suspected there were a few other closet Christians, but no one who really wanted to come out and admit that.

Talk about character builder. I could either do the things that I knew would make me fit in, or I could take a stand and take the heat for it. I'm not really sure why I chose what I did (enter the Holy Spirit), but I decided to make a statement with my life. Maybe it was the impulse to be different. Whatever . . .

The first time I hung up a sign announcing a Wednesday morning Bible study, the guys around me got quiet. Not a word. *Did they hate me or admire me?* I wondered. That was the last time I got invited to the big party on Friday. Here goes, I thought.

The first Wednesday, one other guy showed up. I kind of knew Carlos from a class, but here we were together, reading God's Word and praying. I felt encouraged (but only a little bit).

By week two, a girl showed up. I didn't want to set my hopes too high, so I thought, *Hey, three's a good number.* But we kept growing. Pretty soon all the closet Christians started coming out. Some of them I would have guessed, but some of them actually surprised me. And then when some of the other guys started coming, I thought it was too good to be true. No, I didn't make friends instantly, and I still took a lot of heat for what I had decided to do. But I sure made a statement. My classmates definitely knew where I stood. And I think that by doing what is right, I gave others courage to step up and do the same.

DRUGS

If God made pot, why can't we smoke it?

> And God said, "See, I have given you every herb that yields seed which is on the face of all the earth, and every tree whose fruit yields seed; to you it shall be for food."
>
> Genesis 1:29

There is a verse in the Bible that says God gave us every herb and tree for food. Some people say that means pot is OK because it's a plant that grows in God's creation. You probably know by now that the difficult issues are never that easy. We could use that verse to mean that any kind of poisonous plant is OK to eat. That doesn't mean they won't make us sick. Drugs can feel good because they mess with our system just enough to give us a ride, like a roller coaster. But that doesn't mean we should use them. In the long run we are hurting ourself. He wants to bring us life, not self-destruction. So, yes, God made all the plants, including pot (which, traditionally, was used for making rope). If that means He meant for us to smoke plants, I've got some dandelions out back that are going to waste.

Does the Bible say I can't take Ecstasy?

Do you mean the drug, ecstasy? Of course you know that ecstasy wasn't invented when the Bible was written, so there won't be actual verses about it. And, yes, I know that ecstasy came on the scene before there were even laws to govern it. What we have to look at with these questions is, "Since we're dealing with something that wasn't around when the Bible was written, does the Bible give some overall guidelines that will answer this question?" In this case the Bible does. What the Bible has to say about drunkenness has a lot to do with using mood- or mind-altering drugs. Paul certainly talked about it a lot in his letters to the early churches. Jesus talked about it too. One day Jesus was sitting at the temple with His disciples. It was the same day he saw the widow put in her two coins, if you remember that story. Anyway, Jesus talked to the disciples about the lives they should live while waiting for God's kingdom. He told them not to let their hearts be weighed down with carousing, drunkenness, and the cares of this life. Ecstasy and drugs like it have a lot to do with carousing and drunkenness. It would be safe to say that if you are committed to living life according to God's plan, then ecstasy is not the way to go. God needs us alert and aware. He needs us to bring our lives to Him, not run away from life through drugs.

SEE FOR YOURSELF:. Luke 21:34

70

EATING DISORDERS

00. 00. 29

> Consider carefully what is before you; and put a knife to your throat if you are a man given to appetite. Do not desire his delicacies, for they are deceptive food.
>
> Prov. 23:1b-3

What are the negative effects of binging?

To binge for any reason is to abuse the intended use of food. A variety of emotions could trigger the desire to binge—a great report card, an awful report card, someone really cool asks you out, or everyone leaves you out. Depression, celebration, loneliness, frustration, and anger are some of the feelings that can trigger a massive pig-out. So if any emotion can be a potential reason to eat, then binging has to do with self-control. You can't live your life running from one binge to the next for comfort. Self-control comes from the Holy Spirit. And the Holy Spirit resides in the heart of every believer. You may have already established some really deep patterns in regard to binging. If so, a medical professional or counselor may be the best route to understanding how you got to this place, and how the Holy Spirit can restore control. You shouldn't binge because it's harmful to the temple God gave you and because you are using food to insulate yourself from reality. When you eat instead of dealing with the issues in your life, you stick your head in the sand and hope it'll all go away. When you look up again, the issues are still there, and you still haven't learned to deal with life. Food is a poor substitute for the love and power of God, which are what you really need in order to deal with your life. Learning to run to the Father instead of to food may take a lot of work. But the effort will be worth it. Your life will be changed, and God will be pleased.

SEE FOR YOURSELF: Prov. 13:25; 23:20; 1 Cor. 6:19, 20

FAIRNESS

Why do some people seem to have better lives than me, when they don't love God?

> For the LORD loves justice, and does not forsake His saints; they are preserved forever, but the descendants of the wicked shall be cut off.
> Ps. 37:28

You probably know some people who don't give God a second thought, but they have nice clothes, good grades, lots of friends. There are definitely a lot of famous musicians, actors, athletes, and politicians who don't do a lot of good things, but they're living the "good life" all the same. It's easy to want what they have and to wonder why God let them have things He doesn't give to you. Sometimes when you compare your life to theirs, you think, *Man, where is God, anyway?* Psalm 37 reminds you that the situation isn't always what it looks like. The people who don't care about God have what Jesus called a "house on the sand" (Matt. 7:26). It may be a really nice house, but it can't stand up for long. The people who refuse to obey God have nothing to show for their lives in the end. When it looks like God is blessing them and leaving you to fend for yourself, you need to know that He is still on your side. He will never forsake you. He won't collapse when a storm blows in or run away when things are rough. He's here to stay.

SEE FOR YOURSELF: Deut. 31:6; Matt. 7:26; 18:12-14; 28:20

Does God care if life doesn't seem fair?

As children, we continually watch our brothers and sisters, making sure they never get more than we do. A bigger scoop of ice cream could launch a full-fledged attack of whining. We grow up and hang onto that attitude. In our eyes, no one is entitled to more. No one should be able to get away with anything. The teams should always be equal—the best players evenly distributed. The problem is that we don't always have the whole story. That's where God comes in. He shows up and levels the playing field. He is always fair. He always does what is right. He always rewards those who deserve it. It's just that His ways are different from ours. His timing is perfect. Sometimes you'll get rewarded on earth, and sometimes you won't see the reward until you're in heaven. Next time you think you're being shortchanged, take it up with the Lord. Allow Him to calm your heart and give you eyes to see His fairness.

> The righteous God wisely considers the house of the wicked, overthrowing the wicked for their wickedness.
> Prov. 21:12

SEE FOR YOURSELF: Ezek. 18:20; Amos 5:24; Matt. 25:26

So I'm grounded for doing something my parents did NOT SPECIFICALLY say that I shouldn't do. Is that fair?

Fair? Maybe not. But maybe. Was it something you should have known not to do? Was it just common sense not to do it? Think about your motivation for a minute. Were you trying to get by on a technicality? In court sometimes whether someone is innocent or guilty doesn't matter. Their lawyer can get them freed just based on some rule the police broke or some way the evidence was handled. That's a technicality. It's not about whether the defendant is guilty or not. We all do that sometimes. We don't deal with the real point—did I mess up? Instead we deal with the details—"They didn't say specifically not to go out after midnight. They just said that if I went out for dinner to be back by eleven." You know the games we play to justify our actions. The Bible doesn't let us off the hook on technicalities. It says if you know to do good and you don't do it—it's wrong. Part of growing up is disciplining yourself to do the right thing. You're not a four-year-old anymore that needs your parents to clarify your every action. So, what do you think? Was it fair?

SEE FOR YOURSELF: James 4:17

FAITH

Should my faith make me a stronger person?

David said, "The LORD, who delivered me from the paw of the lion and from the paw of the bear, He will deliver me from the hand of this Philistine." And Saul said to David, "Go, and the LORD be with you!"
1 Sam. 17:37

In some ways it should. We will always have weak and broken places. Part of the strength that faith gives is the strength to face the weaker parts of ourselves. We know God accepts every part of us. There is another kind of strength, though. Our faith in God gives us strength because we know we are never alone. God is always with us, always on our side. Do you remember David from the Old Testament? Goliath ... the slingshot ... When David went to fight Goliath, the people around him said he was too weak. David told them that God had delivered him before and God would deliver him again. David was stronger because of his faith in God. As he lived his life, he saw God help him with the small things. Then, when the big things came along, David knew they would be small to God. David was strong because he believed strongly in God.

Does God reward faith?

Not always immediately. Some people have to go through long, hard times in life before they see the rewards of their faith. But the Bible does say in several places that God prospers people who have faith in Him. Proverbs even says God delivers people who have faith in Him. The trick is holding onto your faith until you see the reward. Weak hearts and proud hearts want to quit too soon sometimes. If we are going to believe, we have to give our whole lives over to it. It's not a thirty-day trial period kind of thing.

SEE FOR YOURSELF: Proverbs 28:25-26

How can I make other people's faith grow?

The truth is, you can't really. Only God can grow faith in people. What you can do is encourage people and teach them. You can love them and let your friendship be a safe place for them to understand God's love. If you will focus on doing those kinds of things, God can use you to grow people's faith in His own way. The Bible talks about it like faith grows in a garden. Some people can plant the seeds. Other people can water the garden, but it's really only God who can make that plant grow. So here's a question for you. If faith was a plant, what kind would it be?

> So then neither he who plants is anything, nor he who waters, but God who gives the increase. Now he who plants and he who waters are one, and each one will receive his own reward according to his own labor.
>
> 1 Cor. 3:7-8

How do you know if someone is a Christian?

You really can't know just by looking at someone whether or not they are a Christian. You might get an idea from watching their actions for a long time, but God works with us at whatever level of faith we come to him. No one else can tell but God whether we have crossed that line of faith. The Bible does give us a criterion, though, to judge ourselves by. You might think that if there were going to be a litmus test for faith it would have to do with keeping rules or not doing bad stuff. The only test the Bible gives, though, is the test of love. Jesus told His disciples that people would know they were His disciples because of their love for each other.

What does it mean to have faith?

It means to believe in something, often when you can't even see it. The writer of Hebrews said that faith is the substance of the things you hope for and the evidence of the things you can't see. God promises to hear our prayers. We can't know that He's doing that until He answers them. But through faith we pray. Our faith is the stuff that tells us to pray or believe even if we aren't sure. We don't know exactly what heaven will be like. We haven't seen it and no one sent us back a postcard (though several prophets tried really hard). Through faith though we have evidence of heaven—because God told us about it and we have faith in Him. Until we see it, our faith is the evidence.

> Now faith is the substance of things hoped for, the evidence of things not seen.
> Hebrews 11:1

How does believing in the gospel change my life now?

The gospel is the good news that God came to earth as Jesus and gave His life so that we can connect with God and experience a relationship with Him like a friendship, only greater. To believe the gospel doesn't only get you a ticket to heaven, it changes your life now! Paul wrote to the Thessalonians about this very thing. He said that the gospel came to them in power, and in the Holy Spirit, and in much assurance. To know that God cares enough for us to seek us out and to sacrifice Himself to build a relationship with us tells us that we are never alone. The Holy Spirit is with us and in us. We are never helpless. God is only the distance of a prayer away. We are also never defeated. The gospel gives us the reassurance that God is working through us, in us, and around us. Believing in the gospel does change our lives.

SEE FOR YOURSELF: 1 Thes. 1:4-5

FAITHFUL–NESS

If you return to Me, and keep My commandments and do them, though some of you were cast out to the farthest part of the heavens, yet I will gather them from there, and bring them to the place which I have chosen as a dwelling for My name.
Neh. 1:8-9

If I turn my back on God, will He turn His back on me?

So you haven't spoken to God in a long time. OK, a really long time. You made this big commitment, told all your family and friends, started going to church, went on a few retreats, sang around a campfire, bought a Bible with your name on it—the whole deal. Then you never followed through. You put the Bible in a drawer, slept in on Sundays, stopped talking to God, and eventually you just turned your back and walked away. It's been a long time—years. The yearning that drew you to God is back, but even bigger, and now there's guilt—the guilt that comes from meeting the Maker of the universe and then trying to live like He doesn't exist. Is God disappointed? Probably. Has He given up on you? Nope. What's next? Return to God. He is kind and compassionate. He will welcome you home. Don't delay—every day lived apart from God is a totally wasted day.

SEE FOR YOURSELF: Joel 2:12-13; Rom. 3:23-24

How do I become a faithful person?

Faithfulness, the way God defines it, is not a stuck-like-glue observance of a bunch of rules you learn in Sunday school. What's going on inside you is more important to God than what you do. So the faithful person obeys, not because he has incredible will-power, but because his heart is turned toward God all the time. When a faithful person fails, she is quick to admit it, talk to Jesus about it, and accept His forgiveness. The faithful person is humble, meaning he doesn't think he can live his life—any part of it—without God.

> He will speak peace to His people and to His saints; but let them not turn back to folly.
> Ps. 85:8

This is the kind of person God promises peace to. Now, having peace doesn't mean everything that happens in your life will be wonderful and you won't ever be sad or get upset. The peace that God gives is a way-down-in-your-gut confidence that everything that happens to you, good or bad, is something He will use to bring you closer to Him and make you more like Him. As your friendship with Jesus grows, this peace will take root in your heart. He promises it will!

SEE FOR YOURSELF: Mic. 5:4-5; John 14:27

Will God leave me if I'm unfaithful to Him?

God had a purpose in mind when He made you. His idea was that you would be His friend, love Him, and do things His way. Somehow, though, it seemed better to you to do things your way. Eventually you found yourself a long way from God. A sheep who wanders astray from the shepherd is in big trouble because the shepherd is the one who keeps him safe and makes sure he has all the things he needs. God is your Shepherd, and when you decided to go your way instead of His, you put some distance between you and the Person who has everything you need. It seemed important to God for you to understand that you have wandered away from Him: "All we like sheep have gone astray." That could be a downer. But this verse is actually part of a very hopeful passage telling what Jesus is like and what He did for the "sheep" who have walked away from God. "He bore the sin of many, and made intercession for the transgressors" (53:12). Now you can find your way back to the Shepherd.

SEE FOR YOURSELF: Ps. 95:7; Isa. 53:6, 12; Jer. 50:6; Ezek. 34:12

Forgiveness or bitterness?
Meet Sareena.

When my mom came home bawling one night, I really flipped out. My mom's an emotional kind of woman, but this time she was crying so hard that she was shaking. She seemed hysterical, and I couldn't get any words out of her. She just kept rocking herself back and forth on the couch, holding her legs tight to her chest, and shaking her head from one side to the other. I knelt beside her on the floor, holding her hand, begging her to tell me. "Mom, please, talk to me. What happened? Where's Dad? What's wrong?" I started crying myself. All I knew was that she and Dad had gone out to dinner (which didn't happen much these days), and Mom came home a wreck and Dad was gone. Something had obviously happened, but WHAT???

The next few hours and days unfolded like a nightmare. At dinner, Dad had broken the news to Mom that "there was someone else." Mom had no idea it was coming. He had been "working late" more and more, but she never suspected this. After twenty-three years of marriage, you just don't do that. It shouldn't happen. I thought it would never happen to me, but there I was, trying to comfort my mom and be strong for her while inside I hated my dad. I hated him.

How could he do this to her? How could he do this to our family? Somewhere between the "I do" and the "till death do us part," it must have gotten old to him. It was pretty simple in my mind. If he treated my mom and me like that, he had no place in either of our lives. Yes, I hated him.

Fast-forward six months. Somehow the stability switch clicked back in place in his head, and Dad came back. He begged my mom to forgive him, and they started counseling with a pastor. It was like one of those warped soap operas where nothing seems real, and all of a sudden, Dad was living at home again. Of course, nothing made sense to me any more, so just add it to the list. Mom took him back? After what he did to her? She forgave him? She let him back in our home? She allowed him back in our lives so he can hurt us again? At this point, my mind went on autopilot, and I stopped feeling.

Do you remember the story about how Jacob wrestled with God? Well that was me, throwing punches, arguing, twisting, screaming, bucking against God. He held me, though. And He started to show me some new things about forgiveness and grace. If God could forgive my dad, and my mom could forgive my dad, well guess whose turn it was.

Talk about a battle of the will. I had no desire to forgive him, none whatsoever. But this choice was not about what I wanted, but about what I had to do. I had to forgive him for his sake and also for mine. I knew that the condition of my heart depended on my choices of attitude.

And so I decided to forgive him. The first time I forgave him it felt so good to let go of that hatred, and it lasted for about ten minutes.

So I forgave him again. And again. And again and again and again and again and again. Jesus said we should forgive up to 490 times. I don't think He really meant that number. I think He was using it to make the point, "Never stop forgiving." And so I forgave my dad dozens of times a day, day in and day out. Over time it got easier, but sometimes those feelings of hatred rose up again. And once again, I'd fight the same battle and have to forgive one more time.

You know, sometimes life is rotten. At those times we find out what we're made of.

FAITHFUL-NESS OF GOD

> Also with the lute I will praise You—and Your faithfulness, O my God!
> Ps. 71:22

Is God faithful even in the bad times?

A mom and dad lose their only daughter two days before her fifteenth birthday. She was riding in a car that was hit by a drunk driver. Devastated, they start the long process of grieving for a child who wasn't supposed to die before they did. Several months later they come to your school and tell how difficult the last few months have been. The pain has been incredible for them. Then they say something that grabs you. "All we have left is God. We couldn't have made it without Him. He has been so faithful." You begin to understand what His faithfulness is. He is helping those parents just make it from day to day. He is giving them hope that they won't hurt forever. He is sending them people to give them compassion. On days when they hurt so much they can hardly breathe, He stays right beside them. He carries them when they cannot walk and gives them smiles when they thought smiles were gone forever. Don't wait for an emergency to find out how faithful He is. He's faithful in your good times, too. Be on the lookout for your faithful Father.

SEE FOR YOURSELF: Neh. 1:5; Ps. 36:5

FEAR

What should I do when life gets scary?

00. 00. 29

There is probably more than one answer to
that question. If you're being chased by a herd
of wildebeests, then you should "RUN! RUN
FOR YOUR LIFE!" Jungle animals probably don't live in
your neighborhood, though, do they? Most things in life that are
scary are not dangerous. They are just overwhelming. They stretch us out of our
comfort zone. We aren't really sure it'll be OK or that we'll succeed. It's stuff like
tests and families and new relationships. There was a king in the Old Testament
that took his fears to God. His name was Jehoshaphat. God told him not to be
afraid because the battle he was facing was God's, not his. That's really true for
you, too. If you're God's child, then He's fighting on your side. Trust Him to fight the
battle and you use your common sense to keep yourself out of the firing line.

> And he said, "Listen, all you of Judah and you inhabitants of Jerusalem, and you, King Jehoshaphat! Thus says the Lord to you: 'Do not be afraid nor dismayed because of this great multitude, for the battle is not yours, but God's.'"
> 2 Chron. 20:15

My mom says, "Face your fears and it'll make you stronger." What's up with that?

Probably because once we face our fears we have one less thing to be afraid of.
Fear can take control of our lives. You might remember the story about the
Hebrews escaping from Egypt. God brought them through some amazing miracles
over and over again. Yet, when they finally got to the border of the land God had
promised them they were afraid to go in! Can you believe that? After all that God
had done right in front of them? That's how strong fear can be. When the people
finally entered the land, they were led by a soldier named Joshua. God reminded
Joshua to not give into his fear. Why? Because it was God's power that was fighting, not theirs. Maybe facing fears gets us to where we can see God's power—and
that makes us stronger.

SEE FOR YOURSELF: Deut. 3:21-22

FEARING GOD

Why should we fear the Lord?

Think about it. Some people worship their money. Some people worship their cars. Some people worship their careers. Maybe you don't see them bow down to these things, and maybe they don't call them "god" but they think about them constantly, and all their effort and energy go into making them bigger or better or both. That's worship, or "fear," indicating what they hold to be most important in life. But the car eventually ends up in the junkyard. The money gets spent. The career ends in retirement. Other people worship things that they think are God. They honor the forces of nature or the stars. Or they pray to a statue or a city. Their rituals make them feel better, but they're still worshiping things. God is totally different. He is a Person. He will live forever. He doesn't rust, wear out, or run out. When everything on earth has decayed or burned up or blown away, He will still be running the show. And the people who chose to worship Him (instead of their cars) will still be singing His praises. Even when the earth has passed away, there will be worship in heaven for all of eternity. Awesome.

SEE FOR YOURSELF: Ps. 22:27; Zeph. 2:11; Rev. 15:4

FEELINGS

"God is Spirit, and those who worship Him must worship in spirit and truth."
John 4:24

Sometimes I feel like I really, REALLY believe in God and other times it feels like He's far away and not real, like a cartoon or a movie or something. Why, and what do I do about it?

Feelings are both good and bad. If we had to base our faith on our feelings, we'd have a different faith every time our mood changed, wouldn't we? It's just a good thing that God's nature doesn't change as much as our feelings do. The Bible says that God is a spirit. That's why it's hard to know whether we're close to Him or not. We're used to people that we can see and touch. We can look in their eyes and know if we're OK with them, or if they are mad, or whatever. It's different with God. We have to believe Him when He says He'll never leave us, and that He will always love us. We have to believe it even when it doesn't feel like it's true. With the way life goes, we definitely feel alone sometimes. The Bible says that we must worship God in spirit and in truth. So what do you do about it when God feels far away? You worship Him not based on how you feel, but on the truth of His Word. He is right there with you. Believe that truth and let your feelings catch up when they are ready.

FORGIVE-NESS

First be reconciled to your brother, and then come and offer your gift. Matt. 5:23-24

If somebody does something wrong to you and then asks God to forgive them, do they still have to make it up to you?

They don't HAVE to. They can choose not to. But, yes, they should. That's what we should all do for each other. When we do something to damage our relationships, we should go back and try to amend the situation. In fact, in one of Jesus' famous sermons, the Sermon on the Mount, He said that if you get to the altar and remember that you have a broken relationship, you should leave the altar and make that relationship right, then come back and do your business with God. Do you get that? God said to deal with your friends and family before you come to Him. That's not because they are more important than God. It's because part of our obedience to God is to love the people around us well. So if you have done something wrong, you should ask forgiveness of God AND go to the other person and make it right. If someone does something wrong to you, they SHOULD do the same thing.

How many times do I have to forgive the same person?

Jesus' disciple, Peter, asked that same question. It sounds like a fair one. Jesus' answer seemed a little less than fair. "Up to seventy times seven." Now in the first place, who can count up to 490, to see when to stop letting someone off the hook. In the second place, what Jesus was really saying was, forever. Seven was a number that the ancient Hebrews threw around the way we say millions. We don't mean literal millions. So the simplest answer to your question is, as many times as you need to. Think about this, though. Are you having to forgive this person over and over because they are trying but messing up? Or are you having to forgive them because they are hurting you and don't care? Don't take Jesus' words to mean you shouldn't confront this person about their sin. It just means that holding a grudge is never going to be the smart way to go.

> Then Peter came to Him and said, "Lord, how often shall my brother sin against me, and I forgive him? Up to seven times?" Jesus said to him, "I do not say to you, up to seven times, but up to seventy times seven."
> Matt. 18:21-22

Why is forgiveness important?

If you've been hurt by a friend, you've probably got some big scars. The truth is, you've only got a couple of options about how to handle your pain. You can look at your scars every day and let them remind you how hurt you've been. You can think about them all the time. You can spend hours plotting revenge or deciding what kind of snide remark to make the next time you see your friend. You can tell everybody else how badly you were treated. You can hold a grudge. Eventually that grudge will turn to hatred and bitterness. And you won't ever be satisfied. You'll just end up rehearsing your pain day after day, and it will finally eat you up. You'll regret how much of your life was spent wallowing in misery. The other option is a combination of two powerful expressions: grace and forgiveness. Grace means forgiving a friend even when he or she doesn't deserve it. After that, live your forgiveness. Your words and your actions will show that you have truly forgiven. The first option keeps you in chains. The second one sets you free. Forgiveness frees your heart to love your friend the way God loves you.

SEE FOR YOURSELF: Eph. 4:32; Col. 3:13; 1 John 4:7

FORGIVENESS OF GOD

> For You, Lord, are good, and ready to forgive, and abundant in mercy to all those who call upon You.
> Psalm 86:5

Why would God forgive me?

Because God is forgiving. It's easy to think sometimes that God loves us or forgives us because we are just so stinkin' nice. But that's really not it. He forgives us because it is His nature to forgive. If He forgave us for any other reason then we might get forgiven sometimes, but not others. God's nature is the only thing that doesn't change. Too bad our nature isn't like that. One of the prayers David wrote, which is recorded in Psalms 86, says, "You Lord are good and ready to forgive, and abundant in mercy." David's comfort was not in his own goodness, but in God's nature. That is our comfort as well. And that is why as long as you go to God and ask His forgiveness sincerely, He will forgive you.

Will God always forgive me?

"Just one more chance, please, please. I promise to get it right this time." Ever said that to your parents, or to your teacher, or to God? While your parents or teacher may tire of saying, "OK, one more time, give it a shot," God never will. Even when you are tired of trying, God will lift you up, give you a pep talk, and tell you to try again. When you don't deserve a second chance, God will let you have one. He loves you so much that He will never give up on you. He longs for you, and He delights in welcoming you back when you've blown it. So if you've given up on God, feel like you've used up all your chances, messed up really big this time—there is great news: You belong to the God who gives you chance after chance. Run to Him.

SEE FOR YOURSELF: Ps. 130:4; Hos. 14:4; Luke 7:48; 1 John 1:9; Job 33:29

Does God have to forgive me or does He really want to?

In Luke 15, Jesus tells the story of a guy who wanted to live his own life. So he asked his dad for the money he was supposed to inherit later and left home. Of course, his money eventually ran out, and he had to get the worst job he could think of—feeding pigs. He was so hungry he wished he could eat some of what they were having. Finally, he got tired of living that way and decided to go home. He didn't expect things to be exactly like they were before he left, but he thought his dad might give him a job as a servant.

His dad surprised him. He saw him coming and ran down the road to meet him. His father was so excited to see him that he threw a big party.

Jesus told this story to give you a picture of just how ready God is to forgive you. He's like that dad, standing on the porch, looking down the road for you—running toward you when He sees you coming. He doesn't forgive you because He has to. He forgives you because, like that dad, He loves you, and what He wants more than anything else is to have you home with Him.

> For You, Lord, are good, and ready to forgive, and abundant in mercy to all those who call upon You.
>
> **Ps. 86:5**

SEE FOR YOURSELF: Ps. 145:8; Mark 11:25-26; Luke 15:11-32; I John 1:9

Can God forgive the sins of my past?

What kind of past do you have? Decent? Wild? Funny? Tragic? Wonderful? Boring? Whatever the case, everybody has a past. No one just sprouts up on earth at forty years old. Everyone you know either has grown up or will grow up. Sometimes people have a hard time with the Lord because of things they've done or said or thought (or things they haven't) in the past. Guess what? It doesn't matter. When you confess your sins to God and ask Him to forgive you, He does. Forever. When you pray to Him, He thinks of you as totally innocent. It's as if you never did any-thing wrong. That's because when He looks at you, He sees Jesus. Never be afraid to go to the Lord because of your past. He's in the business of making bad things turn out good, ugly things turn out beautiful, hurts turn into healing. Start fresh with Him.

SEE FOR YOURSELF: Is. 43:25, 54:4; 65:17; 2 Cor. 5:17; Heb. 10:17; 1 John . 5:17; Rev. 21:5

If God is going to forgive me anyway, does it really matter if I do wrong stuff?

> What shall we say then? Shall we continue in sin that grace may abound? Certainly not! How shall we who died to sin live any longer in it?
> Romans 6:1-2

Yes, yes, yes! It does matter. There's a big hole that people sometimes fall into called "keeping score." When they fall into this hole they think of God as a big, holy scoreboard keeping tabs on their rights and wrongs. Are you in that hole? Hellooooo down there! We'll throw you a rope and pull you up! If it was all about doing right and wrong and seeing how much we can get away with, then, no it wouldn't matter if we obey God or not. But that's not what it's about. It's about having a relationship with a God who loves and expects us to (1) believe in Him and (2) show our love for Him by obeying Him. Think about it this way. Let's say you're dating someone exclusively. You expect them to be faithful to you. Why? Because that's the nature of your relationship. What if they weren't faithful and you found out and confronted them? What if they looked sheepish and said, "Well, I knew you'd forgive me if I got caught anyway. . . . ." It wouldn't work, would it? Because it's about the relationship you have, not whether they got caught. It works that way in our relationship with God. Paul answered this very question. He said, "Should we sin more so we can receive more of God's grace?" NO CHANCE!

Dealing with death? Meet Cole.

I think it was the hardest thing I've ever had to deal with. At fourteen, it's not the kind of thing I felt prepared to face. When we got the news that Kristen had taken her own life, every emotion came crashing in on me—grief, anger, bitterness, depression, pain. But the worst thing I felt was guilt.

Kristen had everything going for her. She was cute, popular, and got good grades. She came from a solid family and seemed to have a happy home life. I'm not sure what made her do it, but I should have known it was coming. We all should have known it. She gave little clues, but why would we think anything of them?

I clearly remember sitting around the lunch table one day, and Kristen just made a little comment about how she didn't want to live anymore. Wouldn't it be great not to have to deal with all this mess and just be away from it all? Somebody laughed, and we all brushed it off. The conversation continued as we talked about Mr. Grey's so unfair math test and how awful it was of him. Who would have known?

Her parents never saw it coming either. I think that might have made it harder for them, and naturally they blamed themselves. I started having nightmares. It started with dreams that she was still alive, and I thought I could even see her face and hear her voice. Then I started dreaming of being there with her, screaming for her to stop. I felt so haunted that I stopped eating regularly and couldn't sleep well at all.

The school brought in a counselor, a nice guy around my dad's age. He talked to each of us, her close friends, one-on-one. You know, for as much as I always made fun of counselors, this guy was really cool. He found a way to get me talking. He helped me process my guilt. He knew that I felt responsible for her death, and we talked through it.

Yes, we should have seen it coming or at least suspected it. But we were only fourteen. There's only so much we can do. If we ever suspect something like that going on, then we can approach an adult, a parent or teacher or youth pastor, and at least tell them what we're worried about. It was my first step toward healing. As my new counselor kept meeting with me, he helped me cope with Kristen's death with the help of Scripture. Suddenly, verses about forgiveness and God's power and death all came alive. This book that had seemed so dead was giving me the answers for life.

No, I'll never forget Kristen. As her friend, her death is seared into my mind forever. But I do know that there is a loving God who left me His Word and His hope, that no matter what happens in this life, we are never separated from the love of Christ.

What if I did something bad right before I died and didn't have time to ask God to forgive me, but I was sorry anyway?

For by grace you have been saved through faith, and that not of yourselves; it is the gift of God. Ephes. 2:8

When we put our faith in what God did through Jesus we receive God's grace. He pours that grace over our whole lives. He accepts not only what we have done, but what we will do. He adopts us as his children. We aren't teetering on the edge of getting kicked out of the family if we don't say the right thing at the right time. Ephesians says we are saved by God's grace through our faith, and even our faith is a gift from God. If you did something bad right before you died, God would have already known you were going to do it. If you're a Christian, then He's already accepted you as His kid and that's not going to change because you messed up at the worst possible moment. Your relationship with God is about faith, glorifying Him, worshiping Him, and enjoying Him—not about keeping a track record of your wrongs and rights.

FORTUNE-TELLING

00. 00. 29   00. 00. 30

Do fortune tellers know as much as God?

Asking soothsayers (fortune-tellers), for advice is listed here as a sinful thing that makes the Lord very angry. It is an insult to God to believe that a human being can look into the future and know the plans of the Lord. His ways and thoughts are so far above our thoughts. (See Isaiah 55:8-9.) Why pay money to speak to someone who will just give you his or her best guess?

Instead, get in touch with the Maker, the Master Designer, the One who *really* knows everything. Ask Him for advice. He's been waiting to help you make sense of it all. His guidance will not be confusing or misleading. He will not stut-ter or fumble. He will clearly lead your steps. So go ahead, stop any time, any place, and ask God for His advice. Listen when He answers you through His Word or in your heart. Then follow through—do what He says, walk where He leads. You can count on Him to know exactly what will happen in your future. He's never wrong.

SEE FOR YOURSELF: Lev 20:6; Deut. 18:10; .20:6; Is. 40:13-14; Rom. 11:33

Ancient kings often used astrologers and magicians as advisors to help them make important decisions. Believe it or not, they tried to predict the future by "reading the body parts of animals they used for sacrifice." Can you imagine bas-ing a major decision in your life on the way a sheep's liver looks?
Genesis 41:8

FRIENDSHIPS

> He who covers a transgression seeks love, but he who repeats a matter separates friends.
> Prov. 17:9

How can I keep from making enemies?

First rule to remember, you can't really control anyone else. So if someone decides to be your enemy for some arbitrary reason (jealousy, superficial stuff, etc.) you can't make them stop. But, it's important to do what you can. The second thing to remember is that the best way to not make enemies is by not being one. Proverbs teaches us that a person who keeps a "transgression" to herself is a loving person but a person that talks about other people's mistakes separates friends. Know what that means? Keep your mouth shut and your nose in your own business. It won't guarantee that you won't have enemies, but it will sure cut down on the number.

How can I be a good friend?

Good people usually make good friends, but one trait that sticks out in great friendships is loyalty. People get to the end of their lives and look back at the friends they've had. The ones they treasure are the ones who have stuck by them all the way. Being a loyal friend can be hard work. It means that you're committed even when it's tough. You look past the little things. You forgive and forgive and forgive. You go the extra mile. Being interruptible is part of being loyal. Good friends are the ones you can call in the middle of the night, the ones who will come pick you up when your car dies, and the ones who would drop everything and rush right over if you needed them. Being loyal means that you keep quiet when others want to gossip, and you defend your friend's honor and integrity. If you choose your friends wisely, being loyal to them will be easy, and your loyalty will be returned. According to Proverbs 3, people will see your loyalty and admire you for it.

SEE FOR YOURSELF: Prov.. 3:1-4; 17:17; 18:24; 27:5

Can true friends cause us pain?

Yes. It's not pleasant. It's not even fair. It's not the way we want life to be, but it's true. Even our closest and truest friends can cause us pain. In fact, the more we love the person who hurts us, the more it hurts. King David must have known exactly what it felt like because in Psalm 55 he wrote it was not his enemy that had hurt him. If it had been he could bear it. "But it was you, a man my equal, My companion." Why do our friends hurt us? Because life gets messy and no matter how much we like someone we are different, and we are sinful, and we are sometimes self-centered. But there is life after pain even if we are a little more distrustful. Real friends will take the risk to sit down and talk about the problem and think of ways to be friends again.

> For it is not an enemy who reproaches me; Then I could bear it. . . . But it was you, a man my equal, My companion and my acquaintance. We took sweet counsel together, And walked to the house of God in the throng.
>
> Psalm 55:12-14

My parents say I can't hang out with the bad kids. Didn't Jesus hang out with bad people and help them be good?

Jesus did do that. In fact He was accused of being a partier because He hung out with—not bad people necessarily—but people who needed His help. I bet I can explain your parents' concern, though. There is a verse in Romans that says something like, "Don't let the world shape you into its mold. Let God shape your heart and attitude." That's what your parents are concerned about. Who will affect who the most? Will your friends affect you or will you affect them? And think about this, what is your reason for having friends? Are you just trying to change them? I don't think your friends would be too happy to think that the only reason you were around is to make them better people. It's important that you know people that you can be a good influence on. It's JUST as important that you hang out with people who can be a good influence on you. Don't use "making a difference" as an excuse to have the friends you want. Be more honest than that. What do you really want out of your friendships? Talk to your parents about that balance and let God have his say as well in your decision. Friends are a much bigger deal than most people give them credit for. We act like making them is no big deal, but THEY really make US.

SEE FOR YOURSELF: Romans 12:2

What should I do if my friends are arguing?

Your friends are arguing? Get out of it. Proverbs 26:17 says it would be better to grab a dog by the ears than to take part in your friends' argument. The middle of your friends' argument is a lose-lose situation. The best that could happen is that they will make up, and only one of them will be mad at you. Politely tell them that you love them both too much to be pulled into their disagreement. No matter what you think, it's best to keep your mouth shut. They have to resolve things themselves. You can't relay information. Refuse to take sides. Let them both know that you want to spend time with them, but until this whole thing blows over, you have to step aside. Let them work it out. You will be spared lots of time and heartache if you allow them to be responsible for making things right.

SEE FOR YOURSELF: Prov. 11:12; 13:3; 17:27; 27:12

> He who passes by and meddles in a quarrel not his own is like one who takes a dog by the ears.
> Prov. 26:17

Since I became a Christian, my friends treat me different, like I'm some kind of holy-rollin' freak. How can I get them to see that I'm still just me?

All you can do is keep on living and being yourself. Even though it doesn't feel good right now, stick to your guns, spend time around them just being yourself. Joke with them. Invite them with you to places. There's a verse in Romans that is very wise. It says, "If it is possible, as much as depends on you, live peaceably with all men." That verse recognizes that some things are out of your control. You can't control how your friends think (If it is possible . . .), you can only be yourself and let them find you out in their own time (as much as depends on you). Eventually either they are going to refuse to see you and you'll find new friends, or they are going to realize that your friendship hasn't changed. If it's important to you to keep these friendships, then don't get frustrated and walk away. Just be true to who you are and hang out even though it's a little uncomfortable right now.

SEE FOR YOURSELF: Romans 12:18

How do I really know if someone is my friend?

They don't walk away when things get hard. Friendship is different than acquaintances. When someone is our acquaintance we socialize with them. We know their name. We can laugh together. But they aren't who we'd call when life falls apart. When someone is your friend, you can call them no matter how bad things are. The Bible says a friend loves at ALL times. With every relationship things get bumpy sometimes. Friendships are no different. Things happen. People get grumpy. Friends say things they wish they hadn't. But a true friend can work through those things and find better times together. If someone walks away from you, you have two options. You can let them go and tell yourself that if they are a true friend they'll come back. You can also go after them, being a true friend, and see if they walk away again. Then you'll know if what you've got is a friendship or an acquaintance.

> A friend loves at all times, and a brother is born for adversity.
> Prov. 17:17

Why do my parents act like my friends are dangerous just because they don't go to church or believe different stuff?

Believe it or not, your parents are probably scared more than anything else. They are probably scared that you haven't become really solid in your faith and your lifestyle yet. If you hang out with people who are making different choices, they could easily think that you might make those choices too. It can seem silly to you for your parents to be worried about that. Remember this, though. Your parents were once your age. They can look back at the choices they wish they had made differently. They want to save you from making bad choices that you'll have to look back on with regret. Your parents know that who you hang out with will influence your decisions. Can you blame them for being a little cautious?

SEE FOR YOURSELF: Deut. 13:6-8

I don't always get along with my friends, but even when we fight, we end up better friends. What makes that happen?

As iron sharpens iron, so a man sharpens the countenance of his friend. Prov. 27:17

The Bible describes exactly what you are saying. It says that friends sharpen each other just like iron sharpens iron. Have you ever seen iron clashing against iron? Sparks fly. Friction happens. In the end, though, the edge is sharpened. If the iron is in the form of a tool, the tool is a better one. That's exactly what happens with you and your friends. People face conflict at one time or another. Even the best of friends get grumpy or have disagreements. But when people care enough about each other to not walk away, to listen to each other, and to be committed to the relationship—they learn something about themselves and about love. They end up better friends. I hope you'll always work through your conflicts with your friends. If you do, then you'll always have friends who will help you be an even better friend than you are right now.

What is a true friend?

Jesus gives two examples of what makes someone a friend. First He says there is no greater friendship than laying down your life for someone. That's for sure because that is exactly what He did for us. He also says that we are His friend if we obey Him. Does that mean we have to be obedient to all of our homies to be a true friend? Yes and no. Our friends are not our authorities. Jesus is. So no, we don't obey our friends like that. But yes, when you're a true friend to someone, what they think matters. You respect who they are and you don't do stuff around them that will make them uncomfortable. In other words, you take your friends' wants, needs and preferences into consideration. So from the big survival issues to the details, a true friend does put aside his own way for his friends.

SEE FOR YOURSELF: John 15:13-15

GENDER

Male or female: Does it really make a difference?

God made two types of people—men and women. He made us with different body shapes, different emotional makeups, and different strengths and weaknesses. He is displeased when someone tries to go against His design. He has told us that it is a plan and a purpose for both men and women, and it's sinful to dress up and pretend to be the opposite of what you are. People do it. Most often these people are confused—maybe rejected or angry or hurt, too. They need God's love. Read Deuteronomy 22:5 carefully. God does not hate a cross-dresser. God hates cross-dressing. It is sin that grieves Him. Be glad that God made you the way you are. He has a plan for you as a strong, godly man or woman. He makes no mistakes.

SEE FOR YOURSELF: 1 Cor. 6:9

> A woman shall not wear anything that pertains to a man, nor shall a man put on a woman's garment, for all who do so are an abomination to the Lord your God.
> Deut. 22:5

How come some preachers wear robes and don't get married?

Probably the robes that some priests and preachers wear came from the original clothes that the original Jewish priests were told by God to wear. A reason that priests or preachers sometimes still wear robes today is so that they can get up and teach with as little distraction as possible. No one's going to be noticing their new suit or whether their shirt is ironed. Hopefully people will just listen to what they say. As for the marriage thing, it's different with different religions and denominations. There is a verse in one of Paul's letters that says that it's easier to be devoted only to God if you are unmarried. That makes sense, right? If you're married you have to be devoted to your spouse and family. The church that made the decision to have its priests not get married was probably thinking about something like that when they decided.

SEE FOR YOURSELF: 1 Cor. 7:32-34

Why do they say girls are the "weaker sex"?

That phrase actually comes from a letter in the New Testament that Peter wrote. He tells husbands to treat their wives with honor as with a "weaker vessel." Peter did live in a time when women were treated as if they were worth less than men. They couldn't own property. They couldn't take part in politics or leadership in the traditional church. So, they were weaker—they had fewer rights and less power. But Peter had walked with Jesus. He was one of the twelve disciples. And Jesus treated women with respect. Jesus didn't buy into the cultural status thing. Notice the point of this verse—"being heirs together of the grace of life, that your prayers may not be hindered." Peter was making men and women equal—a radical thought in his day. He was telling them to worship together!

Don't get caught up in gender wars—look on all your brothers and sisters in Christ as equals, so that your prayers may not be hindered.

> Husbands, likewise, dwell with them with understanding, giving honor to the wife, as to the weaker vessel, and as being heirs together of the grace of life, that your prayers may not be hindered.
> 1 Peter 3:7

Honoring God by caring for myself? Meet Claire.

I'm not quite sure how it all began. What started as a health kick turned in to much more. As an athlete, I tried to stay trim, and as a girl, I was very conscious of how I looked. I guess I had always been considered pretty, and I knew that part of keeping that image meant I had to stay thin. I saw some of my girlfriends struggling with eating disorders. It rubbed off. At first, I just started cutting back at dinner. I ate a little less and a little less each day. Within a month, I had a good "diet" going (so I thought). For breakfast, I might eat half a bowl of Cheerios (but mostly just move them around in my milk). For lunch, it was always the same thing: half a carton of fat free yogurt and a few sips of Dr. Pepper. In the growing body of a fifteen-year-old girl, that's not too much. By 4:00 every afternoon when practice started, I sometimes gave in and ate part of an apple. That might keep me going during practice, I reasoned. It was a lot of running. To be honest, a lot of times I blacked out and got really dizzy while I was running. I was still pushing my body really hard because I wanted to be the fastest girl on the team. When I felt well enough, I was. If I had worked hard enough in practice, I might reward myself with a whole banana for dinner.

Slowly it had gotten out of control, and then I started paying the price. I was obsessed with my eating. I couldn't eat even a small meal without extreme feelings of guilt and an overwhelming desire to work out really hard. I had to burn off the fat. I cried when I thought I might be gaining weight. It was out of control. Side effects started showing up. I was tired and weak a lot and could barely stay awake in class. My hair and nails started to get brittle. I wasn't the fastest girl on the team any more. This was the price I paid to wear a size 2 instead of a 6.

Fortunately, someone was paying attention—my mom. She watched me like a hawk. Of course, I didn't want to hear anything from my mom about my eating, but I came to a point where I needed help and I knew it. I was struggling with control issues and eating issues and felt so overwhelmed that I finally turned to her. She had been praying hard for me. She brought me the most encouraging words of all, the words of God.

As a child of the King, I find perfect acceptance in Him. To abuse my body by not feeding it is a sin against myself and against God. Being obsessed with my weight takes my focus off where it should be, on Christ and on others, and puts it totally on myself. I had been terribly selfish and had gotten caught up in something that doesn't matter as much as I had thought. How I look doesn't change who I am.

Even as I began to pray for help to change, I knew it wouldn't be simple. God used my mom again here, too. She helped me figure out a balanced diet, since I had lost any concept of what a balanced diet was like. She encouraged me and even pushed me to eat well. Not only do I feel better physically and spiritually—now I'm also the fastest girl on the team every practice.

GOD

> And the Lord was sorry that He had made man on the earth, and He was grieved in His heart.
>
> Gen. 6:6

Does God ever get sad?

The Bible does tell us about a time that God was sad. In fact, He actually grieved, like you do after someone dies. It was after the story of Adam and Eve, when sin entered the world. People kept messing up and God kept saying, "No, do life this way." It was sort of like when you see a mom trying to teach her little toddler not to grab the stuff off of the coffee table. God was training humanity. Just before He finally started over with Noah, the Bible says that God was sorry He had made man, that He was grieved in His heart. That must have been a really sad moment for God. He gave people the choice to obey, but asked them to love Him. But they didn't. God made us in His image. This is one way we are like Him. It hurts not to be loved. That doesn't make God weak. He doesn't fall apart over emotions like we do. But He's not a robot. He does feel things.

Is it possible to just forget about God?

In Isaiah 51, the prophet quotes God as saying, "You forget the Lord your Maker." So yes, it seems that people can forget about God. But it's not something that can be done lightly. We usually forget about God when life is going so well that we don't think we need help with anything. We also sometimes forget about God when we keep ourselves too busy and we don't ever sit still. God's voice is one that we hear the best when we are quiet all the way through. If we never let ourselves be quiet, then we can forget what His voice sounds like . . . for a while.

SEE FOR YOURSELF: Isaiah 51:12-13

100

Is listening to my "gut" the same as listening to God?

People talk a lot about doing a "gut check." In one sense it's a great thing to know how you really feel about something instead of doing what everyone else thinks you should do. It's also good to have that quiet moment to let God talk to you. Be careful, though. What your gut says and what God says don't always sync up. When Paul wrote the Galatians, he warned them that our spirit fights against our flesh. That means the spiritual part of us that wants to do right fights with the part of us that wants to do whatever we want. Be sure you go by your "gut" only after you've prayed and listened for God's "gut" on your decision.

> I say then: Walk in the Spirit, and you shall not fulfill the lust of the flesh. For the flesh lusts against the Spirit, and the Spirit against the flesh; and these are contrary to one another, so that you do not do the things that you wish.
> Gal. 5:16-17

Is there anything that God can't handle?

Hard. You know all about hard. It's hard to juggle school, a part-time job, and chores at home. It's hard when the game is tied and you miss a free throw. It's hard when you sit down to take a final and realize you should have paid attention in class all year. It's hard when a grandparent dies. Sometimes, when things are hard for us, we assume they're hard for God, too. They aren't. Nothing is too hard for God. His best stuff happens when all hope is gone. He parts the sea for people who don't have a way out. He gives babies to women who can't have any. He saves the souls of people who deserve death. Think about the hard times, the last second, the darkest hour, the deepest hole. They are "mission impossible" for us. Invite Him into your hard stuff. Every bit of it is "mission possible" for Him.

SEE FOR YOURSELF: Gen. 18:13-14;.Num. 11:23; Matt. 19:26; Mark 10:27

Is there anything God can't do?

Numbers 11 is a powerful chapter! It starts out with the Israelites complaining about their troubles. They were grumbling to Moses that they didn't have any meat to eat. They complained that they had all the fish they wanted in Egypt and that they were sick of having only manna to eat. God heard their cry and told Moses to tell them to purify themselves because He was going to send meat. Moses replied by asking God how such a feat was possible because there were 600,000 men alone to feed. Moses knew that all the meat from their animals wouldn't be enough to feed them. That's when the Lord replied, "Has the LORD's arm been shortened? " In other words, "I can do anything!" Let this verse encourage you today. Nothing is beyond reach with God on your side, because He is the One who can do anything. What's your need today? Do you need a miracle? He's just waiting for you to bring that need to Him. In 2 Peter 1:3 God promises to give us "all things that pertain to life and godliness" to live a life that pleases Him. That includes things that pertain to our spiritual, physical, emotional, financial, and other needs. In fact, if something affects you, God wants to be right there. He is El Shaddai—the God who is more than enough! He is bigger than any problem you can encounter. Begin to seek Him first and watch Him give you everything you need. He promises that He can do anything!

> And the Lord said to Moses, "Has the LORD's arm been shortened? Now you shall see whether what I say will happen to you or not."
> Num. 11:23

SEE FOR YOURSELF: Matt. 19:26; Mark 9:23; 10:27; Luke 18:27; Rom. 8:32

When does God have time to get everything done?

God is outside of time. It's hard for us to imagine, much less, understand. But he is not restricted the way humans are. Who blew the wind through your hair this morning? Who brought the sun over the horizon once again? Who changed the seasons while you weren't even looking? It was God! The One who is always at work. While you slept, He was preparing your day. While you haven't noticed, He is ordering your life. He is strengthening your gifts and giving you ideas about what you really have to do. We have downtime, unproductive days, and mental blocks. We take vacations, and naps, and study hall. We can go for days and not accomplish one thing. Not God. He is always at work. Always creating, always protecting, always loving.

SEE FOR YOURSELF: Job 23:9; Ps. 121:3-4; John 5:17

How is God different from people?

Do you know anyone who has never broken a promise? It's a fact: Somewhere along the line, everyone is going to break a promise. Maybe they didn't mean to and they're terribly sorry, but for some reason they just couldn't keep their word. That can hurt. The Bible tells us that God is not like people. Aren't you glad that He doesn't break any of His promises? God's Word tells us that Christ says yes to all His promises for you. And all we have to do is say Amen (or, literally, "Let it be") to that promise. If God said it, He'll do it. If He spoke it, He'll bring it to pass. God cannot lie. He is not human. He's not going to lie, and He's not going to change His mind. Do you know what that means? All the promises of the Bible are for you. He's not going to forget one of them. You've been promised not only eternal life, but also "all things that pertain to life and godliness" here on earth (2 Pet. 1:3). Personalize every one of His promises for yourself because He is the One who always keeps His promises!

> God is not a man, that He should lie, nor a son of man, that He should repent. Has He said, and will He not do? Or has He spoken, and will He not make it good?
> **Num. 23:19**

SEE FOR YOURSELF: Josh. 23:15; 1 Kin. 8:56; 2 Cor 1:20

Does God want me to be with Him?

You know what it feels like to be chosen. Remember in grade school when your gym class picked teams for sports? Remember when you got chosen pretty close to the beginning? Or maybe you were the last one chosen and you remember that sting. Regardless of what happened to you then, God chose you. And He chose you first. He chose you for just one reason—He loves you. He's crazy about you. He wants you on His team because He doesn't want to be apart from you. That's cool! It's awesome that God chose you. He can choose anybody He wants and He chose you. This shows you how much He wants you with Him. He wants to be with you, too.

SEE FOR YOURSELF: Ex. 22:31; Deut. 14:2; 1 Chr 16; Is. 49:7; 1 Pet. 2:9

Does God care if I put other people or events before Him?

God is a jealous God—that's the bottom line. He wants to be number one in your life above everything: your boyfriend/girlfriend, your job, your family, TV, music, your friends—the list goes on. There's nothing wrong with having things, but don't allow things to have you! You may not bow down and worship a physical idol you've constructed in your bedroom, but once you've placed someone or something above God, that person, place, or thing becomes an article of worship—an idol. Be careful. That idol will even-tually let you down. Nothing can fill the place of God in your life. Remember the story of Abraham and how he put God first in his life. God was so important to him that he was willing to kill Isaac and sacrifice him to the Lord. God has that kind of love for you. You're that important to Him. Where is God on your priority list? Check your heart and make Him first in your life today. He wants to be close to you. In fact, He created you to have fellowship with Him. And His Word says that if you seek Him first, He'll bless you. Be blessed today!

You shall not bow down to [carved images] nor serve them. For I, the LORD your God, am a jealous God. Deut. 5:9

SEE FOR YOURSELF: Gen. 22:1-18; Deut. 4:24; 5:9; Josh. 24:19-20; Matt. 6:33; Mark 12:30

How can I uncover the mystery of God?

To say that God is mysterious is to say that we don't fully understand Him. We don't understand how He creates or how He makes decisions. His timing seems slow to us. Heaven is a big mystery, and all those miracles, well, we just don't get it. There are so many aspects of God that we can't totally grasp. That's where Colossians 2:2-3 comes in. Paul writes that Christ is the key to God's mystery. Jesus physically came to this earth and through His ministry began to unveil the mysteries of God. Paul also writes in 1 Corinthians 13:12 that "now we see in a mirror, dimly, but then face to face." As you grow stronger in your relationship with the Lord, you'll begin to know Him more and more. But even when you're 90 years old and have walked with Him every day, there will still be magnificent mysteries about Him. He's that big. Do you have faith, even in the mystery of God?

SEE FOR YOURSELF: Deut. 29:29; Job 11:7-8; 1 Cor. 2:7; 13:12; Col. 2:2, 3

Does God have favorites?

Imagine everyone different—but equal. No rich, no poor. No one more beautiful. No school better than your school. No house bigger than your house. No one chosen because they have more stuff. No favorites. Everyone accepted the same. Everyone loved completely. It's hard for us to imagine, but that's exactly the way it is with God. He loves the kid you can't stand to sit next to just as much as He loves you. He loves you as much as He loves the most popular kid in your school. The world uses labels like "VIP" or "Executive" to denote status. God is not impressed. He made each one of us different and unique, but loves us all the same.

> [God] is not partial to princes, nor does He regard the rich more than the poor; for they are all the work of His hands.
>
> Job 34:19

SEE FOR YOURSELF: Matt. 7:8; Acts 13:39; Gal. 2:6

Where did God come from? Did he have a beginning?

This is the history the Bible gives about God: In the beginning God. That's all we know. When you read the whole Bible and put all the pieces together, basically it looks like God has always been and always will be. Here in our world we think of everything in terms of time. The earth revolves, and we call it a day. The earth goes around the sun, and we call it a year. But God exists in another dimension where a thousand years are like a day. There is no time clock clicking away. It is always "now." That's difficult to grasp. In our world everything has a beginning and an end. But God is different from us. He is a spirit. No mom and pop. Just a Being. It's one of the great mysteries. According to the Bible, when we enter eternity it will all make sense. For now, though, it's a mind-blower.

SEE FOR YOURSELF: Genesis 1:1

What color is God?

God is a spirit. He doesn't have skin like us. He is not a color. When God created people in his image, he must not have had a specific color in mind because we people come in all shades of brown. Besides our color, we are raised in different cultures. More differences between us. So what does it mean that we were made in God's image? We were made with spirits. We were made with the ability to choose, to love, to live forever even if our bodies won't stick around with us.

> God is Spirit, and those who worship Him must worship in spirit and truth.
> John 4:24

Is there a Mrs. God?

Interesting question. In the story of creation God says, "Let us make man in our image." Huh? Us? Our? Does that mean a Mrs. God? As you read the whole Bible though, you find that we can understand God best in three different ways: God, Jesus (God in human form) and Holy Spirit (God who lives in us, teaching us). In our world everything divides out into male and female. Why? Because the earth would die out if everything didn't reproduce its own kind. But in the eternal "now" in which God lives, that's not an issue. God is like the perfect mom and dad rolled into one. He doesn't need to reproduce. He's not going to die. So, no, there's not a Mrs. God.

SEE FOR YOURSELF: Genesis 1:26

GODLINESS

What does a godly person look like?

Therefore it shall come to pass, that as all the good things have come upon you which the LORD your God promised you,

Josh. 23:15

All through the Bible, God models what good character is, then calls us to be like Him. Here He promises to keep His word. You're a person of strong character if you do what you say you will do—if you keep your promises. Do you normally slide in after curfew? Do you keep people waiting for you? Do you really go where you tell your parents you'll be? If you find yourself always making excuses, it's time for a character adjustment. Look at God and imitate Him. You can be successful at almost anything if you do what you've said you will do. Be dependable, trustworthy, faithful. Those are all attributes of God. He doesn't need to make any excuses.

SEE FOR YOURSELF: Gen. 20.15, Num. 23.19, Deut. 4.31, 1 Kin. 8.56, Neh. 1.5

GOODNESS

What does it mean to be "good"?

For the LORD is good; His mercy is everlasting, and His truth endures to all generations.

Ps. 100:5

Goodness is not a product of God. It is an attribute of God. In other words, it is not something God does; it is something God is. It will never change. Think about it this way. If you were born Hispanic, that's what you are. No matter what you do, you will always be Hispanic. God will always be good. Because He is eternally good, everything that comes from Him is good, too. His will is goodness. He shows us goodness, and He expects it from us. What's good about you? There's nothing geeky about being good. In fact, it takes a really strong and disciplined person to be good. Do other people see goodness in you? Do you give goodness freely? If you do, keep it up.

If you don't, it's never too late to start. What's the worst that could happen? Someone could throw it back in your face, but at least you gave some goodness. Maybe it'll have its impact months or years from now. Someone could return your goodness . . . and the world would be better for a moment. Give it a shot.

SEE FOR YOURSELF: Ezra 3:11; Ps. 145:9; Jer. 33:11; Mark 10:18

Grace in action?
Meet Joe.

When you line up on the football line, anything goes. I've gotten dirt thrown straight in my eyes. I've had guys spit in my face. The guy opposite you swears at you. He wants to kill you. And you're supposed to want to kill him. Your goal is to hurt him so he can't play the rest of the game. You both know every dirty move in the book but have to figure out how to use them without the refs noticing. It's not a gentle sport. When I get ready for a game, every ounce of testosterone boils up inside of me. It's all about adrenaline.

I wouldn't want my mom right there on the line watching me. Would she be proud of her son? Well, maybe not. Besides the fact that the violence freaks her out (she hides her face every time I get hit), she would definitely not approve of the tactics used on the line. I'm just as guilty as anyone else.

Last night I heard a talk on holiness and what it means to be set apart for God. It was one of those moments when I felt like the pastor was speaking directly to me. He talked about work and school and sports. He reminded us that we are to do our best as unto the Lord, working hard and giving our finest efforts. At the same time, we must honor Him in the manner in which we do it. "Holy" doesn't refer to angels or monks. It simply means "set apart for God." That translates into how we handle ourselves.

In football?! No one's nice in football! I reasoned. Whatever. But I couldn't shake the conviction.

The next time the offensive lineman across from me started swearing in my face, I didn't respond. I think it threw him off so much that he lost his grip on me in the next play. When he gave me a few dirty hits, I pushed back fairly. My confidence grew, and I held him. When I knocked him flat on his back and then offered him a hand up, he didn't know what to think of me.

Talk about psyching out your opponent. With a new outlook on sports, I realized that I should never fall for the dirty tactics of the world. I'm called to live up to a higher standard.

What makes me good enough for God?

In many ways, Israel's history is a symbol of the journey that all of Jesus' followers are making. That's one reason the Old Testament is still so important to Christians. You can look in the Old Testament to find wisdom for whatever you're going through and to find out what's coming next. When God said, "I will take you as My people," He wasn't just talking to the Israelites. He was also looking out through time and speaking to Christians today. He knew you would be on earth at this moment and He wanted to be sure you knew that He accepted you as His own. The nation of Israel was God's own because of the faith and obedience of their father, Abraham. Today, you are a chosen person because of the love and obedience of Jesus. Belonging to God makes you worth something. Your brains, your talent, your awesome sports ability—none of it impresses God. Even without all the cool things about you, you'd be worth something because God accepts you as His own.

> I will take you as My people, and I will be your God. Then you shall know that I am the Lord your God.
> Ex. 6:7

SEE FOR YOURSELF: Ex. 6:7; Rom. 1:17; 3:10

What's God's idea of being a good person?

There are a lot of verses in the Bible that give us a piece of the answer to that question. There's not enough space to list them all here. One is the story of the Good Samaritan. The good person in that story was the one who helped a stranger even though two other very religious people wouldn't. We learn from that story that our actions make us good, not our titles or our jobs. The verse we call the Golden Rule also tells us something about being a good person. We should do for others what we want them to do for us. There's a verse in Peter's first letter in the New Testament that gets real specific about that. It says to (1) respect all people, (2) love fellow-believers, (3) obey God, and (4) be a good citizen. That about covers it all, doesn't it? Basically it tells us to take care of all our relationships.

SEE FOR YOURSELF: 1 Peter 2:17

GOODNESS OF GOD

For He is good,
for His mercy endures
forever toward Israel.
Ezra 3:11

Is God good all of the time?

"Good" can be a fleeting thing for us. Some days we think we have it, and sometimes it's hard to hold on to. A misunderstanding can turn really good friends into enemies overnight. We can have a good attitude toward one person and be totally rude to the next. Your favorite ice cream may taste really good, but after six scoops, it's gross. People can even get so confused that they believe that wrong and sinful things are good—like drugs, premarital sex, and pornography. But God is nothing like we are. He is all good. He cannot change His mind because He misunderstood; He is not fickle with people. You can't get too much of His goodness. He is good on every level, all the time. Let those words about God's goodness remind you that everything He does is for your good. You may struggle with good, but God never will.

SEE FOR YOURSELF: Ex. 33:19; 2 Sam. 7:28; Pss. 31:19; 100:5; Rom. 8:28

GOSSIP

What should I do when I hear gossip?

Put away from you a deceitful mouth, and put perverse lips far from you.
Prov. 4:24

Sometimes that can be tricky. It's particularly tricky when you are hearing gossip from someone you really like about someone you really don't like. It can feel harmless, right? Whether the gossip is harmless or not, the character that you are developing inside matters a lot. The Bible is really clear, crystal clear, about gossip. Proverbs 4:24 answers your very question. That answer is something like, "get it as far away from you as possible." Do you have to make your friends uncomfortable? Do you have to come off holier-than-thou? Not necessarily. Maybe you just need to get really good at changing the subject. Whatever you decide, you do need a plan because gossip will come find you; but character you have to build.

GUIDANCE

Does God have a plan for me?

> The LORD of hosts has sworn, saying, "Surely, as I have thought, so it shall come to pass, and as I have purposed, so it shall stand."
>
> **Is. 14:24**

Isaiah gave the nation of Israel a message from God. Much of his message had to do with a Person called "the Messiah," who would bring the nation back to God and restore peace. Isaiah's prophecy came true when Jesus came to live on the earth—even though it didn't happen the way most of the Israelites thought it would. Still, God's plan had been written out, through Isaiah and others, so that they could see it.

In fact, all through the Bible, God tells you about His plans. Many of His plans have to do with you. You have a God-planned purpose in life, which is to know Him and to love Him like a best friend. He plans for you to become like His perfect Son. He plans for you to win out over that part of you that really likes to be selfish. He plans for you to be part of a group of people who love Him and want to see things go His way on planet Earth. He plans for you to change the world, at least your little corner of it. What He plans is going to happen. Let Him use you to get the job done.

SEE FOR YOURSELF: Is. 42:9; 46:10-11; Ezek. 12:25; Dan. 4:35

How do I know what I should do?

Yes, He will. Something will be required of you, though. You'll need to ask. No matter how grown up someone is. No matter how important their job or how old, they still need direction from God. King David was the most important person in his world. He was close to God. He was even called a man after God's own heart. But David didn't always know what to do. He asked God for direction. "Should I fight the Philistines or not?" God answered him, "Yes, go ahead." Hopefully your questions for God won't be at the war level, but they are just as important. Ask God and then watch and see how he'll answer. Sometime it will be in amazing and unexpected ways. Other times it might be just a commonsense thing. One way or another, He'll let you know.

> And David inquired of God, saying, "Shall I go up against the Philistines? Will You deliver them into my hand?" And the Lord said to him, "Go up, for I will deliver them into your hand."
> 1 Chron. 14:10

Does God have a plan for our lives?

Yes, He does. Usually when people ask that question, they are thinking of specifics. What career will I have? Where should I go to college? Who should I marry? God will guide us through those decisions—and He has designed the outcomes of them all, perfectly. But He's not going to tell you what will happen—He doesn't act as a fortune teller. God knows the number of every hair on your head. He knows your comings and your goings. He knows exactly what will happen in your life.

Paul told the Romans that, no matter what happens to us, no matter how hard or bad it seems, God will find a way to use it for our good—to grow us up a little. Trust Him to guide you through life—"For I know the thoughts that I think toward you," says the Lord, "Thoughts of peace and not of evil, to give you a future and a hope" (Jer. 29:11).

SEE FOR YOURSELF: Rom. 8:28-29

What happens when I listen to God's plan?

Jericho belonged to God, and it was time to reclaim it. So He sent Joshua and gave him the plan. "March slowly around the city every day for six days. On the seventh day, go around seven times, then blow the trumpets, and shout. The walls will fall down, and the soldiers can just walk in and take the city." Cool. What a plan! It worked. Do all good plans work? Nope. This plan worked because it was a God-plan. Joshua listened to God's plans, and God was with him to help in everything he did. The same is true for you. When you listen to God and obey His plan, He promises to help you. He will guide you every single day. His instruction will not be confusing. What wall is God calling you to conquer? Are you listening to Him? Then start marching.

SEE FOR YOURSELF: 2 Chr. 14:11; Ps. 33:20; 46:1; Rom. 8:26

> So the LORD was with Joshua, and his fame spread throughout all the country.
> Josh. 6:27

Should I go my own way or will God guide me?

Who was your favorite teacher? Do you remember that person well? You probably do. Maybe he or she took a special interest in you; didn't let you get away with anything; believed in you more than you believed in yourself; made you want to learn; had high expectations of what you could do; actually made school fun. Whatever the reason, you remember that teacher well, and you're so glad he or she was a part of your growing up. God promises to be your teacher—Life 101. He says that He will point out the road you should follow and that He will watch over you. He has the answers to all of your questions. By His Holy Spirit, He'll even guide you to what is true (see John 16:13). So if you were thinking about skipping God's class, don't. Listen to Him and His wise instruction. He's the last guidance counselor you'll ever need.

SEE FOR YOURSELF: Ps. 32:8; Prov. 2:6; Is. 2:3; John 14:26; 16:13

Does God have a special plan just for me?

Do you know what God thinks of you? He thinks you're the best. You belong to Him and are like His prize. He has compassion toward you because He knows your weak places. He created you out of pure love. He *wanted* you to be alive. He has made plans for all of eternity—plans that will never change, because God's thoughts will never change. He's got plans for you. Your heart, your mind, and your body were designed with His plan in mind. You can run from God's plan for the rest of your life, but you will never change His mind or mess with His plan. He knows what you would be great at, and He built you to do it. Ask Him to show you what He made you for. Invite Him to remind you when you forget. Then go for it.

SEE FOR YOURSELF:Jer. 29:11; Dan. 6:26; Mal. 3:6

> The counsel of the LORD stands forever, the plans of His heart to all generations.
> Ps. 33:11

Will God give me good advice?

Has anyone ever given you bad advice? Maybe they told you to take psychology because it was a breeze and then the year you take it, a new teacher makes it the hardest class in school. Maybe someone gave you some bad directions that told you to turn left instead of right. Forty miles later when you run out of civilization, you realize that you've probably gone the wrong way. Bad advice—when you lack the wisdom to know the advice is bad—can ruin a day, a year, or an entire life. God promises to give you wisdom and common sense. He says that you just have to search for Him, take time to ask Him, obey Him, and He will be faithful to give you the help you need. He is the Source of all that is wise and helpful. He waits patiently for you to stop fumbling around and ask Him for His helpful advice.

SEE FOR YOURSELF: Prov. 2:6-7; Mic. 7:7; Luke 11:10; 2 Thess. 3:3; James 1:5

GUILT

What happens to our guilt when our sins are forgiven?

> I acknowledged my sin to You, and my iniquity I have not hidden. I said, "I will confess my transgressions to the Lord," and You forgave the iniquity of my sin.
>
> **Psalm 32:5**

Guilt comes in two forms, the feeling and the reality. When God forgives our sins, He removes the reality of our guilt. In fact, when God as Jesus gave His life for our sins on the cross He removed the reality of our guilt. He took it on Himself. The feeling of guilt is a different matter. Sometimes even though we ask God for forgiveness and we believe He gives it, we still feel guilty. That kind of guilt takes some faith to get rid of. We've got to believe that God does what He says. Psalm 32 says that God forgives our sins. We've got to have enough faith to believe that. How sad for us to have our sins forgiven, our guilt taken away, and yet we walk around like a sad sack feeling guilty. We have to let our feelings catch up with reality. Our guilt is gone.

HAPPINESS

How can I be happy?

The best way to stay happy for the longest periods of time is to base your happiness on things that don't change. You have to look pretty hard for those things. There aren't many of them. Hannah was a woman in the Old Testament who spent part of her life very unhappy. She wanted a child, but had never been able to get pregnant. When she finally did get pregnant (after much prayer), her mood was much improved. But she didn't run around saying, "I'm happy because I'm pregnant." Instead she said, "I'm happy because of God's salvation." She was happy because God had responded to her. It was in his provision that she celebrated. God, and his love for you, is the only thing in life you can count on. If you can base your happiness on that, you've got a much better chance at being a happy person.

> And Hannah prayed and said: "My heart rejoices in the LORD; my horn is exalted in the LORD. I smile at my enemies, because I rejoice in Your salvation".
> 1 Sam. 2:1

Trust God when my world falls apart? Meet Ally.

Did you ever read that book that starts out, "It was the best of times. It was the worst of times." It's by Charles Dickens, I think. I read the Cliff notes for class last year. Anyways, that pretty much sums up my life. *It was the best of times*—that's for sure. My freshman year of college, off on my own, making the best friends ever, and having a great time in life. Everything seemed to be awesome, and I was loving life.

It was the worst of times—I went home for Christmas break. Mom and Dad sat me down and explained to me that they had decided to get a divorce. They hadn't been getting along for the last year and just weren't in love with each other anymore. My dad had actually been living in an apartment for about four months. They felt like this was the best thing for all three of us.

I was totally shocked. I had been so carefree, off at school, enjoying life and not really putting together the clues. I hadn't been home at all, so I hadn't seen them interact. This explained why they had been calling me separately, never together. I had thought they did that just to be nice. This explained why they didn't talk about spending time together or about the other one at all. This explained why Dad had picked me up at the airport but dropped me off for dinner with Mom. This explained why the TV and the couch from the basement were gone. How naïve of me.

My world fell apart. If you've been through a divorce situation, then you know what I mean. Everything seemed awful. I got seriously depressed in about two seconds, and it didn't let up for a full year. The divorce wasn't too messy—after all, with only one, grown kid, they didn't need a custody war. They managed to divide up all the furniture and photo albums and everything that had been in my *home*. Home was destroyed, as was my life, I felt.

In the depth of my despair, I turned to God for help. I started reading the Psalms and meeting with my pastor once a week. I got involved in a women's small group and shared my burden with other believers. I cried out to God, pouring my heart out to Him, and I prayed. I prayed and prayed and prayed. I didn't have specific things to ask for, I just fell in exhaustion on my God.

Who knows how it will end? Will I be a stronger person because of it? Will God find some way to bring good out of a bad situation? I don't know for sure, but I can hope in Someone who is stronger than I am. And I can pray for the grace to get me through each day.

HATE

Sometimes I hate my brother. I really mean hate. Does God expect me to love him?

Beloved, let us love one another, for love is of God; and everyone who loves is born of God and knows God.
1 John 4:7

It can be so hard growing up with someone right in your face. Brothers can be tough. Here's the news. God does expect you to love your brother. Having said that, let's talk about what that means. Loving your brother doesn't mean that you have to feel ooshy-gooshy about him. It doesn't even really mean that you have to like him a lot. But it does mean that you need to choose to show him respect and to look out for his best interests. Why? Because he deserves it? No. Because he wants it? Maybe he does, but that's not the reason. The reason is because God asks you to love other people the way God loves you. Because we have been loved by God, we have to share that love. It's a choice, not a feeling. It's a way of acting, not an emotion that you have to drum up. You might not think of your brother as even human, but God is concerned with what kind of human YOU are. Be civil, whether your brother is or not. And even more, love him.

HEAVEN

How much do people have to pray to get into heaven, or is it different depending on how much bad stuff and good stuff you do?

Getting to heaven is not about how much bad and good stuff you do. Getting to heaven is about believing in God's existence and in the fact that He sacrificed Himself for our sins. A jail warden once asked Paul and Silas, "What do I need to do to be saved?" (Which means to go to heaven and be saved from hell, which means to live WITH God for eternity instead of SEPARATE from God for eternity.) Paul answered, "You need to believe in Christ." Now praying does have something to do with that because prayer is an act of faith. It's one of the first ways we acknowledge God's existence—we talk to Him. But the prayers are not what make the difference. It's that we believe He is there to listen and that He honestly did sacrifice Himself so that we could have a relationship with Him. When we nail that down, we connect with God in a way that lasts forever, even after we die. When we are with Him after we die, we will be in heaven.

If you get to heaven, can they throw you out? What about hell?

In the book of Revelation, John describes our life in heaven. He says that NEVER AGAIN will we hunger or suffer. He doesn't say, unless we do so-and-so we'll never hunger or suffer. He talks about it like it's a done deal. For all the Bible tells us, the best we can figure is that after everything is divided out, we are either in God's presence (heaven) or out of God's presence (hell). Now, God might have chosen not to give us all the information. But according to the information that He gave us, it's a done deal either way.

SEE FOR YOURSELF: Rev. 7:16-17

Forget the *Guinness Book of World Records.* This is the book you want your name mentioned in. Anyone whose name is erased from this book will not be able to spend eternity in heaven with the Lord. Obviously, the Lord doesn't need a book to remind Him who His followers are— He is God, after all. Ps. 69:28

Do people eat or go to the bathroom in heaven? What about God?

> Yes, I think it is right, as long as I am in this tent, to stir you up by reminding you, knowing that shortly I must put off my tent, just as our Lord Jesus Christ showed me.
> 2 Peter 1:13-14

Peter described our bodies as tents—temporary, portable houses for our souls. When we go to heaven we won't have the same kind of physical body. We'll live as spirits. We won't need food the same way. Therefore we won't need bathrooms the same way. God is a spirit, so that's true of Him as well. Now, when we think of food as the fuel for our bodies that all makes sense. But when we think about the flavor and the fun of eating, we'd hate to think that heaven wouldn't include fast food or pot-luck suppers. How could heaven be fun without those things? We don't know yet. That's a big wait-and-see.

What if you're in heaven and you see somebody you hate? What do you do?

Heaven will work differently than earth. We will work differently in heaven than we do on earth. There will be no more death, grief, crying, or pain. The Bible says the old order of things will have passed away. So, to be honest, I don't think there will be hate in heaven. If you see someone you hated on earth, I don't think it will be the same. Heaven will be a place of love. Will you remember that you hated them on earth? Maybe. Will you remember what they did that made you hate them? Maybe. But all that will be changed, resolved, forgiven. It's difficult to imagine now, isn't it?

SEE FOR YOURSELFF: Rev. 21:3-4

Will there be sadness in heaven?

There is one simple and wonderful answer to that question. No. There will not be sadness in heaven. There's more good news, too. No one will die there. That means no funerals. There will be no crying. That means no hurt feelings, no disappointing friends. In fact, in Revelation, John says that God will wipe away every tear. What a great picture that is. In your imagination, how big a tissue would that take? Heaven will be wonderful because we will be with God. But it will also be wonderful because we will be away from the hard parts of life. No more pain, physically or emotionally. No more disappointment or worry. No more troubles.

> And God will wipe away every tear from their eyes; there shall be no more death, nor sorrow, nor crying; there shall be no more pain, for the former things have passed away.
> Rev. 21:4

If earth money won't matter in heaven, why do I care if the streets are made of gold?

In the book of Revelation John describes a vision that he has of heaven and of the end of the world as we know it. It's wild and sort of funky, really. In that way, it's like Ezekiel's visions of spinning wheels and Daniel's visions including the seventy weeks. Each of these men were seeing heavenly things and trying to describe them in earth terms. They say things like "it looked like . . ." or "it seemed like . . ." The earth terms are never enough. If God wants streets of gold in heaven, He can have them. He's God. He gets to do that. But it might be that gold was the closest earth thing that John could find to describe what he saw. He said the gates to the city were pearls and the streets were pure gold, like transparent glass. The point is that God's heaven is a beautiful and glorious place—and that reflects God. It's not about money–it's about God's glory.

SEE FOR YOURSELF: Rev. 21:21

Heaven sounds boring. Is it just all clouds and harps and everybody sitting around with nothing to do but tell God how great He is?

But as it is written:
"Eye has not seen,
nor ear heard, nor
have entered into
the heart of man
the things which
God has prepared
for those who
love Him."
1 Cor. 2:9

There's an awful lot we don't know about heaven. All we know about is what kinds of things are fun here on earth. What do you love to do? Play ball? Hang out with friends? Go to Disney World? Whatever makes life fun for you, heaven will seem un-fun without it. Problem is, we don't have any frame of reference for heaven. We only know earth. The Bible says in 1 Corinthians that we haven't seen or heard or even thought about what God has prepared for us. Jesus described heaven in terms of things we know—houses, even mansions in some translations. We think of worship as sitting around in church singing and praying. You know what? God thinks a lot more broadly than we think or than we can understand. We can trust that if He says heaven will be a blast, we won't be sitting there with a yawn and a pasted on smile.

Where is heaven?

When the Bible talks about heaven it usually talks about a place way above us. In fact, the Bible refers to the sky as "the heavens." The Bible says that God looks down from heaven on us. So we generally think that heaven is a place way farther away than we can imagine. We think of it this way—that as far as our telescopes can see, to the end of space, that is just the size of a little fish tank in the middle of God's reality, heaven. Our world seems so big to us because we are the little creatures living on it. But that doesn't mean there's not a whole bigger place that we haven't dreamed of. There's another way of looking at it though. We think in three dimensions: height, width, and depth. Sometimes we talk about time as a dimension. It could be that heaven is a whole different dimension, a place that we can't even understand the physics of (yuck, physics). From the Bible we know this ... heaven is not an imaginary place like Oz. It's a real place where God exists. Through faith in Him, one of these days we'll be there.

SEE FOR YOURSELF: Ps. 14:2

HELP

Is there anyone who can help me or am I all alone?

Just as God fought for the Israelites when they were stuck between the raging Red Sea and the advancing Egyptian army, Jesus has fought for you. He fought and defeated the power of sin in your life. Big deal, right? Right—that means you can do the right thing even when it's hard. Even the apostle Paul said that he had a hard time doing the right thing because his selfish desires kept urging him to do something else. Everyone who wants to please God faces this problem. But Jesus went up against all of your selfishness and temptations. He went smack up against all the right things that you don't want to do. And He won.

Moses told the Israelites, "You shall hold your peace." That's true for you. You don't have to fight because Jesus has already won your battle. Does that mean you just sit around like mush? No, you just have to stay strong, stay close to Him, and keep believing that He's already won.

SEE FOR YOURSELF: Deut. 1:30-31; 2 Chr. 32:8; Neh. 4:20; 32:8

Will God help me when I need Him the most?

Remember the last time you needed help? Not just help with your homework, but HELP. You were at the end of your rope, no more options; you'd done everything and nothing worked. You were confused, afraid, and lonely all at the same time. What do you do when the answers just don't seem to come? Joshua 1:9. God gives two positive commands here—be strong and be of courage. Don't be afraid. Don't be discouraged. And then, the promise, "The LORD your God is with you wherever you go." That promise gives you strength to obey the two commands. You can rest in the fact that God promises to help. You are not alone. You may not get help at the exact second you think you need it, but He will help you. He knows exactly how much you can take. He'll be right on time.

SEE FOR YOURSELF: Josh. 1:9; Ps. 54:4; Zech. 1:2, 3; John 14:16; Heb. 13:6

Will God always answer my call for help?

The Lord is the protector of Israel—and of everyone who puts his or her trust in Him. He protects you from the enemy of His people, Satan. Satan hates the fact that you want to live for God. He will throw whatever he can at you to get you off track. But as long as you stand under God's protection—trusting Him and obeying Him—Satan's plans don't have a lot of effect. And God doesn't ever let His guard down. He doesn't get bored or tired. Unlike humans, He doesn't need rest to renew His mind and body. That means you can call on Him anytime you feel the enemy's attack. If Satan needles you with doubt at midnight, if he attacks you with fear at three A.M., if he throws you a temptation at high noon—whatever and whenever—the Lord can hear you call Him and will rescue you.

SEE FOR YOURSELF: Deut. 11:12; Ps. 11:4; Is. 40:28

> Behold, He who keeps Israel shall neither slumber nor sleep.
> Ps. 121:4

If I ask, will God help me?

God has a pretty good track record when it comes to helping His children. He helped the Hebrew people escape from Egypt by dividing the water of the Red Sea. He helped David kill Goliath with just a slingshot. He helped Peter by sending an angel to lead him out of jail. Of course, the list could go on and on. God wants to help His people. He wants to show the world His power through the lives of the people who love Him. Has He helped you lately? He's not waiting for you to get into a life-or-death situation before He helps you. He's just waiting for you to ask Him. He wants you to know that you need Him. He wants you to admit that He can do a better job with your life than you can. Remember, His help might come in an unexpected way, but it will always be the best thing that could happen to you.

SEE FOR YOURSELF: Ex. 33:14; Josh 1:9; Is. 12:6; Hos. 14:8, 9; Zech. 1:2, 3

HOLINESS

How can I take holiness seriously?

> I am the LORD your God. You shall therefore sanctify yourselves, and you shall be holy; for I am holy.
> Lev. 11:44

00. 00. 29   00. 00. 30

It's the bottom of the ninth inning, bases loaded, and your team's down 4–1. The best hitter's at bat with two outs and two strikes. The pitch . . . grand slam! Your team wins 5–4. "HOLY COW!" screams the announcer. "Holy cow!" Holiness is taken lightly by a lot of people—not just sports announcers. Let's find out what God says about being holy. First, we must know that we serve a holy God. Psalm 111:9 says, "He has sent redemption to His people; He has commanded His covenant forever: Holy and awesome is His name." Psalm 99:5 tells us that the Lord is a God of holiness. Second, He wants us to strive to be holy as well, so we can be like Him (Eph. 5:1). Do you want to be like Jesus? Live like Him? Talk like Him? Act like Him? Think like Him? That's what being holy is: being devoted to God and obeying His Word. As you spend time with God, He will make Himself known to you. There's nothing greater than spending time in the presence of Almighty God! Spend time today praising Him because He is the One who is holy (Ps. 71:22).

SEE FOR YOURSELF: Lev 20:7; 1 Pet. 1:15-16; 20:7

Everything involved in offering a sacrifice to God was considered holy. What's more, once something had been used for such a holy purpose, it could not be used again. That's why the ancient Israelites threw away their pots and unused food after a sacrifice.
Lev. 6:24-30

HOLY SPIRIT

> But the Spirit of the LORD came upon Gideon; then he blew the trumpet, and the Abiezrites gathered behind him.
> Judg. 6:34

How does God use the Holy Spirit to help me?

In this passage, the Holy Spirit "came upon Gideon," giving him the divine power he needed to carry out God's plan. The assignment was big—rescue Israel. It required one faithful man and supernatural help from the Holy Spirit. One man plus God is mightier than any army and stronger than any opposition. If God is calling you for a big job, you can bet that He will also send the power of the Holy Spirit. You won't be alone. God goes before you to clear the way for you, and He sends the Holy Spirit to take control of the situation—and of you. You'll know what to do. You'll know what to say. You can run to the battle with the total confidence that the Spirit of God is in control.

SEE FOR YOURSELF: Judg. 14:19; 1 Sam. 10:6; Ezek. 2:2

How can the Spirit help us understand God?

This verse is talking specifically about a king who will arise from David's family. This king would be Jesus and He would receive understanding, wisdom, knowledge, and might from the Spirit of the Lord. But does that mean the Spirit won't give those gifts to anyone else? No, of course not. The Spirit of God gives understanding, wisdom, and knowledge to anyone who asks. He is the Source of those things. Read John 14—16 to see what the Holy Spirit's jobs are. You'll see some things that remind you of this verse. When you get in a situation where you need understanding, wisdom, or knowledge beyond your own, ask the Spirit for His help. He'll always be there for you.

SEE FOR YOURSELF: Prov. 2:6; Luke 24:45; John 14:16; Col. 1:9; James 3:17; Is. 11:2

What are you made of?
Meet Brendon.

"It's the little stuff that shows what you're made of," my dad always says. For some reason, out of all the lectures he gives, that one thought really sticks with me. I can hear his voice saying it, and I can picture his face as he looks at me. Those words come to mind right away when all of the "little things" come up in my life. When my sister scratches my car backing it out of the driveway . . . when my brother begs to borrow twenty bucks and never gets around to paying me back . . . when my friend seems to show a lot of interest in my girlfriend . . . when I don't get the grade I think I should from a tough English teacher . . . when each of these things comes up, I have a chance to show what I'm made of. When bumped, I either spill out grace or I flip out in anger and bitterness. Believe me, I still have a lot of room for growth with this.

So there we were, the six of us guys, just driving one Saturday night. Nobody could decide what to do, so we were driving around in Jason's new Land Cruiser (a sweet car with a serious sound system) Blake's riding shotgun, and he thinks it'll be fun to throw a little rap in. Now don't get me wrong. It's not that I think all rap is bad, but I think we can all agree that some of it is. As the well-known voice blasted through the speakers, none of us could ignore what he was saying. I think every other word began with an *f* and the ones in between were pretty graphic. The whole car was quiet (none of us could hear anything else anyways) and a bit uncomfortable. Everyone seemed to be waiting for Mark's reaction. Predictable.

Mark's the "fanati-freak" of the group. Yeah, all of us claim to be Christians, but Mark really lives it out. Some of the other guys are a little sketchy, if you know what I mean. So Mark hit Blake on the shoulder and just spoke right up. "Hey, can you change the music? This stuff offends me. I don't want this trash in my mind."

Every guy knew he was right, but he just has this annoying way of saying it. So Blake, being how he is, decides to turn the music up even louder.

That's when the words "It's the little stuff that shows what you're made of." I thought about it for about two seconds and then faced up to my buddies. I leaned over the front seat and just hit the power button. "Funny, Blake. Mark's right and you know it." That's all I had to say. The car got real quiet for a few minutes. I'm sure all the guys were thinking. I guess it's kind of a guy thing that we don't talk about "how we feel" after a feud like that. But everyone got the picture.

HOMOSEXUALITY

Is homosexuality a sin?

You shall not lie with a male as with a woman. It is an abomination. Lev. 18:22

Yes, along with all types of sexual immorality, like fooling around with your crush. The Bible makes this clear. ". . . God gave them up to vile passions. For even their women exchanged the natural use for what is against nature. Likewise also the men, leaving the natural use of the woman, burned in their lust for one another, men with men committing what is shameful, and receiving in themselves the penalty of their error which was due" (Rom. 1:26-27).

Now this might shock or offend you, but some Christians struggle with homosexuality. Just like with gossip, stealing, rebellion, or drunkenness. They are making a choice to live in sin, and are not right with God if they are practicing that lifestyle. God hates sin. But God loves His creation. Before you call someone a fag or queer, think about the sins you might be living in. Do you gossip with your best friends every weekend? Do you refuse to get along with your mom or dad? Do you feel hatred toward gay people, rather than that lifestyle? "If someone says, 'I love God,' and hates his brother, he is a liar" (1 John 4:20-21).

The homosexual lifestyle is definitely wrong. And if you or someone you know is struggling with this temptation, seek help. Pray. These temptations aren't sin—giving in to them is. And God has promised us power over sin. So, if you are living in this sin, refusing to repent and give it up to God, then Christians are commanded to not associate with you (see 1 Cor. 5:9-12). If you have a friend who is living in this sin, you must confront them. God requires that we speak the truth, in love, to our brothers and sisters who are struggling. Don't back down. Don't avoid it just because it's tough. You've got to let them know what God says about their lifestyle. But, say it in love.

Temptation toward homosexuality may seem foreign to you, or it may be your biggest struggle right now. So, whether you're trying to learn to have compassion for homosexuals (as opposed to homosexuality), or you're trying to break free from the temptation of that lifestyle, know that God will provide for all your needs. Call on Him, and He will give you the strength to defeat your sin—whether it be hatred or sexual immorality.

SEE FOR YOURSELF: Lev. 18:22; 1 Cor. 6:9-10

HONESTY

Diverse weights and diverse measures, they are both alike, an abomination to the LORD.

Prov. 20:10

What does God think of a person with double standards?

God despises double standards. In Proverbs double standards are described as diverse weight and measures. When merchants sold stuff in the marketplace they used scales to measure out how much grain or fish were selling. The dishonest merchants had many different weights and measures. They could cheat that way. So somebody could pay for a whole pound of meal, but they would only get three-fourths of a pound. God hates social double standards too. James wrote in the New Testament about treating people differently according to their wealth. That's just as much a double standard as fake weights. God despises it all.

How can I live my life to please God?

Have you ever told "a little white lie"? You know, what you said was not quite true, but it didn't hurt anybody and it got you out of a tight spot. Or maybe your skill is telling your mom something that is technically true. When you've finished explaining, what she thinks happened and what really happened are two different things. That's the way human beings are—they shade the truth this way and that, turning what's black and white into shades of gray. But God isn't like that. Everything He says is pure and true, not barely sliding by on a variation of the truth. His honesty doesn't depend on technicalities. And God isn't just honest. He's also right. You might make a statement that you thought was true, only to find out later that you were wrong. But God doesn't make mistakes. His Word is so reliable that you can use it for a shield. That's what Jesus did when Satan tempted Him (see Matt. 4:1-11). He used God's words to protect his heart. It's good to know that there are no cracks in the shield. Everything He says is true.

SEE FOR YOURSELF: Prov. 12:19, 26:17; Matt. 4:1-11

What does it matter if I cheat on one stupid test. Does God really look at my report card?

> But as He who called you is holy, you also be holy in all your conduct, because it is written, "Be holy, for I am holy."
>
> 1 Peter 1:15-16

God certainly can look at your report card if He wants to. But that's not what is most important to Him. Worse than God looking at your report card, God can look right into your heart. He sees it all: what you do, why you do it, and whether you feel like it or not. You really can't hide anything from Him. So whether you cheat on the test or not, God will know. But what He will be even more concerned about is why you think it's OK. What does that say about your character? Are you just being lazy? Are you bucking the system? Would you rather make a grade off of someone else's work? Are you scared of failing? All those things: laziness, fear, defiance...those are the things God is concerned with in your life. Why? Because His goal is to make you like Himself. He is holy and clean through and through. He wants you to be holy in every way. So it's not about a single grade, either on a test or a report card. It's about all the little choices that you make that add up to whether or not you have integrity. It does matter whether or not you cheat on one stupid test. That choice to take the shortcut becomes part of who you are. It's not the end of the world, but it matters.

SEE FOR YOURSELF: Prov. 12:19; Matt. 4:1-11; Prov. 26:17.

HONOR

Why should I honor the Lord?

00. 00. 29   00. 00. 0

God spoke everything you see into existence. Incredible. He made you and every person who has ever lived before you. He didn't copy someone else's idea. He didn't improve on an old design. The earth and the heavens and all things in them are totally original and straight from the mind of God.

What a huge concept to process! Doing a science project can seem overwhelming to us, much less creating the whole world. Because of His place as Creator, God

00. 08. 62   00. 08. 83   00. 08. 84   00. 08. 85   00. 08. 86

deserves your respect and your honor. You don't just get physical life from Him. You get spiritual life from Him. He is the Source of the things that make you so alive—the ability to enjoy life, the capacity for love, laughter, peace, joy, work, play, rest. You can go to Him and get replenished when you run low. He is your Life Preserver—life flows freely forever in Him.

SEE FOR YOURSELF:Gen. 1:1; Ps. 95:3-7; 148:5, 6; Jer. 10:16; 51:15, 16 .

> You alone are the LORD; You have made heaven, the heaven of heavens, with all their host, the earth and all things on it, the seas and all that is in them, and You preserve them all. The host of heaven worships You.
>
> Neh. 9:6

What do I do if I don't feel like honoring God?

God makes you who you are. He gave you the talents you were born with. Your personality came from Him, too. All the things that happen to you He uses to help you become the person He wants you to be. He also gives you some discipline and a lot of gentle leading. But God needs your cooperation. If you won't listen to Him or if you're always complaining every time your life isn't going the way you planned, then it's going to take a long time for you to change. But if you let Him do what He needs to do, the change will come quicker. That's the key—let *Him* do it. You can make yourself more patient, more loving, or more thoughtful only by letting God change the way you think (see Rom. 12:2). You can decide to change your actions ("I will not yell, I will not yell, I will not yell"), but unless you change on the inside, it'll fall apart after awhile. Changing your actions is not a bad idea. But ask Him to make the *real* change. That's His job.

SEE FOR YOURSELF: Is. 64:8; Rom. 12:2; 1 Cor. 7:7; 1 Pet. 4:10

How can I honor God?

Ever feel like just one of the guys (or one of the girls)? You know, you go to the same school as all of your friends, hang out at the same places, like the same bands, wear the same style of clothing, watch the same movies, play the same sports, have the same tennis shoes . . . Maybe you have red hair and your friends have brown, but mostly you're all just about alike—regular kids. The Lord doesn't see you as one of the guys. He says you are special—not in a cheesy way. You are rare, one-of-a-kind. When He looks at you, He goes, "Wow." He feels that way about you all the time, not just when you pray or worship. That's one of the ways He honors you. Psalm 34:9 says that you are to honor (fear) Him, too. You don't have to be all stuffy or religious to honor the Lord. You just have to think about Him, consider what He wants, follow His direction, spend time with Him. Thank Him for making you His special treasure and feel the same about Him—that He is your treasure. One of the best ways to honor Him is to look at Him and go, "Wow."

> Oh, fear the LORD, you His saints! There is no want to those who fear Him.
> Ps. 34:9

SEE FOR YOURSELF: Deut. 26:18; 1 Cor. 1:30, 31; Heb. 2:11

HOPE

How do I know things will get better?

So I have come down to deliver them out of the hand of the Egyptians, and to bring them up from that land to a good and large land, to a land flowing with milk and honey.

Ex. 3:8

The children of Israel had been delivered from Egypt and wandered in the desert for forty years before entering the land God had promised them. But you know what? Year number 41 came, and they didn't wander anymore. They entered into the land of milk and honey! Maybe it seems that you are in a desert period in your life. Maybe you feel like you've been stumbling around for 40 years. Don't worry, number 41 is on its way! Look at these examples: Noah and his family were on the ark while it rained for 40 days and 40 nights—41 came, and the rain stopped; for 40 days Goliath showed up every morning and taunted Israel—41 came, and David slew him! God has promised to bring you out of your Egypt as well—if you will hold on to your faith in Him. Whatever situation you are going through right now, don't give up. God is on your side! So if it seems like trouble has been raining down on you, don't worry because 41 is on the way. The rain is going to stop. Whatever giant is in your life, 41 is coming and that giant's coming down! You are more than a conquerer through Christ Jesus (see Rom. 8:37). He will deliver you out of Egypt.

SEE FOR YOURSELF: Gen. 7; 8; 1 Sam. 17; Ps. 34:17, 19

How does God give me hope?

A student's life can feel like a roller-coaster ride—lots of ups and downs. Sometimes you're upside down in a tunnel, wondering which way is out. If you can hang on, the ride is incredible and is a time you'll look back on and smile at. But some students get stuck on the ride during a power failure. They're sitting in the tunnel wondering when they'll get out. Does anyone even know they're there? When will this ride be over? Life can get kind of dark sometimes. The downs seem to hang around too long, and the power is taking forever to come back on. Some students lose their hope in these scary places. Maybe they've never heard about God's promise to them to fill their future with hope. He promises to ride with you, restore power where there is none, and return order when things seem upside down and confusing. He promises that more good is ahead of you. There is everything to live for. Your future is bright and blessed because you belong to Him. Stand on His promise and look toward the future—dream great dreams and hope against the odds. You have everything to look forward to.

SEE FOR YOURSELF: Prov. 23:17, 18; 2 Thess. 2:16; 1 Tim. 1:1; 1 Pet. 1:3

> For I know the thoughts that I think toward you, says the LORD, thoughts of peace and not of evil, to give you a future and a hope.
> Jer. 29:11

HUMILITY

How far ahead does humility get you?

By humility and the fear of the LORD are riches and honor and life.
Prov. 22:4

Actually, humility gets you pretty far ahead.
I know it can seem like the kids that brag
get more attention sometimes. They sure
seem to feel bigger because of it. But that's just
as far as people can see. God sees a lot more. When God looks
at you, He wants to see that you understand that good things come from Him.
Even your ability to accomplish the stuff that you could brag about, those abilities
are gifts that God gave you. The Bible says that when God sees a humble heart
He responds. He gives riches and honor and life. Maybe our humility shows Him
that we know how to handle the good stuff He sends our way. Maybe He knows
that He can trust us with it because we'll use it to serve Him instead of just to get
more attention. Be humble and be patient. Let God bring the honor your way.

HYPOCRISY

What is hypocrisy?

God describes hypocrisy this way. He says it's when people honor Him with their lips, but they keep their hearts far away from Him. Jesus spent a lot of energy in His ministry pointing out to people (particularly the Pharisees who were famous for hypocrisy) that what our faith is when no one is looking is more important than what we do out where people can pat us on the back. If we aren't really building a relationship with God and loving Him, then what good is it to go out and act like we are? Are we just using God to get a good reputation? Our faith should be more important to us than that. But that's exactly what hypocrisy is.

> Therefore the LORD said: "Inasmuch as these people draw near to Me with their mouths and honor Me with their lips, but have removed their hearts far from Me, and their fear toward Me is taught by the commandment of men.
> Is. 29:13

What makes someone a hypocrite?

A hypocrite is a person who says one thing, but does another. Like they might say they like you, but when you are gone they talk badly about you to your friends. They might say they believe they should obey God, but then don't do it. Hypocrites have been around since time began. Jesus talked a lot about the danger of hypocrisy. Even back in the Old Testament, one of the Proverbs warned about hypocrisy. It said that a hypocrite destroys his neighbor. Now it would be one thing if a hypocrite destroyed his enemy. That might be palatable. But to destroy a *neighbor.* No wonder Jesus didn't appreciate hypocrisy.

SEE FOR YOURSELF: Prov. 11:9

Holding your friends up to a standard? Meet Katie.

It was a rainy evening, middle of November, one of those gloomy nights when you just want to curl up on the couch and watch a movie. Unfortunately, I had to do homework instead. I buckled down after school and pounded out this terrible English assignment. It took me three hours to finish, and by the time dinner was over and I ran spellcheck on my paper, I was so sick of homework. Rebecca called me to go to Starbucks, and I was waiting on the porch as soon as we got off the phone. I'll admit it, I'm addicted to lattes. What a great break to reward me for all this boring homework, and Rebecca's always fun to talk to.

After our quick coffee break, she dropped me off again at home. She said she still had a lot of work to do tonight. Probably hasn't even started that English assignment, I thought to myself. Poor thing. It was unbearable. "So did you get your English done?" she asked me innocently.

"Yeah, I finished it right before you called. What a beast. How's yours coming along?" I asked.

"Oh, pretty good," she said. Yeah right. She is such a procrastinator. "I just have a little more to write and then maybe read through it again. Shouldn't take me too long." So she's going to pull an all-nighter on this one? "By the way, can you print me a copy of yours while I'm here? I'd really like to look at it just to make sure I'm on the right track."

Well. I heard what she was saying, but I knew exactly what she meant. I could tell that she hadn't even started and that she had no idea what the assignment was even about. She talks so much in class that she rarely has a clue of what's going on. I had a choice to make. She was my good friend, and it probably wasn't that big a deal. But I definitely thought that cheating was wrong, and it made me mad that I would do all the work and she could just use me for that. Suddenly I saw her real motivation for going to Starbucks, and I got even madder.

"No," I snapped back. "You can't just use my paper. Why would I just let you borrow all my work?" I started to calm down a little. "But here's what I'll do. Come inside for a half-hour, and we'll talk through the assignment together. I'll help you think of some ideas for your writing."

She looked kind of ashamed and tried to cover it up, so she came inside with me. I think our talk was really helpful for her paper. I think my response was really helpful for her character.

INTEGRITY

How does having integrity make my life better?

They could find no charge or fault, because he was faithful; nor was there any error or fault found in him.
Dan. 6:4

Here's an example. Remember Daniel from the Old Testament? He was an Israelite who was taken captive to Babylon (later Persia). Through his integrity he was recognized as a wise person and eventually he became a government official there. As politics will go though, Daniel made some enemies. These guys, called governors and satraps, wanted to dig up some dirt on Daniel so that they could make him look bad in front of the king. They looked really hard, but they just couldn't find anything against Daniel. Why? Because he was a man of integrity. He kept his life clean. People can give you a hard enough time without giving them the opportunity to do it. Living a life of integrity means there are a lot less places for people to take potshots at you.

SEE FOR YOURSELF: Dan. 6:4-5

What does someone look like who has integrity?

> And he did what was right in the sight of the LORD, according to all that his father Amaziah had done.
> 2 Chron. 26:4

Mostly they look the same inside as they do outside. They are people who know what they are about and they would do the same things whether anyone was watching them or not. They are honest and humble. The Bible describes King Uzziah as a man with integrity. 2 Chronicles says that Uzziah did what was right in the sight of the Lord. A person with integrity doesn't just do the right thing because he doesn't want to get caught. He does the right thing because it's the right thing to do. A Christian should do the right thing because it honors God, whether anyone else ever notices or not.

JEALOUSY

What kinds of things does jealousy do to relationships?

And the patriarchs, becoming envious, sold Joseph into Egypt. But God was with him.
Acts 7:9

Jealousy is a destructive thing. It says, "I'm not getting what I deserve and it's because of *that* person." It also says, "See what they have? I should have that." Jealousy leads to bitterness and anger and resentment. One of the most famous cases of jealousy-run-wild is the story of Joseph and his brothers. Joseph was one of those natural born leaders. He had big dreams and ambitions. He was also daddy's favorite. His ten older brothers (the patriarchs of the Jewish nation) resented him terribly. They were jealous. In Acts they are described as envious. Because of their jealousy they almost killed Joseph. They did beat him up and sold him as a slave. How could brother's do that? Their jealousy got out of control; that's how jealousy destroys relationships.

Isn't jealousy just a natural reaction? Why would it be wrong?

Jealousy IS a natural reaction. That's the problem. Just because something is natural doesn't mean it is harmless. Have you ever heard of food poisoning? That's about as natural as it comes. Most often the problem with jealousy is that it causes you to resent people, even to wish them harm. Want to hear a big secret? (The Bible says it, but most people don't talk about it a lot.) When Jesus was arrested even though He was innocent . . . it was because of jealousy. Mathew 27:18 says that Jesus knew His enemies handed Him over because of envy or jealousy. They were jealous because people were listening to Jesus. The religious leaders were losing their admirers and they were jealous. They came to resent Jesus and they wanted something bad to happen to Him. We have the same reaction when we are jealous. Resenting someone doesn't get us any closer to what we wish we had, though. Jealousy can end up destroying everything good that we do have.

SEE FOR YOURSELF:. Matt. 27:18

Doesn't the Bible say God is jealous? Is it wrong to be jealous, then?

For the LORD your God is a consuming fire, a jealous God.
Deut. 4:24

The Bible does say God is jealous. He is jealous over us and our worship. When we think of jealous being a bad thing, we think of a guy who is way too jealous and possessive, or a girl who is jealous of something nice her friend got. That jealousy is bad because those people really don't have the right to the things they are jealous of. God, on the other hand, has every right to us and our worship. He made us! He is the one, true God. What He asks of us is our faith. When we don't give God that, He is jealous and He has every right to be. We are giving away something that should belong only to Him. We are usually jealous out of a sense of competition. God's jealousy is way more righteous than that.

JESUS

What did Jesus' death conquer?

OO. OO. 29   OO. OO. O

> He will swallow up death forever, and the Lord GOD will wipe away tears from all faces.
> Isa. 25:8

When Jesus died and came back to life, He dealt death a mortal blow. He gave notice to anyone who would believe in Him that there was a power greater than death. His friends don't have to be afraid of death because they know that their physical death is not the end. And there will come a day when no one dies anymore.

Something else happened when Jesus died on the cross. He did battle with the spiritual death that had cast a shadow over planet Earth since Adam and Eve had left the Garden of Eden. If you put your confidence in Jesus' goodness rather than your own, the seemingly irresistible urge to go your own way (instead of God's way) doesn't have to run your life.

And Jesus promises that your tears will come to an end, too. That's because all the things that make you sad—someone's parents getting a divorce, people getting sick, even natural disasters—are part of a world that's not perfect because of sin. Jesus has already beat sin, and just like death, sin's days of having any say in our lives are coming to an end. Then we'll see what Revelation 21:4 reports: "The former things have passed away."

SEE FOR YOURSELF: Rom. 8:2; 2 Tim. 1:10; Rev. 21:4

What kind of stuff did Jesus lose His cool about?

Jesus felt passionately about a lot of things. He wasn't this bland, emotionless person that we sometimes see Him portrayed as in made-for-TV movies. He was a real guy and a real God, all in the same body. The Bible doesn't walk us through every minute of Jesus' life, so we don't know all the things that may have "riled" Him, but we do know about one. John's gospel tells us that Jesus walked into the temple one day and found merchants selling animals for sacrifice. What He saw was people doing business with each other at church instead of doing business with God. What did Jesus do? He lost His cool. He used a whip. He got those merchants out into the marketplace where they belonged. For Jesus, God's house was not a place to be tampered with.

SEE FOR YOURSELF: John 2:13-17

> For God so loved the world that He gave His only begotten Son, that whoever believes in Him should not perish but have everlasting life.
>
> John 3:16

Did Jesus have feelings like we do?

The Bible teaches us that Jesus experienced life just like we do. He had to grow up. He was tempted. He had friends and lost them. He got sad like we do. He traveled to Bethany once because His friend Lazarus had died. When He got there He cried. People have spent a lot of time guessing about what was going on in Jesus mind, what actually upset Him. The point is though that He had emotions. He didn't just go through life like a little wooden soldier. He dealt with the same stuff that we deal with every day. The Bible says He has compassion on us because of that.

SEE FOR YOURSELF: John 11:35

Is Jesus really coming back? If He is, then when?

Yes, Jesus is really coming back. Jesus promised it to His disciples before He left. Bible writers talked about it throughout the New Testament. But when? No one knows when. Now, a lot of people study the Bible to see if they can figure out when Jesus is coming back. They read all the prophecies and look at current events. But the truth is, there is a lot of mystery in all of that. And the other truth is that the Bible itself says that no one knows. So the best we can do is live our lives well and look forward to Jesus' return like it's a big surprise party.

> And if I go and prepare a place for you, I will come again and receive you to Myself.
> John 14:23

How come if Jesus was God, He let them kill Him?

"Let" is the right word to use. Jesus IS God. And He did LET them kill Him. It's really what He came to earth to do. Remember all the sacrifices in the Old Testament. People would offer an animal for their sins. That animal would actually be killed on an altar. Its blood would be spilled out. This was a reminder to the people that sin brings death. It was also a reminder that one day God would sacrifice himself for our sins. That is what Jesus came to do. When Jesus was being arrested (a BUNCH of soldiers came to arrest one man), His disciples wanted to defend Him. He said something like, "Don't you know that I could say the word and God would send more angels than you'd know what to do with?" Jesus knew that He needed to go through that whole horrible process in order to make God's forgiveness for our sins complete. He did it out of love for us. As hard as it must be to die, how much harder would it be to die knowing that you could do something about it?

SEE FOR YOURSELF: Matt. 26:52–54

146

Where was Jesus before He was born in Bethlehem?

There's a lot we just can't know about the answer to that question. One thing we do know though, Jesus was around when the world was created. Paul wrote in Colossians that by Jesus "all things were created that are in heaven and that are on earth . . . all things were created through Him and for Him." That's pretty amazing, isn't it? We sometimes think Jesus wasn't even on the scene until the whole manger deal, but that's not true. As God, He's been in on the whole thing since the beginning.

> He is the image of the invisible God, the first-born over all creation. For by Him all things were created that are in heaven and that are on earth, visible and invisible, . . . All things were created through Him and for Him.
> Col. 1:15-16

Has Jesus ever sinned?

No. But was He ever tempted to sin? Yes. Hebrews tells us that Jesus faced the very same temptations that we do. He is like a High Priest who has lots of compassion for us because He walked in human skin. Satan himself tried to get Jesus to sin (Matt. 4). But Jesus didn't ever choose sin over God's way, which is the real definition of rebellion. Now, that didn't mean that Jesus seemed all goody-goody. In fact, most people thought He was a regular guy. They were surprised when He started doing miracles. His neighbors would look at each other and say, "Isn't this Mary and Joseph's boy? What's up with that?" But no matter what they thought, Jesus kept His heart righteous His whole life.

SEE FOR YOURSELF:. Heb. 4:15

So are Jesus and God the same person?

Yes, Jesus was God in human form. He was born as a person, but He was God at the same time. It's one of the greatest mysteries of life. John calls Jesus the "Word." He says that Jesus was with God at the beginning of the world when God spoke the world into being. He says that Jesus was indeed God. The Holy Spirit is also God. God expresses Himself to us in these three ways: as our heavenly Father (God), as our Savior (Jesus), and as the Holy Spirit that lives in us and guides us.

> In the beginning was the Word, and the Word was with God, and the Word was God.
> John 1:1

What did Jesus come to do, really?

Jesus came to give us life in a new way. John quotes Jesus as saying so: "I have come that they may have life, and that they may have it more abundantly." Jesus provided a bridge between us and God. When we connect with God our lives are different. We are in touch with our Creator. We are forgiven for our sins. Not only does Jesus give us eternal life, He makes the lives we are living now so much better. Because of what Jesus did for us, we know we aren't alone. God is always with us, guiding us and leading us.

SEE FOR YOURSELF: John 10:10

Speaking the truth?

Meet Dane.

Some things aren't worth fighting for, and some are. When a person just starts going off about something and no one gives a rip what the guy is saying, well then just let the guy vent. No biggie. But when something's really at stake, I might consider speaking up. I never thought I was brave enough to stand up to someone in authority over me. I'm what you might call the "silent type" in class—never say a word unless called on, just try to blend in and be a wallflower. My theory is that if you're getting a lot of attention from the teacher, it's usually a bad thing.

When Mr. Fischer started our new segment in science class on "The Origin of the Universe," I figured it would be more of the same old, politically correct jargon, lots of different opinions and no real answers. As a Christian, I was glad that the text at least taught the theory of "Intelligent Design." No, they didn't give God much credit, but at least they didn't teach the theory of evolution as *fact*.

But Mr. Fischer was new. He was quite the first-year teacher, very opinionated, very pushy, failing kids left and right. I wasn't that excited to be sitting in his science class, especially since all my friends managed to get Mrs. Rosebrock, whose class was actually *fun*. So when Mr. Fischer started going off on evolution, I just rolled my eyes at first, expecting him to wrap it up pretty quickly and move on to the other theories. Wrong. Imagine how shocked I was when he flat-out said, "You may have heard of other theories before, but let me just put your little

minds at ease. There is no God. Evolution is true, it's scientific, and anyone who claims otherwise is a poorly educated, religious fanatic. For the record, if any of you disagree with me, I won't make you debate me in front of the class now. I'm just interested to know if any of you actually believe in the old God-theory."

Suddenly, the mood in the classroom had gone from boring to really hostile. I knew several other kids were Christians in my class, so I waited to see if any of them would raise their hands. Nope. Silence. No movement. Well, for crying out loud . . . I lifted my hand.

"Dane?" he asked in surprise. I really hadn't planned anything to say. I think God gave me the words. "Well, I do believe in God. He's real, He created the universe and all that I see, and He is alive and active today. I'm no expert on the different theories, but I can bring you a good source defending the Creation theory tomorrow."

Mr. Fischer didn't respond.

Another kid raised his hand. "I agree with Dane." Four other hands shot up and voices echoed, "So do I." I think he was shocked that I had actually spoken that he still didn't say anything.

"All right, Dane, I'll be interested to read that," he said, and he actually had respect in his voice. And I had twenty-four hours to find something for him to read.

Why did Jesus come to earth, when He could have stayed in heaven?

You shall also be a crown of glory in the hand of the LORD, and a royal diadem in the hand of your God. Isa. 62:3

Christians talk a lot about the things God gives them—faith, peace, forgiveness—everything they need, really. That's okay. It's good to think about all the good stuff God has given you and to say thanks. But have you ever wondered what's in it for Jesus? He left the greatest place you can imagine (heaven) to spend years on planet Earth. It was definitely not a step up for Him. And He didn't exactly get the royal treatment while He was here, either. So what's His reward—what does He get out of the deal?

You are His reward. You are what He wants for His trouble. You are His crown—which means your relationship with Him brings Him glory. After everything He gave up to make that happen, He deserves His crown. He deserves you. Let Him have more of your life every day.

SEE FOR YOURSELF: 2 Tim. 4:8; Rev. 14:14

If Jesus was Jewish, why aren't all His followers?

Before Jesus came, God had a special relationship with a group of people who descended from Abraham. Abraham's descendants are known as the Jews. God had promised Abraham that his descendants would become a nation and that the Messiah would come from them. Jesus was that Messiah. But one of the points of Jesus' ministry was that while the Messiah came from the Jews, God didn't send the Messiah just for the Jews. God sent Jesus to sacrifice Himself for the whole world—everybody. Paul wrote about this specifically in his letter to the Romans. He said, "There is no distinction between Jew and Greek." That was BIG news for that day. Some of the Jewish leaders were NOT glad to hear it. But the truth is God's salvation is free to all no matter who their great-great-great-great-great granddaddy was.

SEE FOR YOURSELF: Rom. 10:12

> When Jesus heard it, He said to them, "Those who are well have no need of a physician, but those who are sick. I did not come to call the righteous, but sinners, to repentance."
>
> Mark 2:17

JOY

Can God give me true joy?

00. 00. 29   00. 00

Are you a smiler or a frowner? Do you naturally
notice happy things, or are you a walking
vessel of gloom and doom? How about laughing?
Do you remember the last time you laughed until your
sides hurt, and your eyes watered, and you begged for mercy—you just couldn't
laugh anymore? However long it's been, whatever your natural disposition, God
promises to give you something to laugh about. He promises to walk right into
your most depressing day and turn things around. God didn't put you here to see
how awful He could make you feel. He put you here to glorify Him and to enjoy
life. So invite Him into your day and tell Him you really need something to laugh
about. Watch Him do a miracle on your behalf. No heart is too hard, no day is too
far gone, when the Maker of laughter keeps His promise.

SEE FOR YOURSELF: Sam. 2:1; Ps. 126:1-3

> Behold, God will not cast away the blameless, nor will He uphold the evildoers. He will yet fill your mouth with laughing, and your lips with rejoicing.
> Job 8:20, 21

In ancient Israel, dancing was considered a form of celebration and worship. As an expression of joy, both men and women danced to the music of the tambourines and stringed instruments.
Ps. 149:3

JUDGING OTHERS

> Judge not, and you shall not be judged. Condemn not, and you shall not be condemned. Forgive, and you will be forgiven.
> Luke 6:37

How come it's supposed to be wrong to judge others, but my parents and teachers and churches do it all the time?

You are facing a very sad truth of life. Most of us have an idea of what the truth is, but we are all inconsistent. The Bible does say, "Judge not, and you shall not be judged." You know what is the really puzzling thing about judging? It's so easy to judge other people because THEY are being judgmental. In fact I haven't found anybody that it's easier for me to be hard on than someone who is condemning somebody else. Then I have to realize that I'm making their same mistake. I would tell you to be careful about one thing, though. Sometimes your parents and teachers make statements that sound to you like judgments, snap statements where they are deciding what someone else thinks or feels. But remember that the adults in your life have lived longer than you and (hopefully) have learned some things from their life experiences. What sounds like judgments to you, might actually be some smarts on their part. Ask them questions and find out their thoughts before you judge their judgments.

> Just as a metalsmith working with gold or silver uses fire to purify the good and get rid of the bad, God uses the fire of His judgment to purify people and get rid of the bad.
> Zech. 13:9

153

KINDNESS OF GOD

> For the LORD your God is gracious and merciful, and will not turn His face from you if you return to Him.
> 2 Chron. 30:9

Does God ever pretend to be kind and merciful?

Kindhearted people sometimes make us suspicious. We wonder, *Is she for real? Is he like this all the time? What does she want from me?* Unfortunately, some people have learned how to use kindness to manipulate and charm others for selfish purposes. You don't have to wonder about God's kindness. He is for real. There are no strings attached. He is truly gracious, generous, sympathetic, and tolerant toward you. He cannot be unkind. There's nothing manipulative about God. He owns the whole world, so He won't charm you into giving Him something. He's always got your best interest at heart. He's genuinely gracious, kind, and merciful. You can trust Him because He loves you so purely and so much.

SEE FOR YOURSELF: Ps. 111:4; 145:8; Gal. 5:22, 23; 2 Tim. 2:1

LAZINESS

How do you know if a person's lazy?

> The soul of a sluggard desires, and has nothing; but the soul of the diligent shall be made rich.
>
> Prov. 13:4

00. 00. 29   00. 00. 10

Proverbs 13:4 says that a lazy person wants stuff but has nothing because he's not willing to do anything to get what he wants. Now, that doesn't mean everyone who doesn't have everything they want is lazy. We can't all get what we want. But it does mean that if a person keeps on complaining but doesn't do *anything* about it, they probably have some laziness going on. The opposite of laziness according to that same verse is diligence. A diligent person is the person who sees what they need to do, gets organized, and does it. They don't wait around for someone else to do something for them when they could do it themselves. Proverbs says that kind of person will get rich, but the lazy person won't have anything.

LEADERSHIP

> You shall select from all the people able men, such as fear God, men of truth, hating covetousness; and place such over them to be rulers of thousands.
> Ex. 18:21

What makes a good leader?

Moses had a talk with his father-in-law, Jethro, once about how to pick good leaders. Jethro had come to visit and saw that Moses was way overworked. Jethro suggested that Moses pick some leaders to help him so that Moses was dealing with the really tough problems but his assistants were taking care of the smaller ones. Jethro gave Moses these criteria: able men who fear God, men of truth who hate jealousy. That sounds like a good place to start. A good leader is someone who can do the job, who obeys God, and who has integrity. That's the kind of person that people can trust to lead them. Moses evidently picked his leaders and it paid off for him.

Is God in control of who our leaders are?

King David sure thought so. Do you remember the story about King Saul and him? Before David was king he served in Saul's court. Saul got jealous of David and suspected that David might replace him. Saul basically put a contract out on David. Saul made him a wanted man. Saul made David's life miserable. Yet, each time David had the opportunity to get back at Saul, he didn't. Why? Because Saul was God's anointed king. David took that very seriously. In fact, when Saul died, it was in battle with the help of a passerby. The passerby told David that he had helped Saul take his own life. David hit the roof. Why? Because Saul's leadership was ordained by God. That meant that only God had the right to end Saul's reign.

SEE FOR YOURSELF: 2 Sam. 1:16

Can political leaders influence their people for good?

Absolutely, beyond a shadow of a doubt, yes. If the Old Testament history of Israel teaches us anything it is that the kings had everything to do with whether the people obeyed God or didn't. Take King Josiah for instance. He was a righteous king who heard some of the Law from the Old Testament and realized that his people weren't obeying the Law at all. He committed himself to following the Law and what happened? The people committed themselves to the same thing. Ahab, on the other hand, was an evil king. He didn't even care whether his people worshiped God or not. Know what happened? They didn't. They worshiped the false god, Baal, instead. Political leaders make a lot of difference in how a nation relates to God.

> Then the king . . . made a covenant before the LORD, to follow the LORD and to keep His commandments and His testimonies and His statutes, with all his heart and all his soul, to perform the words of this covenant that were written in this book. And all the people took their stand for the covenant.
>
> **2 Kings 23:3**

How does a good leader make decisions?

Some of that depends on what kind of leader you're talking about. Some leaders are there to represent other people. In their case they have to make decisions based on what their "constituency" wants them to do. No matter what kind of leadership a person is involved in, though, there is a lot of responsibility that goes with being a leader. A wise Old Testament king, Jehoshaphat, trained his leaders to fear God, not show partiality, and not take bribes. Those are good guidelines for any leader. After all, every leader will stand before God one day and give an account of how he used his influence. The leader may as well think about that now.

SEE FOR YOURSELF: 2 Chron. 19:5-7

Why am I always reading about some preacher in a big scandal? Aren't they supposed to be better than the rest of us and set an example?

My brethren, let not many of you become teachers, knowing that we shall receive a stricter judgment.
James 3:1

Yes and no. Yes, because any leader has the extra responsibility of living their life in front of a lot of people. The book of James in the New Testament says that teachers have a stricter judgment because they are leaders. So leaders should set an example. You are right on target with that. It's important to remember, though, that just because someone is a leader doesn't make them super-human. In fact, people in power probably have more temptation thrown at them than regular, everyday people. So, because someone is a leader they have more pressure, but that doesn't mean they have some magic beans that make it easier for them to not mess up. If they do mess up, you can be sure a lot of people will know about it.

Holding my tongue?

Meet Ellie.

"Ugh, did you see how she is dressed today? When is she ever going to get a clue? I could do so much with her if I could give her a makeover. She really has a cute face underneath," Jade started the day off with her typical report on Mackenzie's outfit for the day. Usually I just wait for the conversation to change to the next victim who walks by, but today I had something of my own to add.

Mackenzie was one of those girls I had known all my life. We had been in school together since second grade, and we had been in a lot of the same classes over the years. We weren't friends, though, just acquaintances. We had absolutely nothing in common. She was unique. How she dressed was always a hot topic for conversation. She wasn't exactly geeky or alternative or artsy—kind of a weird mix of all three. She had these thick glasses, fake red hair, several unmentionable body piercings, and brightly colored, random clothes from the seventies. Whenever new people came to our school, they always did a double take at Mackenzie. I guess I had grown used to her over the years.

Yesterday afternoon I had overheard her boyfriend talking with one of his friends. I guess things weren't going so well in their relationship, and he planned to drop the axe sometime this week. I can't even repeat what he called her.

So as Jade turned toward me, the info was on the tip of my tongue. I knew the girls would go crazy over this newest gossip, and it would only take ten seconds before I had all their attention on me. I started to open my mouth.

A feeling of guilt shot through me, and I remembered seeing Mackenzie in class the day before. Her brown eyes had looked sad even through her thick glasses. She was fighting back tears over something. I thought of her as a little girl, remembering how we both looked in fourth grade. I thought of how *I* have felt when other people talked bad about me. So I said nothing.

Jade looked at me again. "Were you going to say something, Ellie?" she asked.

"No, I'm just excited to go to the game this weekend, aren't you?" I asked. She and Rachel quickly jumped on their new topic, and I felt a sense of confirmation sweep over me. I remembered some verses I had read about how the tongue has the power to tear down or to heal. It's something I have to be conscious of.

LIVING IN THE LIGHT

He brought them out of darkness and the shadow of death, and broke their chains in pieces.
Ps. 107:14

How can I live in the light?

In the Bible, the word *darkness* refers to ignorance, hiding, and sin. *Light* indicates truth, openness, and the presence of God. Jesus told Nicodemus, "And this is the condemnation, that the light has come into the world, and men loved darkness rather than light, because their deeds were evil. For everyone practicing evil hates the light and does not come to the light, lest his deeds should be exposed" (John 3:19-20). Because people loved the darkness—their evil way of life—they rejected the light, Jesus. When you made Jesus your Lord, He rescued you from darkness. You are no longer ignorant of the wrong things you do or of God's love for you in spite of them. You don't have to be ashamed of anything. Even sin doesn't have to hold you back from God's love. Instead, Jesus has revealed His truth to you. He's given you the peace and confidence you need to share yourself with others. Most of all, He's become your Friend. Look back to the time before you were a Christian. Look how far you've come. You've come out of the darkness of sin into the light and love of Jesus.

If light and daytime represented goodness and truth, what do you suppose darkness and night represented? If you said they symbolized sin, evil, and death, give yourself a pat on the back.
Job 24:13-17

168

LOVE

Does true love ever stop?

00. 00. 29

Stop what? Does true love ever stop loving?
No. In 1 Corinthians Paul dedicates a whole
chapter to the nature of love. He says that love
bears all things, believes all things, hopes all things,
endures all things. It never fails. Be careful, though, to understand
the nature of love. Some people take this to mean that they think they need to
put up with anything just because they love someone. They end up getting hurt
but doing nothing about it in the name of love. Loving someone doesn't mean
hurting yourself or letting yourself be hurt. Loving someone does mean always
caring what happens to someone and helping them out whenever you can. It
means being a friend for all time, not just when it's convenient or fun.

Love never fails. But
whether there are
prophecies, they will
fail; whether there are
tongues, they will
cease; whether there
is knowledge, it will
vanish away.
1 Cor. 13:8

LOVE FOR OTHERS

You shall not take vengeance, nor bear any grudge against the children of your people, but you shall love your neighbor as yourself: I am the LORD.
Lev. 19:18

Do I have to love people who hurt me?

Here's a great piece of advice from Leviticus. You can use it in all your relationships, not just friendships. Unfortunately, friendships can be tricky sometimes. They can be especially hard at times when you're growing so much so fast—like in your teenage years. People may treat you like their best buddy one day and not even speak to you the next. High schools are famous for cliques and clubs, and sometimes even when you're "in" you get treated like you're "out." God knows about high school. He knows what it's like to be tight with a group and have your back stabbed. Don't play those games. He says not to be angry and not to take revenge. Stuff hurts. So hurt, but don't be angry, and don't start thinking about how you're going to get someone back. The Lord says love. Love that person as much as you love yourself. Whoa. That's big love. The cool thing is that God will help you. You may not be able to muster up one ounce of love on your own, but ask God to help you love and He will. Be quick to love and quick to forgive. That's God's good advice and you'll be happier and healthier because of it.

Hospitality was serious business in ancient Israel. God commanded His people to show kindness to strangers. Often this involved offering food and shelter to travelers and their animals. Since most travelers wore open shoes, hosts were also expected to provide water so that their guests could wash their dirty feet.
Jud. 19:20-21

SEE FOR YOURSELF: John 5:1-3; 15:12; 2 Cor.
Eph. 4:31-32

162

Do we have to love our enemies?

We only have to love our enemies under one condition: if we want to live the life God calls us to. The Bible talks about love over and over again. It's everywhere in there. And specifically, the Bible talks about the difference between loving the people who love us (a big easy, piece of cake) and loving the people who don't. The point is our motivation for loving. If we love only because someone loves us, God loves us and we want to obey Him, then we've done something significant. God says to "Love your enemies." If what God says matters to you, then yes, you gotta.

> But I say to you who hear: Love your enemies, do good to those who hate you.
> Luke 6:27

Does the Bible actually say we should take care of people who have less than we do?

Yes, it does. In the Old Testament God made taking care of the poor and the needy a part of the Law. In the New Testament, Jesus and the apostles spoke of it often. Jesus made a point that when a person gave a party, they should invite people that couldn't give anything back. In doing that, they were showing God's kind of love. He loves us even though we can't repay Him. That's how we should treat the people who have nothing to offer us.

SEE FOR YOURSELF: Luke 14:13-14

LOVE OF GOD

Oh, give thanks to the LORD, for He is good! For His mercy endures forever.
Ps. 136:1

Do I have to be a certain "type" to receive God's love?

This whole chapter in Psalm 136 tells about God's enduring mercy. He loves us with an unconditional love. It doesn't matter what you look like, what your breath smells like, how much money you have, or what your past is like. God loves you anyway! Regardless of anything, God loves you just the same. That's the kind of love we need to have for each other. We need to look at the world through Jesus' eyes. There's a story in Mark 2 about four men who brought a man, crippled with disease, to Jesus. There was not enough room for them, so they ripped a hole in the roof where Jesus was teaching and lowered the man down through the hole. Now that's compassion. When Jesus saw their faith, He healed the man. These four men loved their friend with an unconditional love. They were willing to rip off a roof to get him healed. He was sick with disease, and so he probably didn't look or smell that good. They probably had needs themselves, but the only thing they were concerned about was getting their friend to Jesus! Unconditional love. Next time you've failed and feel like nobody cares, remember that God loves you unconditionally. Like those friends, He's willing to rip a roof off in order to show you the love and mercy you need.

SEE FOR YOURSELF: John 14:21; Rom. 5:5; 1 John 4:10, 16

164

Will God ever take away His love from me?

It's hard to imagine mercy (compassionate, loving concern) that never ends. Your boyfriend loved you yesterday, but he loves someone else today. Your parents seem to love you. You know someone whose dad just left because he doesn't love the mom anymore. Love seems to come and go very easily down here on earth. But there is Someone who is truly in love with you. He can't keep His eyes off of you. He is so proud that you belong to Him. The love of God will never disappoint you. His commitment is forever. There will be no trial separations, no grounds for divorce. He is good, and you are the one He loves without end.

> They lifted up their voice with the trumpets and cymbals and instruments of music, and praised the LORD, saying: "For He is good, for His mercy endures forever."
> 2 Chr. 5:13

Did God love Hitler?

God loves everyone. He gives everyone a chance to hear Him and come to Him in faith. Hitler had that chance as much as anyone else. Early on Hitler had some religious influences in his life. Unfortunately he never connected with God in such a way that caused him to live a life of love. He did some horrible things with his life. But did God love him and want the best for him? Yes. We can separate ourselves from God by refusing to connect with Him. But nothing can separate us from God's love, not our choices, not sin, not ourselves.

SEE FOR YOURSELF: Rom. 8:38-39

> **Ever wonder who introduced music as part of the worship service? It was King David. David's son, Solomon, carried on the tradition in grand style after the temple was built. Nearly three hundred "master musicians" led the four thousand members of the choir and orchestra in carrying out their duties.**
> **1 Chron. 25:1**

Why does God make some people ugly or poor or stuff like that? Doesn't He love us all the same?

> But the LORD said to Samuel, "Do not look at his appearance or at the height of his stature . . . For the LORD does not see as man sees; for man looks at the outward appearance, but the LORD looks at the heart."
> 1 Samuel 16:7

This is one way in which we think very differently than God does. God recognizes that by human standards some people are more impressive than others, but it matters to Him in a whole different way. Once God sent Samuel to find the next king of Israel and to anoint him king. God warned Samuel not to be impressed with the outward appearances of the people he would see. He reminded Samuel that people look on the outward appearance, but God looks on the heart. Samuel ended up anointing David, the youngest and least of all Jesse's sons. David ended up being the greatest king of Israel. God lets life do some things in terms of how we look. Our genetics do some things. God's concern is our character, how we face what life does and who we become because of them. That doesn't feel fair at all

SEE FOR YOURSELF: Rom. 5:8-11; Eph. 2:4-7; 1 John 4:7-1

How does God care for me?

Why does God care about everyone? Because each one of us is His creation, fashioned by Him, and completely loved. How does God care? He provides all that we need. He waits patiently for us to seek Him. He is faithful to guide our steps and order our days. He pours grace all over us. What can we do to get God to care about us more? Nothing. We are already cared for completely just because we belong to Him. When will His caring end? Never. He promises to be with us always. How can you be like God? Care about other people even more than you care about yourself.

SEE FOR YOURSELF: Job 36:5; John 13:34-35; Gal. 2:20;1 John 4:7-11

Does God love others more than me?

Does your teacher have a favorite student—someone she has chosen to be teacher's pet? Does your coach have an athlete who's obviously his choice for MVP? Do you see favoritism in choices made in your church or in your family? Sometimes, the same person will be the favorite everywhere they go. If you're the favored person, you can get to feeling pretty special. If you're not, it can be the pits. God says you are His favorite—His chosen one. There's nobody else on earth He loves more than He loves you. When He sees you coming to pray or to worship Him, He's so glad you want to be with Him. He wants to be with you, too. You aren't just His favorite when you're down or left out and nobody else will give you a second glance. You're His favorite even when your ego doesn't need that kind of boost. No matter where you go or what you go through, you're always God's chosen one.

> Yet hear now, O Jacob My servant, and Israel whom I have chosen. Thus says the LORD who made you and formed you from the womb, who will help you: "Fear not, O Jacob My servant; and you, Jeshurun, whom I have chosen."
>
> Is. 44:1-2

SEE FOR YOURSELF: Job 34:19; Jer. 9:24; John 3:16; Acts 10:34

How long will God love me?

Can you imagine having someone be eternally loyal to you, someone who loves you forever? For most of us, even the thought that there is an eternity just blows our minds. We can't imagine being eighty years old—much less living forever and ever and ever. God loves you so much that He promises not only to let you live with Him forever, but also to love you and be loyal to you. That's the ultimate friendship! God has so much confidence in who you are, who He made you to be, that He wants to spend forever with you. Even if every friend you ever had were to desert you, He would still be there loving you. If you did something and hacked off everyone you know, He would be loyal to you. God hasn't committed Himself to you for the length of your life, but for the length of His life—for all eternity.

SEE FOR YOURSELF: Is. 55:3; Jer. 31:3, 4; Hos. 14:4; Rom. 8:35-39

I know they say that God loves us all, but does He even know about me as one single person or does He just kind of love all of us as a group?

> Are not two sparrows sold for a copper coin? And not one of them falls to the ground apart from your Father's will. But the very hairs of your head are all numbered. Do not fear therefore; you are of more value than many sparrows.
> Matt. 10:29-31

As unbelievable as it sounds, God loves you as one single person. There is a verse that says the "very hairs of your head are all numbered." That's pretty individual, don't you think? Somewhere around that same verse it says two sparrows could be bought for one coin—that meant sparrows weren't worth much to people at that time. But, the verses say, not one sparrow falls to the ground outside of God's sight. Then it says something like, "Don't you know you are more important to God than little birds?" Again, pretty individual, don't you think? It's hard for our human minds to understand a God who can even be aware of all us humans at one time, much less care about us all. That's what makes Him God. He can do that. It's a mystery, but it's good news. He knows about you, and He cares about you.

Should I really do what Jesus would? Meet Luke.

As soon as someone said something, the rumors started spreading like wildfire. You know how high school is. Stories get passed along the grapevine so fast, and you never have a chance to defend yourself. Especially rumors like this. It's the kind of juicy thing that every person listens to and then tells three other people within ten minutes. Even the guys. Usually girls are a lot worse about gossip, I think, but the guys were ruthless this time. But I guess it was so shocking that people just wanted to talk about it.

Supposedly, Matthew was gay.

I don't know if he officially came out of the closet and told his closest friends or if they confronted him on it. I guess he didn't even bother to deny it. It's not like he's hitting on other guys between classes, but then again, no one will go near him now. It's like he's a leper or something.

Yeah, I know what the Bible says about homosexuality. It's perfectly clear that God condemns it as sin. I also know how Jesus wants us to treat other people with love and compassion. If you read about Jesus' life, you'll see Him always loving sinners, welcoming them into His presence, but always challenging them to leave their lives of sin.

It was hard not to just join in the gossip and make Matthew feel even more alienated. But I felt a strong sense of conviction after I heard the brutal gossip going around. I knew Matthew pretty well, enough to hang out every now and then. He was suddenly in desperate need of a friend. *What a bad situation,* I thought. *If I start spending time with him, I'll get blasted too. They'll think I'm the same way.*

I took a risk. I took Matthew on as a friend. We ate together and started hanging out on weekends. At first the other guys felt really uncomfortable around both of us, but I just kept acting natural. Soon they started treating me (and Matthew) normal again.

I didn't ignore Matthew's sin. He knew where I stood on it, and even if I was the only person who would tell it to his face, he knew exactly what I thought and what God thought about it. I made it impossible for him to forget it. He was pretty mystified by how I treated him, but he was my friend, and I was going to love him through his struggles.

MEANING OF LIFE

All things are full of labor; man cannot express it. The eye is not satisfied with seeing, nor the ear filled with hearing.
Eccl. 1:8

Where can I find meaning in life?

A lot of people spend all their lives trying to get satisfied. Cars, clothes, tattoos, body piercing, drugs—whatever the latest thing is to make you feel like somebody. Solomon says in Ecclesiastes that nothing will ever do it. Nothing will ever make you feel satisfied. New clothes may fill you up for a few days. And then you're empty again. The high doesn't last long enough. Without Jesus, nothing matters. There is no purpose in life, and even the coolest stuff only brings momentary pleasure. Solomon says that apart from Jesus you will never enjoy your time on earth or the things you've been given. It's all meaningless without the Savior. Without Jesus, this is all there is—no future, no eternity to look forward to. So when your heart is aching, your life seems empty, and you feel lost, go to Jesus to be filled up and satisfied. He will not disappoint you.

SEE FOR YOURSELF: 1 Cor 15:58; Gal. 6:8; Phil. 3:7, 12-14

Why did God make us in the first place?

We don't know God's exact thought process. There's a famous poem that says that God said, "I'm lonely, I'll make me a man." But the Bible gives us no reason to think that God was lonely without us. He sure has had a headache with us (if He had headaches, which I don't think He does). So if you're asking, "Why did God THINK to make us?" We don't know. But if you're asking what God's purpose is for our lives, we do have some answers for that. God created us for Him, to be in relationship with Him, to bring Him glory, to do good works on the earth. What does it mean to bring God glory? Have you ever heard somebody say, "That kid's just a glorified version of his dad"? It means the kid is just like his dad. We bring God glory when we are just like Him. He created us in His image. We bring Him glory when we live up to that. God created us to be His children.

SEE FOR YOURSELF: Eph. 2:10

> For by Him all things were created that are in heaven and that are on earth, visible and invisible, whether thrones or dominions or principalities or powers. All things were created through Him and for Him.
> Col. 1:16

MEDITATING

I want to learn to meditate. My parents aren't sure. Is it OK?

I will meditate on Your precepts, And contemplate Your ways. Ps. 119:15

It probably depends on what you're meditating on. The Bible actually talks a lot about meditation, particularly in the Psalms. It says that we should meditate on God's Word. That means we should let it roll around in our minds. We should quiet ourselves and open our minds up to God and let Him teach us and change us from the inside out. Sounds simple, right? Then why are people scared of meditation? Because when you meditate you are opening yourself up in a spiritual way. If people meditate on Scripture, then good things can be done inside of them. But many people feel that if you open up your mind and your soul through meditation without the protection of Scripture, that evil spirits can get to you more easily. Does that sound weird? There ARE evil spirits. There is a whole spiritual dimension going on all the time—angels and demons slugging it out. God protects us from that if we'll let Him. So how you meditate makes a difference in whether you can be sure it's OK.

MERCY

Why is mercy important?

When we give mercy we are freed up to receive mercy. It seems to be one of those things, like forgiveness, that God withholds from us if we withhold them from others. Proverbs tells us to bind mercy around our neck and write it on our hearts. That means to do whatever we have to not to forget and not to let mercy get very far from us.

> Let not mercy and truth forsake you; bind them around your neck, write them on the tablet of your heart, and so find favor and high esteem in the sight of God and man.
> Prov. 3:3-4

MIRACLES

Miracles: Were they just for Jesus or does God still do them?

> "Before all your people I will do marvels such as have not been done in all the earth, nor in any nation."
>
> Ex. 34:10

God said that He would do things "such as have not been done in all the earth." He sure kept that promise to the Israelites. He cut a path for them through the Jordan River. He made the walls of Jericho fall down when the priests blew their trumpets. He kept the sun from going down one day. And that was just the beginning. God did a lot of miracles in New Testament times, too. Jesus and His disciples healed people almost all the time. Jesus made blind eyes see. He made crippled legs walk. He made lepers whole. He even raised people from the dead. Today, a lot of people have just quit expecting to see God do miracles. Modern technology has been able to do things that used to require a miracle. Science can explain things that no one understood many years ago. Sometimes even people who do believe in miracles aren't on the lookout for them anymore. We live in a day of miracles. God's miracle-working power is alive and moving all over the world. Be on the lookout. He can do "exceedingly abundantly above all that we ask or think" (Eph. 3:20). He'll do miracles.

SEE FOR YOURSELF: Ex. 11:9; Ps. 77:14; Dan. 6:27; Mic. 7:15; Gal. 3:5

How come you don't see miracles all the time, like back in the Bible days?

> And as you go, preach, saying, "The kingdom of heaven is at hand." Heal the sick, cleanse the lepers, raise the dead, cast out demons. Freely you have received, freely give.
> Matt. 10:7-8

Partly because we don't expect them. Have you ever gone to some big event, walked through a big crowd where you never expected to see anyone you knew, and walked right past a friend before you recognized them? Sometimes we do that with miracles. God answers our prayers all the time. He does amazing things. Jesus never gave us the impression that miracles should stop with His era. In fact, He told the disciples they should be able to do what they had seen Him do, AND MORE! Wow. There is no verse that says, "and after this date, God won't do amazing things anymore." Our world is much bigger now, though, and we are a skeptical group. We don't always hear about amazing things that happen and when we do, we sometimes discount them. There sure are scams around. Don't stop looking for miracles though. If you need one, go ahead and ask God for it. You might be amazed at what you find.

What is a miracle used for?

A miracle is an event that happens in a way that nature doesn't normally work. A car is crushed from every angle, but the driver comes away unharmed. A kid walks in healed after doctors declare that there's no hope. The wildest troublemaker in town gets saved and starts telling everybody what God has done in his life. A Man dead three days in a grave gets up and appears to over 500 people. If you've ever seen a miracle, you can be sure that you were witnessing the hand of God working. You experienced a supernatural event. Only God can do miracles. Sometimes He uses people in the process, but no man can work a miracle by his own power. You've got to have God for a miracle.

The purpose of a miracle is to bring glory to God and to remind us of His amazing love toward us. Miracles force us to stop looking at ourselves and our limitations. We have to look up at God and His mighty power. A miracle is meant to get our attention and cause us to be amazed by our God.

SEE FOR YOURSELF: Ex. 34:10; Ps. 72:18; Mic. 7.15

MONEY

Is it wrong for TV preachers to get millions of dollars for what they do?

Even so the LORD has commanded that those who preach the gospel should live from the gospel.
1 Cor. 9:14

Hmmmm. Let's see. Is it wrong? When we look at it in really black and white terms, it sure looks fishy, doesn't it? I mean, here are people dressed in nice clothes on a TV show asking for money from people who have a lot less than them. It seems like the TV person should be giving money to the poor people doesn't it? Before we make any further judgments, though, we ought to find out what that TV preacher is doing with the money. Is the money going to make meaningful ministries happen? If so, then that TV preacher is allowing his viewers to be a part of something that they couldn't do by themselves. Is the money just going to buy TV time, nice clothes, and fame? Well, that seems a little less honorable, doesn't it? You know as well as I do that there are faithful good-hearted people who send money they can't afford to TV personalities that don't use it well. I'm not defending it...at all. But I know this. God looks at the faithful intentions of those people who share of what they have in the hopes of doing something good in the world. And God will judge the heart of the one receiving the money. The Bible does say that it's OK for a minister to be supported financially by his ministry. It also says that leaders will be judged for what they've done with their leadership (shudder).

What can money do to our relationship with God?

Money can distract us from our relationship with God. When we have money we have to tend to it. We need to manage it and invest it. We try and make it grow into more money. Money can also tempt us to find our security in it instead of God. When we have money we think we can take care of ourselves and so we sometimes forget that God is still the source of everything we need. Once a rich young man came to Jesus and asked how to get eternal life. Jesus tested him by asking him to get rid of all his possessions. The man couldn't do it, even for eternal life. Money does that. It seems more important than everything else, but it isn't.

> Then Jesus, looking at him, loved him, and said to him, "One thing you lack: Go your way, sell whatever you have and give to the poor, and you will have treasure in heaven; and come, take up the cross, and follow Me."
>
> Mark 10:21

Money: Where is it going to come from?

We serve an awesome God! He is so practical. There's nothing that He will not or cannot do for you. It's a fact. God is concerned with every area of your life. Every area? Yes, every area. He's so concerned that He will even give you strength to make a living. He wants to give you creative ideas that will cause you to turn the corner financially. If anybody should be blessed, it should be God's children. Remember, God wants you blessed so you can be a blessing! You are His child, and He gets pleasure when His people prosper. Don't settle for second best. God has equipped you with the goods that you need to make a living. We can learn from Solomon's example. God told Solomon that he could ask for whatever he wanted, and it would be granted. What did Solomon ask for? Money, wealth, power, fame? No! He asked for wisdom; and, boy, did he get it! He received the wisdom of God and this wisdom brought the money, wealth, fame, and the admiration of others. One thing is certain: Solomon didn't have a problem making a living, and neither should you. Begin asking God for godly wisdom today—and meaning it from your heart. He promises to give you the strength to make a living!

SEE FOR YOURSELF: Deut. 8:18; 1 Kings 3:5-14; Job 12:13; Ps. 35:27; Prov. 8:12; Phil. 4:19

MURDER

Does God consider any sin as bad as murder?

If a man acts with premeditation against his neighbor, to kill him with guile, you shall take him from My altar, that he may die.
Ex. 21:14

Yes, He does. In the Sermon on the Mount Jesus went through a series of sins that people commit as actions and He showed how those sins were really attitudes first. For instance, He compared committing adultery to having lustful thoughts. Jesus pushed His listeners to go one step further in keeping their hearts clean as well as their actions. In this part of His sermon He addressed murder. He compared murder to disrespecting someone, treating them like they are worthless, being angry with them without cause, or calling them a fool. It makes you think twice about name-calling doesn't it?

Simple words to save a friend?
Meet Mikayla.

Gillian has always had everything going for her—class president, homecoming queen, and a lot of family money. She's a Conner, after all, and that family could buy the whole state if they wanted. Her parents are high-profile people, and they travel all over the world. I guess it's a little lonely for Gillian then, but she's got plenty of other things to do.

There are about eight of us girls who always hang out together. It makes it fun, you know, since there's always something to do. The girls always say Gillian and I are the most sensitive. We're the ones who cry during TV shows and whenever we see a dead animal on the road (especially dogs). I guess I just sense emotions easily, in myself and in other people.

I started to notice that Gillian hadn't quite been herself recently. For some reason, she's been really tired looking, not eating much, and seeming low on energy. We've had homework, but geez, not that much. She didn't go out with us last Friday, and I wondered what she did at home by herself. Plus she flipped out at DeDe the other day, and that's totally not like her. I started paying closer attention to her.

When Gillian gave me her favorite pearl earrings, I was suspicious. When she pulled DeDe aside for an hour to apologize and to set things straight, I really began to wonder. She was showing all the classic signs of depression, and I wondered if she might be thinking suicide. Her parents had been gone for six weeks this time and weren't due back from Hong Kong until next Thursday. I started to get scared for her, and I didn't think anybody else noticed.

I called her that night and asked if I could come over. Her aunt was asleep in the guest suite, so we just hung out in the basement. I kept making small talk but prayed that God would give me the right words to ask. I knew it was something I had to do. "Gillian, you've seemed kind of depressed lately. Are you dealing with something I don't know about?" I asked hesitantly.

"Yes," she whispered, her eyes locked on the floor.

"Are you really depressed?" I asked. She nodded. "Are you thinking about hurting yourself?" She started crying. She talked to me about her loneliness and emptiness inside. She poured out the dark feelings and the doubt that she felt. She felt like no one cared about her. Her self-worth had dropped really low. She felt she had no reason to live. We talked for about an hour, and mostly I just listened. We prayed together and then made a plan to go see the school counselor together in the morning.

By having an outlet, I think Gillian felt reconnected to her life. Her parents came home early, and I noticed they haven't been traveling much lately. Praise God He protected her from herself. All I can say is, I'm glad He gave me the courage to get involved.

Is violence and killing wrong if it's just in a video game or a movie?

Is it wrong for digital signals that appear on the screen to appear as if they are destroying the other digital signals that appear on the screen? It would be hard to apply morals to that. Instead of talking about digital signals, let's talk about you playing the game. Have you heard the phrase, "Garbage in, garbage out"? It applies to a lot of things. On a computer, you'll only get something useful out of it if you put good information into it. It's how it works with the human heart and mind too. Jesus said it's not what we put on that makes us moral. It's what comes out of us. The danger of the violence and killing in games and movies is that it affects us. It sharpens our appetite for that fatal kind of excitement. It affects the way we think. It's not the digital signals, it's how much time we spend thinking about and participating in killing and violence, even just in our minds. What kind of balance is your life in?

SEE FOR YOURSELF: Mark 7:20-23.

> I say to you that whoever is angry with his brother without a cause shall be in danger of the judgment. . . . But whoever says, "You fool!" shall be in danger of hell fire.
> Matt. 5:22

MUSIC

I can turn on my favorite song and instantly feel better. Why is music so powerful?

And so it was, whenever the spirit from God was upon Saul, that David would take a harp and play it with his hand. Then Saul would become refreshed and well, and the distressing spirit would depart from him.
1 Sam. 16:23

Music somehow touches our souls. It expresses our feelings even when we can't. We can't exactly explain how that happens. It has always been true, though. In ancient times there was a king named Saul who was a little bonkers. When he would go into one of his dark times, his servants would go get a young man named David to play his harp for Saul. This was before radios, recorders, and certainly CDs. They didn't have music at the flip of a switch. They had to ship in actual musicians if there was going to be music. David's playing comforted Saul and helped him get his wheels all in the same direction again. Music has that same power today. We are so used to music being everywhere that we can take it for granted. Every store we walk into has some kind of music playing. Music is one of the amazing gifts of God that He just leaves laying around for us to use any time we want to.

SEE FOR YOURSELF: 1 Sam. 16:23

My parents won't let me listen to rap, not even Christian rap groups. How can they say it's bad when it's Christian music?

00. 00. 29   00. 00. 0

If there is any virtue and if there is anything praiseworthy— meditate on these things. Phil. 4:8

I'm not sure trying to explain parents to their children is any more possible than explaining kids to parents. I will say that association is a strong thing. Because so much rap music has negative lyrics, your parents would probably rather you not develop a taste for it. For all they know, you'll like the music so much you'll want more, and you'll be willing to listen to worse lyrics to have the music you like. Sometimes parents are scared, but they just don't show it. Maybe you could sit down with them and show them the lyrics to the music and let them know that the words you are listening to ARE important to you. You can read them Philippians 4:8, that verse that tells you to think about good and noble things. Let them know that you aren't going to listen to lyrics that don't pass the test of that verse just because you like the music. It might not seem like it now, but your relationship with your parents is more important than listening to a CD. This is a good time to learn to work things out together.

SEE FOR YOURSELF: Phil. 4:8

The ancient Israelites preferred stringed instruments for their worship services and percussion instruments for their parties and celebrations. The instruments the Israelites played were probably quite different from our instruments today. Held by handles at the bottom, sistrums were used to create a rattling sound. 2 Sam. 6:5

What should we use music for?

There are probably a lot of answers to that question. The Bible does give one answer specifically, though. Paul wrote to the Colossian church that they should use psalms, hymns, and spiritual songs to teach and encourage each other. That doesn't mean that we can't enjoy music just for the beauty of it. But music has such a capacity to touch our souls. We can't let that power pass by without using it. That's why music is and always has been such an important part of the church. Even when Jesus met with His disciples just before His death, they ended their time together by singing a hymn.

SEE FOR YOURSELF: Col. 3:16

And He said to them, "Why is it that you sought Me? Did you not know that I must be about My Father's business?"

Luke 2:49

OBEDIENCE

Do I have to obey everything God says?

Samuel said: "... Behold, to obey is better than sacrifice, and to heed than the fat of rams."
1 Sam. 15:22

The right thing is always to obey God. Saul proves in this passage that you can't just do whatever you want, even if it seems OK or harmless. God wants you to obey Him. Saul thought he could just take over and revise God's instructions to suit himself. God was really disappointed with Saul's disobedience and took away his title as king. The Bible is God's word of instruction to us. It helps us live so that we can be safe, happy, and blessed. It is not up for revision. You can't just pick the parts you like. God wants you to obey Him. All of Him and all of His Word.

SEE FOR YOURSELF: Ex. 19:5; Deut. 10:12, 13; Is. 1:19

Fasting—that is, going without food for a certain period of time—was a common practice in ancient Israel. Usually it was done as part of a religious ceremony or as a way to show grief or repentance. Officially, the Israelites were only required to fast on the Day of Atonement. Sometimes, though the leaders of the country would call for a voluntary fast during times of war.
2 Chron. 20:3

Do I really need to obey my parents' rules?

The difference between what you want and what your parents want is all about perspective. You see what everyone else is doing and long to be a part of the fun. Your parents see a much bigger picture—the part that you don't want to think about—the stuff you know will never happen to you. When you say, "Why can't my curfew be one hour later; what's the big deal?" they see the reality—the later it gets, the more drunk drivers on the road, violent crimes increase, fatigue causes people to make poor decisions, and the list goes on. Your parents' years have brought them wisdom. And they are responsible for you to God. Proverbs says that wise sons and daughters heed their parents' instructions. Your parents are the instruments through which God builds your life and gives you direction. Even if you have a hard time accepting their judgment, learn to respect their authority. Do not be the stubborn child who ignores his parents and grows up to be a fool.

SEE FOR YOURSELF: Prov. 12:1, 15; 13:1, 10; 20:20

> A wise son heeds his father's instruction, but a scoffer does not listen to rebuke.
> Prov. 13:1

THE OCCULT

DD. DD. 29

The occult: Harmless games or dangerous practices?

> There shall not be found among you anyone who makes his son or his daughter pass through the fire, or one who practices witchcraft, or a soothsayer, or one who interprets omens, or a sorcerer, or one who conjures spells, or a medium, or a spiritist, or one who calls up the dead. For all who do these things are an abomination to the LORD.
> Deut. 18:10-13

God calls those things an abomination. As a believer, it's your job to imitate God and to think His kind of thoughts. So the next time you're at a slumber party or sleepover and someone wants to turn off the lights and levitate somebody or contact a dead person, be the brave one who says, "No. That's disgusting and stupid. It's fooling around with Satan; and if he's invited to this party, I'm outta here." That's what séances are—an invitation for Satan to come in and use his power on a game board or whatever else you ask him for. He'd love to come to your party and play tricks with a bunch of young people and hang out all night messing with you. Come on, there are plenty of other fun, innocent things to do at slumber parties. (We don't need to give you any ideas!)

SEE FOR YOURSELF: Ex. 22:18; Lev 19:31; 20:6, 27

Is Halloween an evil holiday?

Halloween (which means All Hallow Even, like Christmas Eve) has some evil connotations. Originally it did involve a celebration of evil. Today, for some it still does. It has become a custom though. There are a lot of people that don't even think about the evil beginnings of Halloween. They just think of it as a fun time for kids to dress up and get candy. Once something, even one that has some bad things about it, becomes a custom, it's difficult to know what to do about it. In Paul's day there was a custom that Christians struggled with. They would go to someone's house and be offered meat for dinner. A lot of the meat in those days was offered to idols. Should they eat meat that had been dedicated to an idol? Paul said something like, "Don't get me wrong, idols aren't anything. We aren't saying they have any power over the meat. In Romans 14, Paul urges the believers not to judge one another. Whatever you do, whether it is eating or celebrating a holiday, celebrate it unto the Lord. God knows each one of our hearts, and He knows our motivations, and we need to be judged by Him alone.

You cannot drink the cup of the Lord and the cup of demons; you cannot partake of the Lord's table and of the table of demons. Or do we provoke the Lord to jealousy?
1 Cor. 10:21-22

The Israelites had some bad neighbors, most of whom practiced witchcraft and magic. Witchcraft involved trying to see the future with the help of a pagan god. Magic involved trying to expand one's knowledge through mind-altering drugs. All forms of witchcraft, magic, and fortune-telling were strictly forbidden by God.
Deut. 18:10,11

Witches: Are they harmless or Satan's followers?

> You shall not permit a sorceress to live.
> Ex. 22:18

"You shall not . . . practice divination or soothsaying"! That's what Leviticus 19:26 says. Don't even think about it. The world of witchcraft and black magic is very real and totally controlled by Satan. Experimenting with spells and curses is asking Satan to use his power on you. He will, but not without a trade. He'll want something from you in exchange for his power. People who experiment with witchcraft can really get messed up because they start out by just letting Satan have a tiny part of them. But the next time he requires a little more; then before they know it he's moved in and he's running the whole place. Stay away from witches, Satan worship, black magic, animal sacrifice, even "white witchcraft"—anything that promotes darkness and evil. Some forms are easy to spot, but others are sneaky. Look out for movies, books, music—anything that goes into your head. Satan is happy if he can even get you to think about him. The old saying is still good: "Hear no evil. See no evil. Speak no evil."

SEE FOR YOURSELF: Lev. 19:26; 20:6; Phil. 4:8; 1 Thess. 5:21, 22; Rev 21:8

The right circle for my love life?
Meet Scott.

I thought everything was right about this girl. I couldn't think about anything else besides her. Autumn was everything I could ever want—and more. She was one of the most popular girls in our class, and every guy was dying for a date with her. She seemed like a good girl, too, not like some of the sketchy girls you wouldn't trust. To top it off, she was just gorgeous—big blue eyes, light blond hair, tall and elegant. Needless to say, when we first went out, I was in awe of her. After a couple of weeks, I had discovered that she had an amazing personality, too. She was so fun to be around, and I looked forward to the weekends with her so much. I'll admit it, I was whipped.

There was one issue I kept avoiding. In my mind, I was in total denial. When my parents asked, I kind of shaded out with some vague answer about what a great girl she was. But in my mind, I kept coming back to the same reservation. I didn't think she was a Christian.

Now you might be thinking, what's the big deal? Well let me just tell you—this was a big deal. My parents had always forbidden me to date unbelievers, and I had thought I agreed with their reasoning. It made sense what they said, about how being yoked to an unbeliever will pull you down in your walk with the Lord. My mom always brought up the long-term danger. What if you start dating an unbeliever and fall in love with her? Then what? The Bible's pretty clear about that being a bad match, a formula for trouble in your life. And what if you can't share your faith, the most important thing in your life, with the person you love?

Yeah, I knew the arguments, but I had no desire to stop dating Autumn. I thought it was so unfair. I thought that maybe I could witness to her and try to convert her. I thought that she was perfect for me. I kept thinking about her and how much fun we have together. But I couldn't shake my concern.

If you're a Christian, then the Holy Spirit has such a power in your life. He kept reminding me that it wasn't right. He kept convicting me that I was taking the wrong path. He didn't let me forget what I knew in my heart to be true. He kept pestering me so much that I couldn't gnore His message any longer.

Doing what's right is usually pretty hard. It seemed like I was giving up the best thing ever, and I kept arguing with myself. When I stopped seeing Autumn, I explained to her what I had been dealing with, and much to my surprise, she seemed to understand. What a painful situation for both of us, I thought. And I knew whose fault it was for letting it go this far. I trusted God to bring someone better into my life. I'm waiting to see who He has planned for me.

189

There's a girl in my class who says her mom is a real witch, like a black magic kind of witch. I know it's just fake, so does it matter if I go to one of their "witch meetings" with her?

Also he made his son pass through the fire, practiced soothsaying, used witchcraft, and consulted spiritists and mediums. He did much evil in the sight of the Lord, to provoke Him to anger.
2 Kings 21:6

There are a lot of things in this world that are fake. This woman might be all talk. You need to understand though that there really is evil in the world. It's not about pulling rabbits out of hats. It's not all about potions or spells. But there are people who align themselves with evil, just like there are people who align themselves with God. Be careful. It does matter if you go to the meeting. You could be opening yourself up to some dangerous stuff. Curiosity is one thing. When it comes to evil, you don't want to taste the real thing. Manasseh was known as one of the wickedest kings of ancient Israel. He consulted spiritists and mediums. He used witchcraft and even practiced child sacrifices (YIKES !). The occult was real in Manasseh's day. It's real today. Stay as far away from it as you can.

My friends all play "Magic," the card game. My Mom says it's evil, but it's all just pretend. Which games are OK?

Beloved, do not believe every spirit, but test the spirits, whether they are of God; because many false prophets have gone out into the world.
1 John 4:1

Moms are cautious, particularly about anything that might hurt their kids. Does your game fall into the category of mystical stuff like finding out the future or getting insights from spirits? Is that why your mom's all in a wad about it? I'd just say, be careful. Yes, it's just a game. Yes, it's just pretend. But, you know what? Evil is a real thing in the world. There really is a spiritual war going on, and Satan wouldn't be opposed to using a pretend game to get a little hold in your life. The Bible says to test the spirits. Maybe you need to test the game. What is the atmosphere usually like when you and your friends play? Is it just fun or is it a little spooky? Does it feel like you're all on the up-and-up or does it seem like you're getting away with something? Do you come away forgetting about it, like you would any other game (like if you played Scrabble, I doubt you'd dwell on your third from the last word) or do you think back on it a lot? Be careful with yourself. Make good choices.

OTHER RELIGIONS

> So the scribe said to Him, "Well said, Teacher. You have spoken the truth, for there is one God, and there is no other but He."
> Mark 12:32

I heard where the God that Jews and Muslims and all the other religions talk about is the same as our God. Is that true?

There is only one God. There is no other one. Some religions worship false gods. The Jewish religion worships God, but doesn't accept Jesus as God's Son. Christianity worships God and accepts that Jesus is God come into the world as a human. That's what sets Christianity apart. When you hear about other religions, use that as the test. Do they believe in Jesus and His sacrifice for our sins? Do they worship the one true God that came to the world to make a way for us to connect with Him? All religions really aren't the same. Most of them are based on people trying to be good enough to win God's favor. Christianity is not about people being good enough to reach God. It's about God reaching down to us and us letting Him do that.

The foreign gods Jacob referred to were small idols made from wood, metal, silver, or gold. An idol could be anything that stands in the way of a personal relationship with the one true God.
Gen. 35:2

What about Mormons and Amish people? Are they really Christians? How can you tell which churches are Christian and which aren't?

00. 00. 29

For if he who comes preaches another Jesus whom we have not preached, or if you receive a different spirit which you have not received, or a different gospel which you have not accepted, you may well put up with it.

2 Cor. 11:4

00. 00. 10

Anyone is a Christian who believes in Christ's sacrifice for our sins. That's why we're called "CHRISTians," because our faith is in what God did for us through the life of Jesus Christ. You can talk about groups of people, but what it comes down to is every individual, no matter what label they wear. Does a person believe that only faith in God through Christ is the way to have a relationship with God? That's the key. Paul wrote to the Corinthian church about this very thing. He was concerned that they would believe any old gospel that came along instead of the true gospel. He gave them the Jesus litmus test. If anyone preached to them about anything other than faith in Christ being their connection to God—he said it just wasn't true. That's how you know if a church is a Christian church.

PAIN

Where is God when my heart is broken?

The LORD is near
to those who have
a broken heart,
and saves such
as have a
contrite spirit.
Ps. 34:18

God is right beside you when your heart is broken. David wrote a Psalm that says that very thing: "The LORD is near to those who have a broken heart." Our hearts can get broken about a lot of things, some of them big and some of them not. *Why* our hearts are broken is not the issue. God is with us. Sometimes it doesn't feel like it. Sometimes when we are hurting so badly all we can feel is the hurt. That's when God seems far away. That's when we have to have faith that God is right there. Your broken heart matters to Him.

It feels like my life is screwed up and it's never going to be OK again. I can't just cheer up and get over it. How can I make myself feel better?

There are a lot of things you can do and you might need to try all of them. The first thing you need to try is giving yourself a break and some time to feel better. Once your life feels *that* bad, it takes a while to feel better. Another thing is to know that you are not the only one to struggle with this kind of thing. In fact, David, who was king of Israel and a writer of part of the Bible, was down and out more than once. Several times in the Psalms he asked himself, "Why are you cast down, O my soul? And why are you disquieted within me?" In other words, "What's wrong with me? Why am I so messed up?" David comforted himself with knowing that even though he felt alone, God was right there loving him. He also reminded himself that no matter how bad life felt, it would get better one day. That doesn't mean life got instantly better. It sounds like you might want to talk to somebody you trust and let them know how bad you feel. Whether or not you have a friend on earth you feel that comfortable with, you can always trust God, and He's a good listener. At least you know that you and King David have this struggle in common. Just like with David, God is with *you*. Things will get better eventually.

SEE FOR YOURSELF: Ps. 42:11

194

Does God care when I hurt?

Yes, beyond a shadow of a doubt, without hesitation. God cares when you hurt. You are His child. He doesn't want you to hurt. Nehemiah was a Hebrew leader in the Old Testament. One of his prayers for his people shows how much God cares. Nehemiah was reminding God of all the good things He had done for the Hebrew nation. Nehemiah said, "When they cried to you, You heard from heaven." In this case, what was true for the Hebrews is true for you as well. God cares about your struggles. He might not fix them. He definitely might not fix them right away. But He won't leave you alone in them. He's right there, seeing you through.

> Therefore You delivered them into the hand of their enemies, who oppressed them; and in the time of their trouble, When they cried to You, You heard from heaven; and according to Your abundant mercies You gave them deliverers who saved them.
>
> Neh. 9:27

Will God make my hurt go away?

Ever been through a time when it seemed like your heartache would never go away? The tears keep pouring out. The suffering seems endless. You're convinced you'll never be happy again. After a while you wonder if God even notices your broken heart. If He does, then surely He will do something—quick. God says that He has stored each one of your tears in a bottle. God knows you intimately, and He has not turned His back on your suffering. Even when you feel completely alone, God has not abandoned you. He sees your tear-stained pillow. He hears you cry yourself to sleep. It breaks His heart to see you hurt. Do not be afraid. He is there—close enough to catch each one of your tears.

Grief was a much more public emotion in ancient times than it is today. People demonstrated their feelings of loss and sadness by tearing their clothes, putting ashes or dust in their hair, and wearing really uncomfortable clothes called sackcloth. These outward signs were used both for mourning a death and for repenting of sin, and they were often continued for several days.
2 Sam. 3:31

PATIENCE

Who is a perfect example of patience?

> The LORD is gracious and full of compassion, slow to anger and great in mercy.
> Ps. 145:8

Patience should be put on the "endangered character trait" list. You rarely see patience anymore. Maybe everyone has already used up all their patience. No one wants to wait for anything—ever. Overnight mail moved too slowly, so someone invented the fax machine. But sometimes it takes a while for the fax to get through; so, thank goodness someone invented e-mail. One push of a button, and your friend immediately has your message or very important document. Who knows what's next? Maybe think-mail, where you just have to think and your thoughts are instantly processed around the world. So to say that God is "slow to anger," means He's patient with us—and we do try His patience! This is not to say that God is outdated in our fast-paced, we-need-to-know-now society. He's not. It's just that in our rush to know more and do more we have forgotten how to wait. God models the virtue for us. He is very patient, especially about important things, like waiting for the people He loves.

SEE FOR YOURSELF: Neh. 9:30; 2 Pet. 3:9

PEER PRESSURE

> And you shall know that I am the LORD; for you have not walked in My statutes nor executed My judgments, but have done according to the customs of the Gentiles which are around you.
>
> **Ezek. 11:12**

00. 00. 29

When is peer pressure bad?

00. 00. 0 0

Peer pressure is bad when it pulls you away from God. God dealt with the Hebrew people in the Old Testament about peer pressure all the time. They moved back to their homeland after hundreds of years away. When they moved back other people had moved in, people who didn't worship God. So He warned the people to not be influenced by their neighbors to worship false gods. The prophets that preached to the Hebrews, men like Ezekiel, warned them over and over to not give in to the customs of the people around them.

SEE FOR YOURSELF: Ezek. 11:12

Why is "following the crowd" dangerous?

Josh was fourteen years old. After he died, people talked about his football ability, his great personality, his good looks, and his love for God. One night he was at home and accidentally killed himself by "huffing" fluorocarbons. His friends said he was just experimenting and wasn't a habitual user. He didn't mean to do it. He was just "messing around." Josh didn't use good sense. Getting a "buzz" from huffing seemed pretty harmless. He probably didn't even think it was dangerous. But it was a tragically unwise choice that ended his life after fourteen short years. Whether it's huffing, or drag racing, you have to separate yourself from the potential "thrill" and ask, "Is this wise? What could the consequences be? What is the absolute worst thing that could happen? Could I hurt myself or someone else?" Make sure you know how much damage could be done to yourself or other people. The Holy Spirit will give you direction. But you have to follow through and do the right thing. It takes guts not to follow the crowd. God will provide the guts—all you have to do is ask Him.

SEE FOR YOURSELF: 1 Cor. 6:19, 20; Col. 3:5; 1 Pet. 1:13-16; Prov. 19:8

POWER

How strong is God's power?

OO. OO. 29   OO. OO. OO

Ever tried to look at the midday sun? You
can't—and you're not even supposed to try.
It will damage your eyes. The sun is thousands
of miles away from the earth, and yet you can't look at
its brightness. If we were to travel to the sun, we would burn up long before we
got there because of the intensity of the heat. There is nothing on this earth to
compare with the power of the sun. Job says that the power of God is even
brighter than the sun. Imagine that. To God the sun is probably like a nice campfire. It's a fire that God built Himself and hung in the heavens. We sometimes forget how awesome God is. The next time you watch a sunset, think about God and
remember that His power is even stronger.

SEE FOR YOURSELF: Deut. 10:17; 1 Chr. 29:11, 12; Ps. 47:2

> Even now men cannot
> look at the light when
> it is bright in the skies,
> when the wind has
> passed and cleared
> them. He comes
> from the north as
> golden splendor;
> with God is
> awesome majesty.
> Job 37:21-22

A sensitive response?
Meet Chloe.

Talk about a sticky situation. Unbelievable. At first I thought she was joking, but then I could tell she wasn't. I tried not to show the shock on my face, but I'm sure she could tell something was shady about the whole thing. How could I be gracious in that situation? Definitely the worst situation ever.

So I've had this major crush on this guy Caleb for like six months. We finally have a class together this semester, but I still didn't know if he ever noticed me. Every day I was secretly checking him out and so pumped when we would actually talk or do a group project together or whatever. But I never really got my hopes up. So on Sunday, I get this random phone call, and you'll never believe who it was—Caleb! I was totally shocked and so excited. So we talked for a little while and then he asked me out for this Friday. Yes! So I'm thinking, life is awesome, how could it get any better than this? Then I went to school Monday morning.

So Riley and I were talking during study hall, and I was so stoked to tell her about my date with Caleb on Friday. All of a sudden, Riley leans toward me and says very quietly, "Chloe, I have something to tell you. I haven't told anyone else yet, and I just need to tell someone."

She continued in a whisper. "Chloe, I really like Caleb. For like the last month I've totally been thinking about him all the time, and you know what? I actually think he likes me, too. I just had to tell someone. Plus, I know you used to like him last year, right? Isn't he such a cool guy?"

By this point, my mouth was just hanging open, and I had not a clue what to say to her. I thought she was kidding. Nope. "Huh" was all I said.

Monday passed, and Tuesday rolled around, and I knew I had to say something to her. But what?!! This was the worst situation ever, and I knew someone's feelings would get hurt. Riley was my friend, but I was so crazy about Caleb! This whole thing was just stressing me out.

I knew what I had to do, and I prayed about it. It was time for me to set this whole thing straight. These were words I just did not want to say. "Riley, I have something to talk to you about. It's about Caleb," I started. She looked up, startled. "Well, before you ever told me you liked Caleb, I had been planning to go out with him this weekend. I don't really know him that well, but I think he's a great guy. So I didn't mean to do anything behind your back. Your friendship is more important to me than Caleb is, so just be honest with me. What are you thinking? I think I should just cancel with Caleb and end this whole situation." Thank God the words were out.

Riley took a deep breath. Slowly she started to talk. "Chloe, I know you've liked Caleb for a lot longer than I have. I don't blame you for wanting to go out with him. I think you should do it. And you know, like you said, our friendship is more important, and even if guys come and go out of our lives, our friendship should be a constant."

I was very impressed. She handled herself with such poise and unselfishness. I guess he hadn't meant as much to her as I had thought. Anyway, that day taught us a lot more about our friendship than about anything else. And I'm sure we'll look back someday and laugh about the whole thing.

PRAISE

How can I praise God?

When God's people come together, they
usually praise Him. That's what He expects.
Because of that, people spend a lot of time
trying hard to praise the Lord—with the right music,
the right words, the right posture. You may even be sitting or standing in the pew
trying to work up the frame of mind that will please God and make you feel
good, too. If that's the case, there's nothing wrong with your motives or the
motives of the people who plan the songs and the prayers and the standing and
sitting. But David had a different idea about how he was going to praise God. He
was determined to praise God—no matter what. He knew that when he did his
part by *choosing* to praise that God would fill him with praise. The happiness that
David had in God's presence came straight from God. So when you get together
with other people who love God, make up your mind that you're going to praise
God. Think about His goodness, His power, His awesome love. Ask Him to fill your
heart with praise like He did for David. And He will.

SEE FOR YOURSELF: Ps. 4:7; Is. 61:11; Rom. 15:13

> My praise shall be
> of You in the great
> congregation; I
> will pay My vows
> before those who
> fear Him.
> Ps. 22:25

PRAYER

Do you need to kneel to pray?

`00.00.29`   `00.00.10`

No. You can pray in any position at all, riding in a car, walking on the side of the road, laying in bed at night. Do you remember Nehemiah from the Old Testament? He was a cupbearer for the king. He did some butler-y type stuff, and he also tasted the king's wine to make sure it wasn't poisoned. One day Nehemiah was heartbroken about some news he had gotten from home. The king must have been able to tell because he asked Nehemiah what was wrong. Right then and there, as Nehemiah was going about his duties, he prayed about how to answer the king. God honored Nehemiah's prayer. The king let him take a leave of absence from his work to help out back at home. Prayer is just connecting with God. While we certainly want to show God respect when we interact with Him, we can do that in our heart attitude as well as our posture when we pray.

> Then the king said to me, "What do you request?" So I prayed to the God of heaven.
>
> Neh. 2:4

How can I pray with power?

Some high school kids meet once a week before school to pray. Last week they prayed for a job for one of their dads, for a grandmother to be healed of cancer, and for a friend who had a hard exam coming up. This week they met and as soon as they got together, the reports began: "My dad got a job the very morning we prayed!" "My grandmother's doctor can't find any trace of the cancer." "Our friend thinks he did well on his exam and thanks you for praying." They all were looking at each other in amazement. "Wow," someone said, "God really answered our prayers!" Sure, God answers your prayers, but we sometimes pray with so much doubt that we're totally shocked when He does. Pray with assurance that God promises to answer. Expect Him to work and watch for His action. Remember that God will answer in one of three ways—yes, no, or wait. Praying is not holy manipulation. God will choose in His wisdom how to respond.

SEE FOR YOURSELF: Deut. 4:5-8; Job 22:27; 23:9; Ps. 28:6; 40:1-17

Does God hear my prayers?

Your best friend is lying in a hospital bed She was in a car wreck over the weekend and the doctors have said she probably won't live through the night. You remember when your parents used to make you go to Sunday school. You remember God. You pray for the first time in years and beg God to let your friend live. He does.

Do you believe God answers your prayers? Not "Do you believe because you think you're supposed to?" But do you really believe it? When you pray, do you just hope your prayer makes it all the way up to heaven, or do you know in your heart that God is listening to you? God says He will answer your prayers before you even get through praying. Now *that* is awesome! He knows you so well that He gets to work on your request before it even gets out of your mouth. Remember, not all prayers have the same "yes" answer. God is totally wise, and He knows exactly what's best for you. It's important for you to pray according to God's will, and you can find that in His Word. Sometimes He says, "Not yet." Whether your answer is yes, no, or not yet, He hears you and goes to work before you finish praying.

SEE FOR YOURSELF: Deut. 4:5-8; Job 22:27; Ps. 28:6; 91:15

> It shall come to pass that before they call, I will answer; and while they are still speaking, I will hear.
>
> Isa. 65:24

Should I pray to Jesus or God or the Holy Spirit? Or should I pray to certain ones about some things and the others about other things?

The prayer that Jesus modeled for us started with "Our Father," so Jesus prayed to God. Since God is this mysterious three-in-one spirit, we are praying to Him whether we say the name "God" or "Jesus" or "Holy Spirit." The names we use probably don't matter as much to him as they do to us. God hears our prayers. Jesus paid the price to give us access to Him. The Bible calls Jesus our Mediator with God, our go-between. The Holy Spirit helps us know what to pray. So in that whole prayer process, God is helping us along. So if it helps, just copy Jesus and say "Our Father . . ." then go for it. Pour your heart out. That's what God wants.

SEE FOR YOURSELF: Matt. 6:9

Does it matter if I start a prayer "Our Father" or "Yo, wassup God?" Doesn't God understand what I mean however I say it?

Likewise the Spirit also helps in our weaknesses. For we do not know what we should pray for as we ought, but the Spirit Himself makes intercession for us with groanings which cannot be uttered.

Romans 8:26

God listens to our hearts more than our words. So, yes, He does understand what you mean however you say it. As you get quiet and face Him to have a conversation, He being God and you being you, you can address Him as personally as you want to. But keep in mind that He IS God. He deserves our love, obedience, devotion, and respect. Respect is found in your attitude. Out of that comes your words. The Bible says that the Holy Spirit helps us know how to pray. In fact, the Bible says that the Holy Spirit sort of prays for us. It's called "interceding." Even when we are praying about stuff that we don't have the right words for, we can sit with God and just let Him read our hearts. The Holy Spirit speaks for our hearts. The important thing is that we don't rush through our lives, never taking the time to sit with God, talking to Him, hanging out with Him, giving Him a chance to talk with us.

Do I have to talk when I pray or can I just think it?

You don't have to talk. In fact, sometimes when we pray, we don't even know what to say. We just know that we need to connect with God. Sometimes prayer is just sitting there quietly, doing that, hoping to do that. Other times we pray as we are going. In fact, the Bible tells us to pray all the time. If we had to talk in order to pray, what a loud world this would be. In the Old Testament, there is a story about a man named Nehemiah. He needed to ask off of work to do some important stuff for God. One day his boss (the king) asked him what was up. It was the perfect opportunity for Nehemiah to talk to the king about it all. The Bible says Nehemiah prayed right then and there. Now, that probably doesn't mean he said a prayer in the king's face. It probably means that he silently said, "God, help me not mess this up." Prayer happens in all those ways as well as when we try to put our thoughts into words. The important thing is that we pray.

SEE FOR YOURSELF: Neh. 2:4-5

PREGNANCY

My friend got pregnant. Her Mom says that she should finish school and not drop out and get married. Isn't it a sin to have a baby when you're not married?

But fornication and all uncleanness or covetousness, let it not even be named among you, as is fitting for saints.
Eph. 5:3

Having a baby isn't a sin. Ignoring God's warnings about sex before marriage is a sin. The great scariness of that sin is that a brand new life can come out of it. That means a whole lifetime of choices come out of that one choice. Your friend made her mistakes before the pregnancy ever occurred. Whether your friend drops out of school, whether she gets married, whether she gives the baby up for adoption or not, those are all difficult choices that are going to follow her for the rest of her life. Those choices aren't sin, though. They are just the consequences of the choice she made to ignore God's guidelines in her life. It's a good thing for all of us that even though we mess up, God is still willing to help us face the consequences. He doesn't write us off or give up on us.

PRESENCE OF GOD

> I will walk among you and be your God, and you shall be My people.
> Lev. 26:12

Is God always with us?

You may have heard the story called "Footprints." It's the story of a man who had a dream. In his dream he was walking along the beach with the Lord. Scenes from his life flashed across the sky. For each scene, he noticed two sets of footprints in the sand—one belonging to him and the other to the Lord. When the last scene of his life flashed before him, he looked back at the footprints in the sand. He noticed that many times along the path of his life there was only one set of footprints. He also noticed that only one set appeared during the lowest and saddest times in his life. This really bothered him, and he questioned the Lord about it. "Lord, You said that once I decided to follow You, You'd walk with me all the way. But I have noticed that during the most troublesome times in my life, there is only one set of footprints. I don't understand why You weren't there when I needed You most. You said You would never leave me." The Lord replied, "My son, My precious child, I love you and I would never leave you. During your times of trial and suffering, when you see only one set of footprints, it was then that I carried you."

Can you catch what this story is saying? No matter what kind of situation you go through, the Lord is going to be right there with you. Don't forget it. You never have to walk alone again. He's the One who walks with you.

SEE FOR YOURSELF: Ps. 23:4; Prov 3:23-26; Heb. 3:23-26; 13:5b

Here's a word you can throw around the next time you want to show someone how much you know about biblical times: theophany. It means a visible appearance of God. Job witnessed a theophany when the Lord came to him in the whirlwind. Job didn't actually see God; he saw the effects of God's presence.
Job 38:1

Does God ever come to earth in person?

Well, I'm sure you realize that Jesus was God come to earth as a person. The Bible says that He lived among us. It's a mystery that Jesus could be all the way a human and all the way God at the same time. God probably made appearances in the Old Testament as well. There are several times that angels appear to give good news. Some experts think that sometimes the messengers weren't just angels but were God Himself. God "appeared" other times not in person, but in voice. For instance, He spoke to Moses out of a burning bush. He spoke once out of a storm. One time He even gave a donkey the ability to speak. When you think about it, humanity has experienced God's presence in a lot of ways. After Jesus went back to heaven, God's presence came to the earth in a new way, the Holy Spirit, to live inside of Christians. In that way God comes to earth as a person by living inside of us.

> And the Word became flesh and dwelt among us, and we beheld His glory, the glory as of the only begotten of the Father, full of grace and truth.
> John 1:14

Will God always be by my side?

Do you remember the fears of your childhood? Monsters in the closet. Thunder in the night. Being left alone. You run through the house screaming, "Mommmmmm!" Fearing that she has suddenly vanished, you begin to check everywhere, look in every room. Your heart is racing as your little imagination runs wild. Maybe everyone is gone. You've been deserted. You'll have to fend for yourself in this big old world. You'll have to cook and clean and earn money. Oh no. You're about to cry. Finally you hear her voice from the garage, "What is it, honey?" "Nothing, Mom," you reply in your calmest voice. "I just couldn't find you." "Well, I'm right here," she reassures you. And so is God. He will never desert you or leave you. Even when you're an adult and feel afraid, rest assured that God is as close as the air you breathe.

SEE FOR YOURSELF: Ex. 33:14; Deut. 31:8; 1 Kings 6:12-13; Ps. 37:28; Ezek. 11:16

Does God ever leave me?

When you're about to go into unfamiliar territory—a new school, your first date, standing up for yourself for the first time—you probably feel a little shaky. Everyone understands that new situations can be a little scary. But if God told the Israelites not to be afraid of their enemies, you can bet He doesn't want you to be afraid of anything either. He certainly doesn't want you to be afraid of something just because you're not used to it. He is with you all the time. You can't get rid of Him. In these days of convenient relationships, children disowning their parents, divorce everywhere, it's easy to think that no one will ever be truly committed to you. God will. In the good times and the bad, in the familiar times and the new experiences, God is totally with you. No matter what you do or where you go, He is there. He doesn't take a break, doesn't blink for a split second. When God says He will not leave you nor forsake you, He is telling you He is with you all the time. You are never alone.

> And the LORD, He is the One who goes before you. He will be with you, He will not leave you nor forsake you; do not fear nor be dismayed.
>
> Deut. 31:8

SEE FOR YOURSELF: Josh. 1:5; Matt. 28:20; Heb. 13:5

How close does God get to me?

God watches you constantly. He's not peering down from heaven so He can whack you on the head when you blow it, but to give an extra measure of strength to people who are being faithful. He gives strength and support to those who are obedient—to those whose hearts belong to Him. If you've ever tried to be obedient, you know that most of the time it takes more courage to do the right thing than to follow the crowd. He promises to see you and your efforts. He will make your weak knees strong. He will give your voice power and authority. He will sense your fear and cast it out. Your job is to be faithful. God promises to never miss a thing.

SEE FOR YOURSELF: 2 Chr. 16:9; Ps. 34:15; 139:1-6; 1 Pet. 3:12

How do I know God is near me?

In this passage, Job ponders the hugeness of God. His miracles are beyond our understanding. His creativity is awesome, and we are part of it. His justice is supreme and fair. He is so amazing that He moves right past us, and we don't even know it. He is closer than we could imagine, so why do we doubt His wisdom and His power? We have mistakenly believed that God is up there somewhere, far away, looking down. He seems remote and out of touch. Distant. But God is here. Intimate. So close. He moves right past you. Are you willing to trust the One who is beside you to care for you and to love you? His presence is real. His patience is incredible. Since He has already been with you all this time, why keep ignoring Him?

> He does great things past finding out, yes, wonders without number. If He goes by me, I do not see Him; if He moves past, I do not perceive Him.
> Job 9:10, 11

SEE FOR YOURSELF: Ps. 119:151; 145:18

Will God leave me when the going gets tough?

Ever had someone stick up for you? They walked right into the middle of your conflict and took your side? Awesome. Did you ever have someone decide to do more than watch? They cared enough to get involved, to actually stick their neck out and speak up for you. It's an incredible feeling to have someone help you fight your fight. All of a sudden you feel stronger, the enemy seems weaker, and your confidence gets a boost. God is ready to fight for you. He is on your side, ready to intervene and do battle. You are not fighting alone. All the power of the supernatural is right beside you. So look ahead with hope and assurance that the strongest Warrior fights for you.

SEE FOR YOURSELF: 2 Chr. 13:10-12;. 32:7-8; Zeph. 2:7

What if no one's watching?
Meet Jason.

Thursday night—most boring night ever for me, not quite Friday, and always lots of homework. I think my teachers must have no lives outside of school, cause if it even takes them a fraction of the time to grade my work as it does for me to do it, there go their Saturday nights. I think the worst is this computer-based calculus course I'm doing for college credit. It requires me to spend at least an hour a night on the computer. At least an hour, if not more, and Sundays included. I should have waited for college. My brother tells me it's easier than high school anyway.

So on this particular Thursday night, I was procrastinating that dumb calculus work and just browsing the Internet. Sports, music, anything besides doing homework. I clicked on what I thought was a homemade site for NCAA basketball picks. Much to my surprise, something graphic popped up on my screen.

The body of an almost naked woman filled the screen, and she was bent in a very suggestive way toward me. At first I was so shocked (college basketball?). The image was very erotic, and I caught my breath. With the mouse in my hand, I looked over my shoulder but realized I was the only one home. If I wanted to, I could keep looking. After all, it was an accident. It's not like I tried to find a porn site; I was innocently browsing for basketball. It wouldn't be too bad just to keep looking for a few minutes, would it? Just enough to satisfy my curiosity.

I hit escape and left the site. I knew that Satan was tempting me, and he uses very powerful tactics. Pornography is a dangerous sin that can quickly lead to addiction. I also know what God wants me to fill my mind with: pure images that honor Him. That site definitely didn't qualify. I prayed that God would clear my mind of that image and renew the purity of my thoughts. It's a powerful realization that even when no one else sees me, God certainly does.

Can I hide anything from God, even my thoughts?

Do you ever wish you could hide from God? Maybe you really want to do something you know He wouldn't approve of. Is it easier to go against your conscience if you pretend that God doesn't know what you're up to? But the truth is, you can't hide from God. When you run a red light, He's there. He's there when you sneak a look at someone else's paper during a test. If someone made you mad, and you flip them off behind their back, He sees it. If you talk bad about someone when they're not around, He hears you. You can't even hide from God what's going on inside you. He's spirit, and He's everywhere—even inside your head and heart. He knows what you think and feel. He sees it when you're jealous or angry. He knows when you're lonely or sad. You can't get away from Him. And once you realize what He's all about, how much He loves you, why would you want to? It's okay for Him to see all about you. He knows you're not perfect, and He's working on you.

SEE FOR YOURSELF: Jer. 23:23

> If I ascend into heaven, You are there; if I make my bed in hell, behold, You are there.
> **Ps. 139:8**

Where is God when I feel all freaked out?

He is right there with you. He never leaves. He is holding you and facing whatever is freaking you out right along with you. There's a Psalm that asks where we can go to get away from God. It says we can even make a bed in hell and God will be there with us. That's pretty extreme, wouldn't you say? It's no fun to be freaked out. It feels like everything is out of control and falling apart. Life can go very wrong sometimes. But at the core of it, you are not alone. God is with you and will help you through the very worst stuff that life sends your way.

SEE FOR YOURSELF: Ps. 139:7-8

PRIDE

What does God do with arrogance?

OO. OO. 29

OO. OO. 10

He punishes arrogance. God values humility. He wants His children to be kind and meek and humble. When God encounters arrogance, whether it is in people or in nations, He deals with that arrogance. In the prophecy of Ezekiel, God speaks to Jerusalem as a way to speak to the Hebrews. He calls Jerusalem back to a life of obedience. He explains why He destroyed Sodom and Gomorrah by saying that they were "haughty," which is another word for arrogant. Arrogance is an insult to God. It is a person or place saying that they are as important as God. It is the reason Satan was thrown out of God's service. It's not something God takes lightly and so neither should we.

> Look, this was the iniquity of your sister Sodom: She and her daughter had pride, fullness of food, and abundance of idleness; neither did she strengthen the hand of the poor and needy; . . . therefore I took them away as I saw fit.
>
> **Ezek. 16:49-50**

PROBLEMS

Man who is born of woman is of few days and full of trouble.

Job 14:1

Is it possible to have a life without problems?

Sadly, no, it isn't. The problems in life come in all shapes and sizes. Sometimes we bring them on ourselves. Other times they just happen. Think about Job, the guy in the Old Testament who had everything go wrong at once. Job said we have "few days and full of trouble." When things are going wrong, it's easy to think, "If I was doing this right, would it be easier?" Sometimes it's also easy to think, "If God was doing His job would this be easier?" But the truth is God never promised convenience. He only promised His presence. The two things that you can be sure of are (1) problems will come, and (2) God will be with you every step of the way.

Why doesn't Jesus take away our trials?

You know what? Sometimes He does. The real kicker is why doesn't He take away our trials all the time. Only He can answer that question. While He hinted at it, He didn't give us a direct answer. He did ask us to do something for Him, though. He asked us to switch roles with Him. He said, "let your trials become Mine. Let Me carry the stress. Take My yoke and let Me have yours." How do you do that? Well, it's a constant giving it over kind of thing. It's trusting God to not give you more than you can handle and believing that, one way or another, things will be OK eventually. It's believing that He never leaves you alone and you'll be better somehow when it's over.

"Lord, if you just get me out of this mess, I promise I will. . ." Sound familiar? Like us, people in ancient times made all kinds of promises to God about what they would do if He helped them. For example, a person might have promised to make a certain kind of sacrifice if God heard his prayer. This verse serves as a reminder that God doesn't take such promises lightly.
Eccl. 5:4

How do I solve impossible problems?

Ever get in a situation where your back's against the wall and you have no clue what to do? Ever need to make an important decision about your circumstances, but the problem is bigger than you are? Those are the times you need wisdom. You need to look at things from God's perspective and know what to do—that's wisdom. You know you need it, but how do you get it? Proverbs 9:10 says that the beginning of wisdom is "the fear of the LORD." In other words, wisdom starts with respect for God. The more you learn to respect and obey the Lord, the more wisdom you'll gain. Remember that respect and obedience are two separate actions. To respect the Lord is to know that He knows best and to care about what He thinks. It is to consult Him when you're in a tough spot. Obedience is a step beyond respect. To obey the Lord is to act on what He's told you. The verse goes on to say that to have understanding, you need "knowledge of the Holy One." Knowing God is much deeper than knowing about God. Knowing Him won't happen overnight, and no one will ever know Him completely; but as you spend time with Him, you'll eventually begin to know Him more and more. He will give you wisdom. Just respect Him, obey Him, and know Him.

> "The fear of the LORD is the beginning of wisdom, and the knowledge of the Holy One is understanding."
> Prov. 9:10

SEE FOR YOURSELF: Dan. 2:21; Eph. 1:17; James 3:17

Why did I have this terrible, horrible, worse than ever day?

If I could tell you the answer to that I'd be a millionaire. The most common question of humankind is, "Why is this happening to me?" There's nothing like a horrible day to set off a new round of that question. But while I can't tell you the exact reason for the circumstances you faced, I can tell you something else. As bad as this day was, something meaningful happened in it. It may not be obvious right now. Correction . . . it's definitely not obvious right now. But God saw all your days laid out before you like a yellow brick road even before your body was fully formed as a fetus inside your mom. He saw this day. Only He knows why it unfolded the way it did. But He was there with you in it. Somehow, if you'll trust Him, He'll bring something good out of it.

SEE FOR YOURSELF: Psalm 139:16

PROFANITY

I don't see why everybody gets all freaked out about the profanity comedians use. They are just funny words. God wants us to laugh, right?

> Let your speech always be with grace, seasoned with salt, that you may know how you ought to answer each one.
>
> Col. 4:6

Yeah, God does want us to laugh. God wants a lot of things for us. Mostly He wants us to be like Him. God is creative and joyful. He wants us to be that too. He is also holy. He spent most of the Old Testament teaching people what that meant by teaching them the difference between clean and not clean. Part of the reason that certain words are funny is because they feel "bad" to us. People call certain words "dirty." They're funny because when we hear them or say them we feel like we're getting away with something. That's what makes us laugh. And that's why some comedians won't use certain words just to get a laugh. It's like a shortcut to humor instead of the real thing. The Bible says our speech should be "with grace, seasoned with salt." That means whenever we speak, our words should reflect God's nature and make things better around us. A lot of the language "everybody" gets all uptight about doesn't pass that test.

PROMISES OF GOD

It shall be, when I bring a cloud over the earth, that the rainbow shall be seen in the cloud; and I will remember My covenant which is between Me and you.
Gen. 9:14

00. 00. 29   00. 00. 30

Can I really trust God to keep His promises?

God had just done something pretty amazing and probably pretty scary. He was so angry that He wiped out the whole world with a huge flood. Every person and every animal on earth drowned. Only the people and the animals on Noah's ark were saved. You can imagine what they might have been thinking. *Will He ever do this again? Maybe next time we won't live through it.* God calmed them down by promising that He would never destroy the world by flood again. To help them understand, He gave them something they could see. He put the rainbow in the sky as the sign of that promise. Did God need the rainbow so He could remember what He'd said? No, the rainbow was for Noah and his family. It was for all his descendants who would live after him (Gen. 9:9). Today, it's for you. It lets you know that God does remember what He said. After all these millions of years, God still remembers a promise He made to a group of people on an ark. He knew that as long as the sunlight hits the raindrops, people could see the rainbow and know that He remembers His promise.

SEE FOR YOURSELF: Gen. 9:13-15

God's promise to give the land of Canaan to Abram is one of the most important events in the Old Testament. The modern conflict between the Palestinians and the Israelis can be traced back to this promise. As for the mysterious smoking oven and burning torch, we can only assume that they are symbols of the unusual meeting between God and Abram. Gen. 15:17

215

Does God always do what He sets out to do?

Yes, God does. But he works with us along the way. God is powerful. He is sovereign, or "in control." But He is not a puppet master. We don't have little strings on our arms and legs that He pulls to make us get His business done. It's a little difficult as humans to understand how He can do both those things—accomplish His purposes and give us choices. There's a book in the Old Testament called Lamentations. It was written by the prophet Jeremiah when everything was going wrong with his country. His people were being taken captive and the future was bleak. But even in the midst of all that Jeremiah wrote, he could say, "The Lord has done what He purposed." Jeremiah recognized that no matter how he or his people felt about it, God accomplished His will.

> The LORD has done what He purposed; He has fulfilled His word which He commanded in days of old.
> Lam. 2:17

Will God back out on His promises?

Broken promises. Nothing stings more. They tear you up and rip your heart out. Friends who tell your deepest secrets. Being stood up by the girl you finally ask out. Dads who walk out on moms. Promise made, promise broken, heartache. When someone breaks a promise, it feels like a punch in the gut—all the wind gets knocked out of you and all your energy is drained. Because we've felt this pain so many times, we assume that God could treat us the same way. He might pull out at any turn. He might say He didn't really mean it—we just misunderstood Him. Not a chance. He promises never to break His promise. He'll always keep your secrets, always be there when you need Him, and always do what He says He will do. You can stake your heart on it.

SEE FOR YOURSELF: Num. 23:19; Josh. 23:15-16; 2 Sam. 23; 1 Kings 8:56

PROPHET'S

And though I have the gift of prophecy, and understand all mysteries and all knowledge, and though I have all faith, so that I could remove mountains, but have not love, I am nothing.
1 Cor. 13:2

How come we don't have prophets now like they did in the old days?

00. 00. 29   00. 00. 30

In a way we don't, but in a way we do. Most of the prophecies of the Old Testament either had to do with the future of Israel, Jesus' arrival, or the end of time. It's true that we don't have prophets who go around foreseeing the future in fuzzy half-tones and visions. But the prophets were also just truthtellers. They were the public conscience of Israel. The New Testament describes the gift of prophecy as understanding all mysteries and knowledge, in other words a very, very, very wise person. Some of our great preachers like Billy Graham function as prophets today. They help people make decisions and teach the Scriptures in a way that people can understand. They give messages to large groups, whole nations, like the prophets of the Old Testament did.

A prophet was a person who received messages form God and passed them along to the people. Sometimes these messages told of future events. There was no use in arguing with a prophet, since his authority came directly from God. Rich people, poor people, young people, and old people alike delivered God's messages. No special training was necessary to become a prophet.
Num. 11:26

217

PROTECTION

Does God protect His children?

Yes, He does. Does that mean nothing bad ever happens? No, it doesn't. Who knows what might happen to us, though, if God didn't protect us. God described His role to Abraham once as a shield. In the old days shields were made of metal or wood. Warriors carried them in front of their bodies so that weapons couldn't get to them. Today policemen still use shields but they are often made of Plexiglas. No matter what a shield is made of, it is something that stands in the way of anything that would hurt us. God does that as well. Nothing can reach us that doesn't first go through God's hand.

After these things the word of the LORD came to Abram in a vision, saying, "Do not be afraid, Abram. I am your shield, your exceedingly great reward."
Gen. 15:1

Who should protect the helpless?

God has given every one of us the responsibility to help those who can't help themselves. Whether it's a child, an animal, or even a grown-up person, God always expects us to show compassion on whoever crosses our path just as He has shown compassion for us. In fact, God made this a part of the Law that He gave to the Jews. It was an actual command. Asaph made it a part of one of his Psalms. There is never room, as far as God is concerned, to turn our backs on people that need us. Think about the story Jesus told of the good Samaritan. We are supposed to love our neighbor, and that means anyone who crosses our path.

SEE FOR YOURSELF: Ps. 82:3-4

Should I give up on a friend?
Meet Emma.

When Julie started acting a little shady, Emma began to suspect that her friend was dealing with something. She had read enough stuff on eating disorders that she noticed the signs right away—bloodshot eyes, headaches, slipping out after meals, weird eating patterns, and leaving by herself at night. Still, Emma wanted to give her the benefit of the doubt. So she just kept watching her very closely. Emma started finding other clues, like the candy bar wrapper and an empty cracker box in Julie's purse. Sketchy.

Emma still didn't know what to think, though. After all, everyone needs a little personal space, so she couldn't blame Julie for going out on her own. Besides, she thought, maybe I'm imagining the whole thing. Emma started praying and reading whatever she could get her hands on.

An article on bulimia by a Christian writer gave her some fresh insight. Physically, Julie was destroying her body. She risked never being able to eat normally again and also seriously screwing up her metabolism. But emotionally and spiritually, her bulimia revealed that she had much deeper struggles. She was wrestling with a control issue and with her self-image and spiritual health. As much as Julie tried to "hide" her habit, she had to know that her friends noticed. Emma couldn't ignore the situation.

Emma kept praying. Julie kept throwing up. Emma kept asking. Julie kept denying. Emma kept watching. Julie kept hiding. Despite her denial, Emma stuck with her friend and loved her. Finally, Julie collapsed. Her body just couldn't take all the cycles of binging and purging. She couldn't continue with what she was doing. She finally admitted she needed help.

Together the two friends went to a counselor from church, and she connected them with a woman who specialized in eating disorders. Emma took Julie to see her one Wednesday morning, and she talked with her for over an hour. They started meeting together weekly, and Julie began to heal.

If there was one thing Emma learned from all this, it's that even Christians struggle with some really ugly stuff. doesn't make us immune to the dangers of this world. But Jesus has a better life for us. Never grow weary in doing good. Never. Never tire of stooping to pick up your brothers and sisters in Christ. Never stop leaning on each other and on your Father. You never know when you'll need to be peeled up off the floor.

Will God always come to my rescue?

God is "a very present help," always ready to aid His children. When the nation of Israel found itself face-to-face with an enemy, God didn't have to go recruit an army and buy some weapons. He already had an army of angels—and enough power in His little finger to wipe out the enemy. Sometimes God used the men of Israel's army; sometimes He used a bunch of trumpets; but whatever He did, Israel came out on top—as long as they obeyed Him. Well, that same power, the "refuge and strength," is for you, too. God is always ready to help you. When you ask for His help with a tough decision, He doesn't have to go research the problem. He's got more knowledge and wisdom than even Albert Einstein could get a handle on. If money is what you need, He doesn't have to go to the bank and get a loan. Everything on earth belongs to Him anyway. Everything you need is wrapped up in God. He doesn't have to get it together before He can help. All He needs is for you to ask.

> God is our refuge and strength, a very present help in trouble.
> Ps. 46:1

RSELF: Josh. 1:9; Prov. 2:4-7; Is. 35:3-4

During wilderness battles, soldiers often hid behind rocks for protection. In the Bible, God is often compared to a rock because He protects the people who obey Him.
2 Sam. 22:2

What does God do to protect me?

Only in heaven will we know how many times God has rescued us from harm. The list probably fills books: family car delayed in traffic to avoid three-car pileup; grounded from the big sophomore party and kept from the lure of drugs and a police raid; army of angels sent to protect unsuspecting students from attempted mugging on campus. Sometimes we can look back and know that God put His hand on us, directed our steps, and protected us. But most of the time we walk around totally unaware of His divine intervention on our behalf. Time after time He keeps us safe from things we can see, and even the things we can't. Take a minute to thank Him for keeping watch over the big and the little things in your life and for guarding every move you make.

SEE FOR YOURSELF: Ps. 7:10; Nah. 1:7; 2 Thess. 3:3

> He shall deliver you in six troubles, yes, in seven no evil shall touch you.
> **Job 5:19**

How does God watch over me?

Sheep are the only animals that need a shepherd for outside care. They would wander off, starve to death, or fall off a cliff if it weren't for the shepherd. The Lord calls us His sheep because, in the same way, we need Him to guide us, to protect us, and to provide for our needs. Sometimes a shepherd will carry a helpless lamb in his arms, and a wonderful thing happens during that bonding process—the lamb finds security and learns to trust his shepherd. When the lamb begins to walk, he will never stray from the shepherd's side again. Are you a wandering sheep? God as your shepherd will coax you back into the flock time and again, and He will hold you close to encourage you to stay with Him.

SEE FOR YOURSELF: Ps. 95:7; 100:3; Is. 53:6; John 10:1-16

PROVISION

Will God give me everything I want?

> I am your portion and your inheritance among the children of Israel.
> Num. 18:20b

God is faithful. You can count on Him. God has always been faithful to keep His Word. He has supplied all of our needs. Most of the time we have much more than we could ever use or appreciate. We doubt God's provision when we confuse our needs with our wants. Need says that you need clothes. Want says that you can only put the hippest, coolest things on your body. Need says that you need to eat lunch every day. Want says that you have to go out with your friends because they'd laugh if you ate in the cafeteria. We live in abundant times. A lot of people have a lot of stuff, and they want more. Think about your needs. Learn to separate them from the things you want. What do you really need in order to live? Has God provided? Take some time to thank Him. He's given you all you need.

SEE FOR YOURSELF: Matt. 6:31-33; Luke 12:29-30; Phil. 4:19

Why can I have confidence that the Lord will give me everything I need?

> The LORD is my shepherd; I shall not want.
> Ps. 23:1

David had a rock-solid confidence in God. He didn't wonder whether God was going to give him food to eat, clothes to wear, or a place to live. Part of that confidence came out of David's experiences. In spite of all the scrapes and tight places he found himself in, God had never let him be hurt or go hungry. And part of that confidence came from the fact that David knew God very well. He knew Him like a best friend. He knew that God was–and is–kind, loving, and powerful.

There was another reason that David could say, "I shall not want." All of David's hopes and dreams were caught up in the Lord. Even if he had been forced to go without some of the things that people consider necessities, he wouldn't have missed them much. David's relationship with God meant everything to him. As long as he knew that God was leading him and that their friendship was where it was supposed to be, David had the thing he wanted most. All the rest was extra. As you grow toward having the same attitude that David did, you'll see–like David did–that God never lets you go without the things you really need. He is the one thing you need most.

SEE FOR YOURSELF: Is. 49:10; Luke 12:29-3

The Year of Jubilee was designed to keep Israel from developing different classes among the people. Imagine having the opportunity to start over again economically and socially! God wanted His people to be free . . . The Year of Jubilee was a way of reminding the Israelites of this.
Lev. 25:14, 15

223

PSYCHICS

Does God use psychics to speak for Him? 29

> And the person who turns after mediums and familiar spirits, to prostitute himself with them, I will set My face against that person and cut him off from his people.
> Lev. 20:6

How many times have you flipped through the channels to see somebody trying to convince you to call a 1-900 number that will put you in touch with your very own psychic? We live in a world today that is fascinated with the supernatural, but rather than turning to God or His Word for answers, a lot of people want to turn to "mediums and familiar spirits," that is, to psychics, fortune-tellers, witches, channelers, and others. God's Word calls this kind of stuff an abomination, and in this particular verse, He says that He is against (the enemy of) those who even visit someone like this. Don't even associate with such people. Instead, turn to Jesus. He really is the only answer! You don't need to go looking to someone else for answers about your future. God speaks to you through His Word and through His Holy Spirit. Don't settle for a cheap imitation. All the answers you need are in the Bible, and if you read the end of it you'll see that you are a winner. In fact, you're more than a conquerer (Rom. 8:37), and God is on your side. Your power isn't counterfeit. It's real. "He who is in you is greater than he who is in the world" (1 John 4:4).

SEE FOR YOURSELF: 2 Chr. 33:6; Gal. 5:19-21

PURITY

How can I be pure hearted?

Purity doesn't come really easily to most people. We are, by nature, sinful and self-absorbed. Those two things are not good breeding ground for purity. The only way we can have pure hearts is to get to know God as much as possible. You know how when you rub elbows with someone you tend to become like them? You pick up their habits and thoughts. That's why we read the Bible and get to know God. We want to become like Him. He is pure hearted. It is only from Him that we can learn to be as well.

Why wait?
To stay alive. In the Old Testament times, it was against the law for a woman to lose her virginity before marriage. If anyone could prove she had lost her virginity, the woman faced a possible death penalty. This punishment did not apply to women who had been raped.
Gen. 34:2-7

225

RELATIONSHIP WITH GOD

Now it came to pass, when Rehoboam had established the kingdom and had strengthened himself, that he forsook the law of the LORD, and all Israel along with him.
2 Chron. 12:1

Why is it harder sometimes to stay close to God when things are going really well?

Probably because we get confident in our own abilities instead of His provision. That very thing happened to a king of Israel in the Old Testament. Rehoboam was Solomon's son. Solomon was the king who was very wise and made Israel wealthy and prestigious. In the end, though, he didn't maintain his own character and integrity, at least in terms of worship. When Rehoboam took over he actually did very well at first. He made some good choices. But then he changed one thing. He started trusting his own goodness and success instead of God. Things went downhill from there for him and for Israel (and when I say downhill, I mean *really* downhill). We can all get a false sense of security when things are going well. The truly successful person remembers even at his best, that God makes it all possible.

Can God speak to me differently than He does to someone else?

God can speak to us in as many ways as He can imagine. He is very creative when it comes to getting our attention. He can whisper to us while we are still, or shout to us in our busyness. We can read the Bible and know that He has just spoken directly to our situation. A teacher may teach from the Scripture and God speaks through him or her. He uses billboards, phone calls, hugs from friends, successes, failures, and ordinary humdrum experiences. He will do whatever it takes, intervene whenever necessary to get you to look up and know that He is God. Do you have eyes to see? Do you have ears to hear God speaking to you?

SEE FOR YOURSELF: Job 33:14; 1 Cor. 2:13; 2 Pet. 1:21; Rev. 2:7

How do I get closer to Jesus?

Think about a tree growing beside a river. Would it be a dry, ugly tree with brown, cracking leaves? No, that tree would always be alive and full with lush, green leaves. Even in the middle of a drought, that tree would thrive because the river would give it all the water it needed. "He shall be like a tree planted by the rivers of water." The word "he" refers to the godly man described in verses 1 and 2. This individual doesn't listen to friends or other people who tell him to go against what God wants. He doesn't make fun of God, even if it seems like everyone else does. This man is delighted when he thinks about what God says, so the man does what pleases Him. If you've made up your mind to follow Jesus, ask yourself if you fit that description. You are like that tree growing beside a river. God's Spirit is the river that flows by you and offers you all the life and strength you need. When you get your life from His Spirit, you're always able to succeed in God's eyes, even if everything around you seems out of control.

> He shall be like a tree planted by the rivers of water, that brings forth its fruit in its season, whose leaf also shall not wither; and whatever he does shall prosper.
>
> Ps. 1:3

SEE FOR YOURSELF: Num. 24:6, 7; Ps. 52:8; Jer. 17:7, 8; Zech. 14:8

Does God know me better than anyone else does?

Have you ever thought, *There are millions of people in the world. How can God keep up with all of us? How can He pay any attention to me? How can He hear my prayers when everybody else is talking to Him, too?* Thoughts like that will blow your mind, but God is so much bigger than your mind. Psalm 43:5 has two words that will help put your mind at ease: "my God." In order to have a close and growing relationship with God, you have to make Him personal. You have to know that He is *your* God. Here's a suggestion: When you pray, just say to the Lord, "You are *my* God." Put the emphasis on the word *my.* Even though there are lots of Christians in the world, your relationship with God is not like anybody else's. He made you to stand out from everybody else. Those things that set you apart from other people are the things that give you a unique place with Him. When you feel like a dot in the middle of a swarm of Christians who need God's love and attention, just remember that He is *your* God.

SEE FOR YOURSELF: Ps. 43:5, 63:1; 118:28; Is. 25:1; Jer. 31:20

How can I really focus on God?

Are you a genuine seeker? When you're with other people who are worshiping the Lord, where is your heart? In other words, do you *worship* when you worship? Is your mind participating in the things that are being said? Or are you just pretending? Eyes closed, mind wandering. Bible open, words blurry. Singing songs because you know them, not because you mean them. Don't answer these questions out loud and don't start feeling guilty if you know that all the answers are "yes" in your life. God already knows the condition of your heart. The point is that God takes care of everyone who truly worships Him. Do you long to be cared for by God? Then worship Him from your heart. Even if you don't feel superspiritual, tell Him what you think and how you feel. Think about how awesome He is, and then tell Him about it. When you sing a song, really pay attention to the words and sing them like you believe them. Pray a lot. Read the Bible so you can get to know God better. The more real He is to you, the more true your worship will be. Don't be lazy or distracted. No one can take care of you the way God can. Just be a genuine seeker.

SEE FOR YOURSELF: Is. 29:13; John 4:23, 24

> The hand of our God is upon all those for good who seek Him, but His power and His wrath are against all those who forsake Him.
> Ezra 8:22

How long will it take for me to know God?

It seems the apostle Paul knew God better than anyone. But even he found God too awesome to imagine. "Oh, the depth of the riches both of the wisdom and knowledge of God! How unsearchable are His judgments and His ways past finding out!" he wrote to the Romans (Rom. 11:33). In another letter he wrote, "For now we see in a mirror, dimly, but then face to face. Now I know in part, but then I shall know just as I also am known" (1 Cor. 13:12). Trying to understand God all at once is like trying to count the stars in the sky. It's just too big of a job. The more you learn of His power to create, to save, to change; the more you see of His forgiveness, His grace, His love; the more you understand of His incredible intelligence (after all, the principles of math and physics were all His ideas); the more you realize that you have a long way to go. Knowing Him is a journey that takes a lifetime. It's worth it.

SEE FOR YOURSELF: 2 Chr 2:5; Job 33:12; John 14:28; 1 John 3:20

> Great is the LORD, and greatly to be praised; and His greatness is unsearchable.
> Ps. 145:3

How well does God really know me?

Read all of Psalm 139 to find out how God knows you. Totally. There's nothing you can ever think or do that God doesn't know about. He even knows what you're going to do before you do it. That could be scary if you think of God as the "Man Upstairs" who's just sitting around waiting to catch you doing something wrong. Relax. God isn't like that. Because you're one of His children, you can be glad that God knows you inside and out. He knows and appreciates what you're good at. He knows exactly what He's got planned for your life. He understands the things that are hard for you. He won't let you face a temptation that you can't stand up to. Since God knows you so completely, you don't ever have to be afraid to share your whole heart with Him. He won't laugh at you or reject you. The fact that God knows you says a lot about His enormous mind and His limitless love. But it also says something about you. It says that you are so important that God spends His time thinking about you. He's in love with you!

SEE FOR YOURSELF:
1 Chr 28:9; Job 23:9, 10; Ps. 139:15, 167; Acts 15:8; Rom. 8:2

RELATION-SHIP WITH OTHERS

Hatred stirs up strife, but love covers all sins.
Prov. 10:12

Sibling tensions: How do I build bridges for a good relationship?

It's going to happen just by virtue of being sisters. Maybe the next time it'll be you. You're running late for school. Nothing is ironed. You look over at her closet, and there's the perfect shirt to throw on. You put it on and think, I'll explain later. I'm sure she wouldn't mind. Some things in life are worth getting upset about, and some things are best overlooked. Borrowed clothes between sisters is not a big deal—even when she didn't ask, even when you don't ask. You could do the mature thing next time and say, "It's okay if you wear my clothes. But when it's not an emergency, I'd really appreciate it if you would ask me." Give your sister the same respect. Build bridges toward her. A sister is an awesome gift from God, even when she gets on your nerves. Love her and try to overlook the little stuff.

SEE FOR YOURSELF: Rom. 12:9, 10; 1 Cor. 13:4; Eph 4:1-3; 1 John 4:7

Speaking the truth in love?
Meet Erik.

What a hypocrite. I cannot believe him. He puts on such an act, and I can't believe that anyone would fall for it. But then again, everyone falls for it. He's so two-faced, and if only they could see the real Wes. His parents are so clueless about what he's up to. Everyone seems to think he's just the greatest Christian guy. All the other parents want their sons to be like Wes. That kid is smooth. Sometimes I can't stand him.

But still, he's my friend. I guess I'm one of the only guys who ever sees both sides of him. Everyone at church thinks he's a model child, and all our friends at school know his bad side. But they don't see both sides of him, so they just think he's an average guy with a terrible mouth. Only I know that he claims he's a Christian and puts on a show on Sundays, only to walk out the door and curse everything and everyone he says he believes in and loves. The kid has issues.

Like yesterday in church. Wes seems to have the right answer for every question. He knows when to talk and when to listen. He acts so respectful to our leaders. Yesterday he spoke up in our small group and talked about how important it is for us as believers to be pure and to show Christ through our lives. What an act! As soon as we left the church, you wouldn't believe the words that came out of his mouth.

Today on the way to school, with just the two of us in the car, Wes mocked the leaders, every one of them and their idealistic teachings, and he started in again with his swearing. I didn't say anything then. Maybe I should have. I just can't stand that kid.

All day I thought about it. I thought about his hypocrisy and about how he brings down the other guys at school. I thought about his deception and how he's lost sight of the truth. Most of all, I wondered if it's my place to say something. Maybe if someone got in his face and nailed him with the truth of what he is, he'd start to see it, too.

Well, my opportunity came. On our way home from school, Wes started going off about stuff, and his language was filthy. So I said it. Everything I had been thinking for a long time but just hadn't told him. I did it with the right motivation, to help him as my friend, not to tear him down. I talked about his image and what people thought of him and about how he acts around the guys. I brought up his language and how offensive it is. In my mind, it would be better for him to just be himself, bad as it might be, rather than putting on a false image. He got really quiet.

We never talked about it again. It was one of those one-time blowup deals, where I vented all my frustration with him, and he took it in shock. I don't think he ever put it together just how out of control he'd gotten. I began to see a change in Wes, and it's made an impact on all the guys. He began living a consistent life, not terrible one minute and perfect the next. He let go of that fake image he had and started building something of substance. I can see the impact God had on him, and I can't tell you how much that's impacted me.

Why is it so hard to tell people things you know they don't want to hear but need to?

> But as we have been approved by God to be entrusted with the gospel, even so we speak, not as pleasing men, but God who tests our hearts.
> 1 Thess. 2:4

One reason is because we want other people to like us and to be happy with us. There's nothing wrong with that. God made us that way. The important thing is that we keep it in a balance. Several times in the New Testament Paul reminded his readers that they should worry more about pleasing God than pleasing other people. Why? Because Paul knew that it is so hard to tell people what you know they don't want to hear. But when you're dealing with the truth, sometimes you have to. That's the thing about the truth—it's always good for us, but it doesn't always feel good.

How should I treat unkind people?

Here in Proverbs and later in the New Testament, the writers give us some wisdom about friends who tell lies or treat us badly. The advice is to do exactly the opposite of what your friends do. Even in your disappointment and anger, you are supposed to be Christlike. Luke 6:28 says to "bless those who curse you, and pray for those who spitefully use you." By loving those who hurt you, "you will heap coals of fire on his head" (Prov. 25:22). Wow, that's pretty hard advice. Your reputation has been shattered. Your pride has been wounded. Your heart is broken. And God wants you to do what? Yep, He says to love them anyway—even give food to them if they are hungry. Oh yeah, and pray for them, too. By doing so, you prove the strength of your character. That's God's way.

SEE FOR YOURSELF: Prov. 25:18, 19, 21, 22; Matt. 18:21, 22; Luke 6:28; 17:3, 4; Col. 3

Why do people join gangs?

People feel stronger in groups. The Bible even says that. Proverbs says that two are stronger than one, and three are even stronger. Also we enjoy associations with other people who are similar to us in some way. That's why there are clubs galore in the world. Golf clubs (not the metal sticks you play with, silly), chess clubs, girl scouts, boy scouts, moose lodges, shriners, bowling leagues, yadda, yadda, yadda. Gangs really function in much the same way. They usually are grouped around the territory they claim. Being in a gang provides protection and a sense of belonging. But you know the reputation of gangs. They have reputations for violence. I'm sure not every gang member is this way, but think about how scared or lonely a person would have to be to join a gang. Which would be the scarier situation if you lived in a dangerous neighborhood, to be in a gang that could be attacked by another gang, or to be in no gang and be up for grabs? Thinking about that makes you feel a little more compassionate for them, doesn't it?

> Though one may be overpowered by another, two can withstand him. And a threefold cord is not quickly broken.
> Eccl. 4:12

If you're married, would you still be married in heaven? What if you were divorced or married three times or something?

Some people asked Jesus that very same question. They were trying to trick Jesus, but we got the answer anyway. They asked, "If a man dies and his brother married his wife (this was a custom in those days to make sure the wife was cared for), then that brother dies and the next brother marries her . . . who will she see as her husband in heaven?" Jesus said that Heaven doesn't work like that. He also said that when we get to heaven we won't marry. We'll be like the angels. So that also gives us the answer of whether there is a Mr. or Mrs. Angel.

SEE FOR YOURSELF. Matthew 22.29-30

233

RELATIONSHIP WITH PARENTS

> Whoever curses his father or his mother, his lamp will be put out in deep darkness.
> Prov. 20:20.

My parents are so embarrassing, what should I do?

Ashley's mom got this new device that you put on your car. It plays forty different songs through your horn. One day in the junior high carpool line, Ashley's mom decide to play "parking lot DJ" and started playing songs through the horn. They were old songs, geeky songs—"Oh Susanna" and "Tea for Two." Really hip stuff *cannot* be played through a car horn. Mom thought it was a riot. Ashley thought it was the most humiliating thing that could possibly happen. Ashley tried to figure out what she could do that would be equally embarrassing to her mother, but nothing came close to that musical horn. Finally, Ashley decided to take the high road. She sat down and told her mom how mortified she was, that it was not funny, and that she wanted her to stop. Mom apologized for being so goofy. She really had thought it was funny. Now she just entertains construction workers as she drives by and the school parking lot is quiet. Parents can be really embarrassing, intentionally or without even knowing it. When it gets to you, work through it. Talk it out. Tell them how you feel. Be honest and don't try to get even. Your parents will appreciate your maturity.

SEE FOR YOURSELF: Matt. 5:9; 1 Cor. 13:4-13

Why should I respect my parents when I don't like their decisions?

In the military, new recruits are taught that above everything else they must respect their commanders. They may disagree with their decisions or their lifestyles, but they are required to respect their positions of leadership. In much the same way, God requires that you respect your parents. He chose them to lead your family and to train you. In His wisdom, He made a perfect decision. Even when you disagree with your parents, you are called to respect them just because they are your mom and dad. Respect means that you obey their instruction—let it guide you and protect you. God influences your life directly through the leadership of your parents. It's the way He set things in order. It's the design that works best. It glorifies God when you respect your parents.

> My son, keep your father's command, and do not forsake the law of your mother.
> Prov. 6:20

SEE FOR YOURSELF: Matt. 15:4; Eph. 6:1-3

Why should I respect my parents when I don't agree with them?

What do I do if my mom is always on my case about the way I dress? The answer to this question lies in the big principle of Exodus 20:12—honor your father and your mother. It's amazing how rational parents can be when you confront them with respect and honor instead of rebellion. The next time the clothes thing comes up with your mom, try something like this: "Mom, I know you don't like this outfit. This is what I like to wear when I'm around my friends. I want to honor you even with my clothes, so when we're going somewhere and it's really important to you that I dress less weird, just let me know." Major life events like weddings and funerals will probably rate pretty high on the "please dress less weird" list. Growing in your faith means that you're always trying to live your life according to the truth in the Bible. Go ahead and talk it through with Mom. You'll be surprised by the respect she'll give you when you give it to her. God will be honored because you honored her.

SEE FOR YOURSELF: Ex. 20:12; Eph. 6:1-3; Col. 3:20

I'm sick of my parents throwing it in my face that I'm "rebellious"! Does God really have a problem with me trying to be my own person like my parents do?

For rebellion is as the sin of witchcraft, and stubbornness is as iniquity and idolatry. Because you have rejected the word of the LORD, He also has rejected you from being king.
1 Sam. 15:23

If your parents are calling you rebellious, then you're probably having a hard time at home. What feels to you like "trying to be your own person" might feel to them like you're trying to be anything but like them, like you're rejecting them. Remember when you were little and it *really* mattered what they thought about you? Ever stop to think that it's important to your parents how YOU feel about THEM? They want to be connected to your life and know you love them, even when you disagree. This kind of conflict is not new. I hate to tell you, but in the Old Testament days, kids who were proved to be rebellious were sometimes stoned (Deut. 21:18-21). It was serious business. Rebellion was considered as bad as witchcraft. The answer to your question is, no, God doesn't mind you trying to be your own person. He wants that for you. He made you unique. But, how you get there matters to Him. This tug-of-war that is probably going on with you and your parents will keep on until somebody drops their end of the rope. You can be your own person and still show respect to your parents. You'll probably get a lot farther with them that way.

So if I'm not supposed to yell back at my parents, what am I supposed to do when they go off on me?

> He who disdains instruction despises his own soul, but he who heeds reproof gets understanding.
> Prov. 15:32

It depends on what you mean by "go off." Most often, if you yell back, you won't get anything different than more yelling, so yelling back is not often the best option. If what you mean by "go off" is that your parents give you a "piece of their mind" and you don't want to listen to it because it feels like they are imposing their opinion on you, maybe you should rethink that. Just because you listen respectfully to someone's opinion doesn't mean that you are taking on that same opinion. The truth is that even if you don't agree with the opinion, you might learn one thing by listening and hearing how your parents came to their conclusions. Maybe you could ask them questions about how they made choices for themselves. Let them tell you their story instead of spouting opinions.

Why would God want me to listen to my parents go on and on when I know they just don't get it?

God puts a high priority on listening. In fact there are a lot of verses in the Bible about it. The book of Proverbs talks a lot about listening and responding to what you hear instead of just turning someone off. Sometimes your parents don't seem to make sense because they see stuff that you don't see yet. You think, "Why are they getting so bent out of shape? It's a simple thing really." But they've lived longer and even if they can't say it in a way that works for you, they probably know some things that you might not "get." The important thing for you is to listen and learn what you can. Just because you listen doesn't mean you have to agree. But God put you there with those people. Look for what He might be able to show you through them.

SEE FOR YOURSELF: Prov. 8:33

Why are my parents always going ballistic about MTV and stuff I like?

> Test all things; hold fast what is good. Abstain from every form of evil.
> 1 Thess. 5:21-22

There's a verse in the Bible that says hold on to the good and stay away from every form of evil. I can't know REALLY what your parents are thinking, but one thing that a lot of parents think is that MTV type stuff flirts with evil a bit. It feels dark and exciting in a not-so-pure way. You gotta admit, it's not what the censors would classify as family viewing. The important thing is that you are doing as much to fill your mind with stuff that draws you to God as you do everything else. What kind of balance do you have?

Why do my parents think I'm going to do stuff just 'cuz my friends do?

It seems like ever since there were bridges parents were afraid that, if their child's friends jumped off of one, their child would follow. It's really not that your parents think you don't have a brain in your head. (It's really not.) It's just that they know how easy it is to get influenced by other people. Not just because they were kids once, but because that never changes. Paul (who was an adult) wrote about that very thing when he reminded the Corinthians that bad company corrupts good character. It's true that what your friends do will affect what you do. Find a way to be OK with your parents being cautious while proving to them they don't need to worry.

SEE FOR YOURSELF: 1 Cor. 15:33

What if my parents ask me to do something that's a sin ?

That's a toughie. First, talk with your parents and make absolutely sure that you are understanding them correctly. If they really are asking you to do something wrong, pray really hard about it. Ask God to help you find your way through the situation. Then try offering solutions that will still accomplish what your parents want but will let you off the hook. For instance, if they are asking you to lie to Aunt Bessie that you have plans so that you don't have to go to a family dinner at her house, maybe you can find another way to get out of it. If on the other extreme, you are being asked to steal or be involved in something indecent or unethical, you'll have to search your heart, pray, and see if God can show you a way to refuse that will still leave the relationship with your parents intact. As always, see if you can find a safe adult to talk this over with. Following God and obeying Him is the most important thing in your life, and sin is to be avoided at all costs. If your parents are asking you to sin—respectfully explain to them why you cannot obey their command

> Children, obey your parents in all things, for this is well pleasing to the Lord.
> Col. 3:20

My mom had an affair. How do I forgive her?

Let's talk about forgiveness. Forgiving your mom doesn't mean acting like nothing happened. It doesn't mean you have to pretend it doesn't bother you or that you aren't hurt. Forgiving your mom just means treating her horrible lack of good judgment the way you'd like your lack of good judgment to be treated. The Bible says that God forgives us like we forgive others. How do you want God to forgive you? He's not going to act like it doesn't hurt Him that you sin even when He asks you not to. He's not going to pretend like nothing happened. But He is going to stay in relationship to you. He's going to love you the same because you are covered by Jesus' blood. You can still speak to your mom with kindness. You can still treat her with at least as much respect as you would like to receive. You can let her know that it will take time before you are over this. You can let her know how you feel. But you can let go of the responsibility to punish her. You don't have to do it. You just have to trust your God and ask Him to show you the meaning of forgiveness.

SEE FOR YOURSELF: Matt. 6:14-15

REPUTATION

What does it mean to have a good reputation?

OO. OO. 29   OO. OO. 10

Therefore be careful to observe them; for this is your wisdom and your understanding in the sight of the peoples who will hear all these statutes, and say, Surely this great nation is a wise and understanding people.
Deut. 4:6

It means that the people who observe your life think well of you. Some of that is out of your control. As you know, people see things from many different perspectives. You might do the right thing, and still someone could disagree with you. But overall, after people get to know you, they get the idea of whether you are selfish or generous, kind or cruel, trustworthy or two-faced. In Deuteronomy, God, through Moses, gave the Hebrews some instructions for having a good reputation. Moses told the people to obey God's law, and the nations around them would say, "Wow, they're wise." That's good advice for you and me, too. While we can't make the people around us think well of us, obeying God will make us the most decent, loving people we can be. That's the best protection for a good reputation.

Free for the taking? Meet Zoe.

"Just take it. It's not a big deal," Kris said. At first Zoe didn't even catch what was going on. She was so blind to the whole thing that she didn't even put it together what Kris was doing. With a swift move of her hand, Kris brushed the lipstick down into her purse. By the time the girl who was helping them came back, Kris was smiling sweetly and standing up to go. "Thanks for all your help. Wow, this is a lot of makeup. Can you hold that powder for me so I can come pick it up later? My name's Julie. Thanks." With a quick wave, Kris stood and walked right out of the department store. Zoe followed her in shock, trying to process what she had seen. "Wasn't that smooth? She doesn't have a clue," Kris bragged.

"Kris," Zoe finally found her voice. "That's terrible! Why did you do that?"

"Do you really think I could afford all this stuff without helping myself to some of it?" she asked innocently, waving at her brand-name clothes and full shopping bags. "The stores have so much stuff, they'll never know the difference." Was this really happening? Zoe brushed it off for a few minutes, trying to figure out what to say. For now, she said nothing.

Inside Marshall Field's, the girls both found some cute stuff to try on. Zoe kept thinking back to the lipstick incident and meant to bring it up with Kris later. For now, though, she was trying to figure out if she looked better in blue or gray . . .

"Take both," Kris whispered. "You need them. Besides, they look so good on you!" Kris looked right into Zoe's eyes, and then turning, she slipped a sweater into her big shopping bag. "Ready to go?" she asked.

"Kris, no! There's no way I'm taking this!" Zoe said to her, getting right up in her face. "What you're doing is wrong, it's shoplifting, it's stealing, and you know it's wrong," she said with some force behind her voice. Zoe had always been a bit in awe of Kris, but the more Zoe got to know her, the less impressed she was.

Kris took the sweater out of her bag. But she stormed right out of the dressing room before Zoe could stop her. Let's just say that the whole thing damaged their friendship. But if nothing else, at least Zoe came to a realization of what Kris was really like. What Zoe saw was just not appealing. Their friendship slowly faded, and Zoe felt sorry for her.

Just how much am I supposed to care what other people think about what I do?

For if anyone sees you who have knowledge eating in an idol s temple, will not the conscience of him who is weak be emboldened to eat those things offered to idols?
1 Cor. 8:10

There's a really important word to remember when you're trying to decide about this. That word is "balance." Have you ever seen one of those scales where you put one thing on one side and another thing on the other side. If you have the same amount of each thing, then the scales balance. When you're thinking about what other people think about you, you have to keep it in balance. On one side of the scales you have the fact that God is really the only person you have to please. On the other side of the scales is the fact that God wants you to influence the world around you for good. In Paul's day people worried about whether the meat they were served had been offered to false gods. Some people got all uptight about it. Other people said, "False idols don't mean anything. Who cares if the meat was offered to them?" Paul said, "Don't do something that's going to make someone else struggle in their faith" (like eating that meat in front of young Christians who would freak out about it). That's an example of doing something because of how it will influence other people. Think about what God thinks first. Then give a thought to how your actions will affect the people around you. Keep it in balance.

Why does it seem like the bad kids get called "cool," and the ones of us trying to be good get called "geeks"?

But Daniel purposed in his heart that he would not defile himself with the portion of the king's delicacies, nor with the wine which he drank; therefore he requested of the chief of the eunuchs that he might not defile himself.

Daniel 1:8

Now THAT'S a good question, isn't it? It's an unfair thing. Why does a person who seems to not care about right and wrong come off looking better than someone who does?

Particularly when it takes a lot more guts and courage to do the right thing. I don't think it's a new problem, though. There were several real stand-up guys in the Old Testament that didn't always get their due. One was Joseph. Another was Daniel. Daniel got dragged to a foreign country. The first thing that happened is they offered him, and the other prisoners, some great food that was totally off the Jewish diet (you know, the whole kosher thing). Daniel asked for healthy foods instead of all the rich food they wanted to feed him to fatten him up. Can you see that? Daniel with his salad greens while the other guys ate their steaks and potatoes? Daniel grew into a leader in that country, but instead of being honored for his beliefs there were some guys that constantly tried to find ways to trip him up. Daniel could have felt some of the same feelings that you feel. I don't know that you'll be able to change the fact that sometimes the outlaws get more prestige than the stand-up guys. Know this, though . . . it matters to God that you try to do the right thing. You make the world a little better place by being that way.

REVENGE

Can I take revenge into my own hands?

00. 00. 29

Sometimes it seems like people can get away with anything. They cheat and steal and lie and curse God. They get other people to go along with them. Sometimes it goes on for years, and they just seem to be getting richer and more powerful by the minute. You look at them and think, *What good is it to obey God? I'm over here trying to live the Christian life, and I'm struggling day by day, and that guy is doing great!* Then BOOM, God takes revenge on His enemies. Everything goes to pieces for the other guy. You realize that God calls us to make choices for Him. God calls us to be responsible for living His way. You see that He may tolerate stuff from His enemies for a while, but not forever. Read the book of Revelation. You'll see that He will take revenge on His enemies. It is worth it to be on His side. He wins.

SEE FOR YOURSELF: Is. 1:24; Ezek. 25:17; Nah. 1:2

> For I lift My hand to heaven, and say, "As I live forever, if I whet My glittering sword, and My hand takes hold on judgment, I will render vengeance to My enemies."
>
> Deut. 32:40, 41

Is it wrong to want to get someone back when they do something really bad to you?

You know, nothing feels more natural than to "get somebody back." It feels fair to us. It feels like the necessary thing. But, the truth is that the "getting back" is not our responsibility—it's God's responsibility. It's one of those mysteries of life. When somebody hurts us or betrays us, we feel like it's up to us to do something about it. The truth is we don't have to. Ultimately, we trust God to take care of us, not that other person and not ourselves. It's up to us to be the best person we can be. It's up to God to deal with the other person. God says several times in the Bible, "Vengeance is Mine." He can't be much clearer than that, can He? And when you think about it, it makes our lives easier. We don't have to spend our energy planning out what we'll do. We can leave that up to God.

SEE FOR YOURSELF: Heb. 10:30

RIGHTEOUS- NESS

> The LORD is righteous; He has cut in pieces the cords of the wicked.
>
> Ps. 129:4

Is God still righteous when bad things happen?

God always is righteous. That doesn't just mean that He follows the rules. Of course He does—they're His rules. But He goes beyond that. He does what is right for you. He knows you inside and out, and everything that comes into your life from His hand is the very best thing that could happen in your life. He gives you what you need to become the person He wants you to be— someone who's more and more like His Son. But don't think that everything that happens to you is something God does. When you or someone close to you sins, that has an effect on your life—but sin is never God's will. Or sometimes Satan hurts you. God allowed that with Job—the bad things that happened to Job did not come from Him, but He knew what Job was going through. Here's what's cool—God can even take people's mistakes and Satan's wicked plans and turn them into something good. Romans 8:28 says, "And we know that all things work together for good to those who love God, to those who are the called according to His purpose." He is so good at doing right, He takes even the crummy stuff in your life and turns it into something great—something that makes you stronger and brings you closer to Him.

SEE FOR YOURSELF: Ps. 7:9; 119:137; Is. 30:18

RULES

I get overwhelmed with all the rules of Christianity. What does God really want from me?

He has shown you, O man, what is good; and what does the LORD require of you but to do justly, to love mercy, and to walk humbly with your God?
Mic. 6:8

If you feel like there are a lot of rules to Christianity, take a few minutes and look again. Christianity is about a relationship with God made possible because of Christ's sacrifice. Because we have that relationship we try to live clean lives. In order to describe the kind of clean lives we live, some people have written down the dos and don'ts. Understand this though. The relationship comes first, not the rules. Several places in the Bible God gives us a bottom line of what He wants. One of those is Micah 6:8: "He has shown you, O man, what is good; and what does the Lord require of you but to do justly, to love mercy, and to walk humbly with your God?" Be fair and merciful to people. Walk humbly with God. The rules will take care of themselves.

The firstborn son had extra responsibilities and privileges. When the father of a family died, the firstborn son was responsible for taking care of the family. When it came time to divide up the family's inheritance, though, the firstborn son received twice as much as everyone else.
Ex. 4:22

It seems like the rules change from the Old Testament to the New one. Why is this? Are they still changing?

Do not think that I came to destroy the Law or the Prophets. I did not come to destroy but to fulfill. For assuredly, I say to you, till heaven and earth pass away, one jot or one tittle will by no means pass from the law till all is fulfilled.

Matt. 5:17-18

You're very perceptive. Faith did look a lot different after Jesus came and did His thing. Jesus, Himself, said that He didn't come to destroy the Law or the Prophets (which means the Old Testament). Instead He came to fulfill the Law. Everything about the Old Testament (the sacrifices, the temple, the prophecies) pointed to the coming of Jesus. They pointed to the change that would come when God sacrificed Himself as punishment for our sins. Once God did that through Jesus, the Law was fulfilled. No more sacrifices were needed; God had done that. The tabernacle/temple didn't hold God's presence anymore; He lived in the hearts of His people. The prophecies were still testimonies of Jesus, but the real thing had come. Suddenly faith didn't mean believing in something that was coming eventually. It meant believing in something that had already been done. All the reminders built into the Old Testament way of living faded away because we can now remember Jesus' life and base our faith on that. There are other prophecies of the Old Testament that haven't been fulfilled yet. In the same conversation, Jesus said that the rules won't change again until they are all fulfilled; then when God builds a new heaven and earth, the rules will be thrown completely out, and we'll live the way God intended for us to live before the mess began.

SADNESS

What should I do when I'm sad?

00. 00. 29

First of all, you should just be sad. If you're sad, there is a reason. Hopefully you know what that is. Maybe you lost something important to you: a friend, an opportunity, etc. Whatever it is, give yourself some time to grieve that loss. Emotions have to work their way out a bit; so be sad. Nehemiah did this very thing. He was an Old Testament government official. He was Hebrew but he worked in Persia. He heard that some things were going very wrong back home, and he felt so sad for his people. What was the first thing he did? The Bible says he "sat down and wept, and mourned for many days." The next thing he did was pray and fast before God. He sought out not only God's comfort but His guidance. Nehemiah ended up getting to take a leave of absence from his job and helping his people out of a tight spot. But he took time to be sad and figure things out first.

> So it was, when I heard these words, that I sat down and wept, and mourned for many days; I was fasting and praying before the God of heaven.
> Neh. 1:4

Sackcloth was a coarse material made from camel or goat hair. Because no one would wear such an uncomfortable cloth under normal conditions, it was an obvious sign of mourning. If you saw someone wearing sackcloth, you knew someone had died or that something bad had happened.
Gen. 37:34

SALVATION

I know salvation is really God's doing, but don't I have to do something in the process?

Then Peter said to them, "Repent, and let every one of you be baptized in the name of Jesus Christ for the remission of sins; and you shall receive the gift of the Holy Spirit."

Acts 2:38

You are right on both counts. It is God's power that saves us. But, yes, we do have to do something. We have to repent of our sins. "Repent" means, basically, to make a U-turn. We turn from our sin and to something else. Of course, what we turn to makes a big difference. When we repent of our sins and turn to faith in Jesus as the payment for those sins, then we enter into an agreement with God. He grabs hold of our souls and promises to keep us with Him forever. We live our lives in the awareness that we belong to Him. Some people call that "getting saved" or "becoming a Christian." It's not something we can do by ourselves, but we do have to make some choices in the process.

How long will I be God's child?

Can you imagine belonging to someone forever—even way after you're dead? God has chosen Israel to belong to Him forever. As a Christian, you are a part of Israel. One of the most awesome things about becoming a Christian is that "forever" becomes a real part of your life. Even though your body will eventually die, your spirit will live forever. When your life on earth is over, you will enter into a new kind of life in heaven. It's mind-blowing to think about, but you really will live forever with God. Just because you are a Christian, you won't always be perfect. You'll make mistakes, have regrets, and wish you'd made different choices. Through all those times, you still belong to God. When He says you belong to Him forever, He means forever—even when you do stuff He wouldn't be pleased with. He's chosen you to be a part of Israel. And you'll belong to Him from now on. Forever never ends.

SEE FOR YOURSELF: Ex. 2:23-25; 1 Chr. 17:22; Is. 43:20-21; 1 Pet. 2:9-10

How do I get to God?

Thousands of years ago, before Christ, the process of "getting" to God seemed a lot more complex. It involved sacrifices and priests. In those days the Hebrews believed that God lived in this little room at the center of the tabernacle. When Jesus came, He streamlined the process of getting to God. In fact, when Jesus died (as a substitute for us) the curtain that blocked off that little room at the center of the tabernacle ripped open—all by itself (wouldn't you like to have seen THAT?). What did that mean? It meant that nothing would stand between us and God's presence. God wants us to believe that He is and that He has made a way to forgive us for our sins. Believing that is how we get to God.

> And Jesus cried out with a loud voice, and breathed His last. Then the veil of the temple was torn in two from top to bottom.
> Mark 15:37-38

If somebody, like in Africa or somewhere, dies without ever knowing about Jesus, will he go to hell?

I think only God knows how He will work all that out. It seems unfair to think about, doesn't it? In theory, you think, how can a person be condemned to live eternity separated from God if he never got the chance to hear about Him on earth. While I don't have a black and white (or any other color) answer for you on that, I can tell you a couple of things that might have some bearing. There is a verse in the Bible that says that before the end of the world (as we know it) the gospel will be preached to all of the nations. Also, as experts study other cultures, even remote tribe kind of cultures, there is almost always some idea about God within that culture. True, they need to hear about Jesus, but it says to me that there is something in all of us that reaches out to God—it's our souls. It's that God made us to want Him. So I don't know the particulars, but from what I've seen so far, I know God can be trusted to have a plan, even if we don't exactly understand it.

SEE FOR YOURSELF: Matt. 24:14

Showing leadership with your friends? Meet Jared.

Our senior year has been a blast. First of all, it's nice to have a lot easier classes, and then the whole thought of getting out of school is so cool. It seems like people have been a lot more open this year, easier to get to know, much more fun. I had always hung out with these four other guys, and that was fun, but this year our group has gotten a lot bigger. We met some other guys and then some cool girls, and there's nothing between any of us, so there's no tension. It makes the weekends more interesting.

Typical weekend night: meet up at someone's house, sit around and laugh for a while, try to figure out what to do. This time some of the girls really wanted to see a movie. It's not always the guys' idea of fun for the evening, but fine, we gave in. As long as it's not a chick flick.

When we got to the theater, we were all freezing outside in line, trying to figure out what movie we should go see. Emily suddenly shouted out this horror film that has been advertised as the scariest movie of the year. Obviously it was rated R and for good reason. Everything I had heard about it was bad—bad violence, lots of sex, horrible language. But it was supposed to be the best scare. Some people agreed, and others were quiet. Since nobody else was speaking up, it looked like this would be it.

These are the kind of moments you avoid, you know, the moment of truth when you know what you *should* do and then you also know what you *want* to do. I knew, very clearly, that I should not see that movie. Regardless of what my parents or anyone else thought, I knew it was trash and bad for me. But I knew what I wanted. I was half-intrigued with the scary movie idea, and the other half of me just didn't want to let everyone else down. It was like I had the little devil on one shoulder and the angel on the other, just whispering in my ear.

"I'd rather go see that football movie," I said firmly. (The angel won out.) It was the first movie I thought of. It was supposed to be an intense drama, pretty clean, and I always love a good sports movie. Hard to tell, though, how they would react.

"Come on, Jared, let's just all see a good scary movie together." Apparently, Emily wasn't going to drop it.

"No thanks, that movie looks terrible. You guys can go see it if you want, but I'm not going to. I can just meet you outside afterwards," I said, standing my ground. End result: six for the horror movie, five for football.

SATAN

Is Satan completely evil?

00. 00. 29

> He was a murderer from the beginning, and does not stand in the truth, because there is no truth in him.
> John 8:44

00. 00. 30

At one point he wasn't. The Bible teaches that Satan was once an angel of God. But he decided that he could be as powerful as God. It was in that pride that he fell. When he fell he chose to be against God's purposes. From that point on, yes, he was and still is completely evil. He wants any loyalty we feel for God. He wants any worship we give to God. He wants to take God's place in our lives. He is bent on destruction just as surely as God is bent on salvation. Jesus describes him as a murderer and a liar. In fact, Jesus says that there's not a speck of truth in him anywhere.

Why doesn't God stop the devil from doing bad things?

I don't know why God's timetable works the way it does. According to some passages in the Bible, God and the devil do interact. The first chapter of the book of Job describes what sounds like a precinct meeting among the spiritual dimension. Angels are checking in. God is having conversations. Satan evidently is allowed. It seems like there is an order to things in the spiritual realm that we aren't aware of. In the midst of all that, God must have some reason for delaying His judgement on the devil. Possibly because the evil in this world will make us aware of the holiness of God? We don't know, but He has proved Himself trustworthy over and over again. We'll have to trust Him on this one.

SEE FOR YOURSELF: Job 1:6-7

It sounds like the devil has it made—all those people have to do what he says and he has like his own kingdom. Plus, it sounds like he's doing God a favor, punishing the bad people. Am I missing something here?

> You are of your father the devil, and the desires of your father you want to do. . . . When he speaks a lie, he speaks from his own resources, for he is a liar and the father of it.
> John 8:44

There are two things you might be missing. The first one is Satan isn't spending his time punishing bad people. He spends his time destroying good people. Do you think that because you think Satan created hell to throw people into? No, hell is the place where Satan will be punished. It is the place where God's presence will not be. That is the horror of hell, way beyond any other description. God is not anywhere to be found there. The second thing you might be missing is life is about more than having your own kingdom where people do what you say. Satan champions evil. He destroys every person that he can. His native language is a lie. He's not a little guy in a red suit with a pitchfork. He's a liar who is against anything good. Don't look at this like a fairy tale with mystical little powers. And, understand that, in the end, Satan will be beaten down by God. "Having it made" is not the phrase that most accurately describes Satan's future.

SCHOOL

What's the benefit of being involved in activities at school?

> Two are better than one, because they have a good reward for their labor. For if they fall, one will lift up his companion. But woe to him who is alone when he falls, for he has no one to help him up.
> Eccl. 4:9, 10

Chances are your parents are more concerned that you get hooked up with a good group of friends than about your passionate commitment to the Latin Club. It's important for you to do things you enjoy with people you enjoy. Activities at school or church are cool, 'cause you can develop the ability to get along with other people and to build your leadership skills. They give you a place to focus your energy and increase your talents and abilities. They're great practice for life later on. Life is all about living and working with other people. Some of the most successful people in the workforce are those who were very involved in high school. On the other hand, kids who isolate themselves or spend a lot of time alone often get into trouble. Get involved. Learn to be a part of a group. Learn to work with other people. You'll be glad you did.

SEE FOR YOURSELF: Prov. 22:24; 1 Cor. 15:33

Is it important to God that I go to school...really?

It's important to God that you be the best you He created you to be. In our culture, that probably involves going to school. Schools were different in the days when the Bible was written. There aren't any verses that say, "You should graduate from high school." They didn't even have high schools back then. But there are plenty of verses that tell us to learn what we can, when we can. Today, that means getting a certain amount of education. Think about why you might not want to finish school. Are you tired? Are you not doing well? Are you trying to get away from home sooner? Are you scared of something? If you leave school to escape something, that's the worst mistake you can make. Deal with whatever is troubling you without running away from it. Solve whatever makes you want out of school without making your life twice as hard by quitting school.

SEE FOR YOURSELF: Prov. 4:13

SELF-WORTH

Can I really make a difference?

> For if you remain completely silent at this time, relief and deliverance will arise for the Jews from another place, but you and your father's house will perish.
>
> Est. 4:14

That's a million-dollar question that everyone asks one time or another. We all feel like we're just living our lives. We wonder if what we do will really matter. Esther, from the Old Testament, was that way too. She was living her life, taking advice from her cousin, Mordecai. She entered a beauty contest and ended up queen of a nation. That's amazing enough, but then she got the opportunity to save her people from destruction. Problem was, she'd have to risk her life to do it. Mordecai gave her some good advice. He said something like, "Don't you think God could have brought you here for a moment like this?" That's the question you have to ask yourself as well. Whatever situation you are facing, maybe God brought you and only you to that situation so that you can make a difference, whether it feels like it or not. Yes, you can make a difference. God is working through you just like He worked through Esther.

How can I measure my worth?

In this psalm, David is amazed that the awesome God of heaven would use people to rule the earth. David says that we seem like weaklings, not worthy of such a place of honor. Has anyone told you lately that you are worth a crown of glory? Worth a place of honor? Well, you are. And David says that's the way God thinks of you. Sometimes it may seem like your worth comes from your report card or your batting average, but it doesn't. Accomplishments are great, but they don't make you more acceptable to God. You couldn't get God to love you more, even if you tried. He has loved you completely from the first time He thought of you. He's your biggest fan. He adores you. You hold a place of honor in His heart. He's so proud of you and so in love with you that He's put a crown of glory and honor on you.

When it was time for Perez and his twin brother to be delivered, Perez's brother stuck his hand out first. After a few minutes, the hand disappeared back into the womb, and out popped Perez, followed by his older or younger brother (depending on how you look at it).

SEE FOR YOURSELF: Ps. 8:5; Luke 2:32; Rom. 2:10; 2 Tim. 2:10;

SERVICE

Is there anything I can do for God?

And you shall be to Me a kingdom of priests and a holy nation.
Ex. 19:6

00. 00. 29   00. 00. 0

When you hear the word *priest,* what do you think of? Maybe you picture a person standing before a congregation wearing a robe or a special collar—something that identifies the person as holy. You probably think of that person as someone who has a hotline to God. You may even think that person loves God more than you do. Since most people have this exalted idea of what a priest is, it's kind of a shock that God told Moses to tell the whole nation of Israel that they would serve Him as priests. Later God appointed men to wear special clothes and to lead religious ceremonies. But He didn't leave the rest of the population to be just "regular" people. In some way, God wanted every one of the Israelites to serve Him as a priest. Because much of what happens to Israel is a shadow, or a picture, of what God intends for all Christians, what God told Moses applies to you, too. In fact, 1 Peter 2:9 says, "You are a chosen generation, a royal priesthood." But don't think you have to go to seminary just yet. Being a priest isn't about wearing special clothes or conducting a religious service. It's about dedicating your whole life and heart to God, no matter what you decide to do for a living. It's about serving Him out of a pure heart. It's about knowing that— because of Jesus—you've got your own hotline to heaven. So even if you don't become a pastor or a missionary, you still have the privilege of serving God as a priest.

SEE FOR YOURSELF: Pet. 2:5, 9; Rev 1:6

In ancient times, hospitality wasn't a courtesy; it was a duty. When a weary traveler stopped at someone's home, the people of the house were expected to welcome the stranger with open arms and care for his needs. It was considered rude for a host to ask his guests questions or carry on conversation with them before they were given a chance to clean up and eat.
Gen. 18:1-5

What does it mean to "serve" God?

The Bible describes our service in a lot of ways. We serve God by obeying Him and by helping other people in His name. As far as God is concerned, though, our attitude in life is as important as our actions. The priest Samuel once told his people to fear God and to serve Him in truth considering what God has done for them. That's a good guideline for us today in serving God. We serve Him with our attitudes first; then out of those attitudes we serve Him with our actions. We always serve God out of grateful hearts because of what He has done for us.

> Only fear the LORD, and serve Him in truth with all your heart; for consider what great things He has done for you.
> 1 Sam. 12:24

How can God use me when I'm so weak compared to Him?

It seems weird for David to say that we humans are only a vapor, that, like a puff of air, none of us is truly great. After all, when he was a teenager, he killed the giant Goliath with a *slingshot!* Then he led Israel's army to defeat the mighty Philistines in battle after battle. He became the greatest warrior and king in Israel's history. But David knew that everything he did was nothing compared to God. He had a grip on just how huge God is. Look at Psalm 62:11-12. David tells us that power and mercy belong to God. When a person begins to really understand (in his or her heart) how powerful and how kind the Lord is, it's impossible to be cocky. When you begin to see yourself as you really are before the Lord, you're amazed at how awesome He is and how little you are. God uses little people. He uses humble people—people who are seeing how small they are compared to Him. He doesn't want us to go around thinking we're dirt. He wants us to go around thinking about how enormous He is.

SEE FOR YOURSELF: Job 14:2; Ps. 62:9; Eccl. 6:12; Is. 40:6-8; James 4:14

SEX

Cybersex is OK, right? I mean, nobody's really doing anything.

But each one is tempted when he is drawn away by his own desires and enticed. Then, when desire has conceived, it gives birth to sin; and sin, when it is full-grown, brings forth death.
James 1:14-15

Before I answer, I want you to understand something. God gives us overall guidelines for living life and loving Him. He then expects us to build a relationship with Him based on those guidelines. When we think about right and wrong, we can't make a new little rule for every new situation that comes along. When people do that, they start thinking that living a life of faith is all about trying to obey a bunch of little rules. They miss the whole point. One of the guidelines that God gives us is to live a moderate life, to not let any one of our appetites (sex, food, approval, etc) become the most important thing to us. Why? Because when we do that (and we all do from time to time), we trust that appetite to comfort us instead of God. The Bible says that there is a process to the building of our appetites. We have a desire (which is natural) but then we go overload on it. We get enticed by it. We feed it. Then it grows into behavior, then compulsive behavior, then sin. Cybersex is a way to fill our appetite for sex that doesn't really involve intimacy or the kind of relationship that God wants sex to happen in. So, it really does feed your appetite for sex in a way that isn't healthy. It's like you should be waiting for dinner, but you're spoiling your appetite with a snack that really is not good for you. It's a substitute.

Is there such a thing as "casual sex"?

Our culture tries really hard to believe that there is such a thing. They do this by saying, "It's not a big deal. It really doesn't matter." And they keep saying it louder and louder and LOUDER. Who are they trying to convince. God says sex is a big deal because it has to do with our bodies. In the Old Testament God lived in the tabernacle or the temple. But after Jesus' ministry God's home became us. What we do with our bodies became even more important then because our bodies had become God's temple. Every other kind of sin is outside of us. But sex has to do with inside of us. Inside the context of a marriage it's a great thing. But, outside of that, there's nothing casual about it. To God, it's a big deal.

SEE FOR YOURSELF: 1 Cor. 6:18-20

> Flee sexual immorality. Every sin that a man does is outside the body, but he who commits sexual immorality sins against his own body. Or do you not know that your body is the temple of the Holy Spirit who is in you?
> 1 Cor. 6:18-19

Why can my mom watch sexy soap operas all day long but I can't watch nighttime TV because of all the sex in it?

Well, first of all, I can't tell you why your mom does anything that she does. Moms aren't perfect, but they are the moms. But you are on target that if there is anything wrong with too much sex on TV, it is just as wrong in broad daylight as it is in prime time programming. It's no secret that the media, daytime and nighttime, tends to send us a message that love is all about sex. The truth is that sex is often separate from love and, at best, is only part of a loving relationship. The other truth is that love takes a lot more work than it looks like on TV. Just because your mom is watching shows that she shouldn't doesn't mean that you should, too. The Bible says a lot about what we should think about. That's where TV affects us. It fills our heads with images and thoughts that we sort of absorb without thinking about it. Make sure you're not soaking up lies about important stuff and calling it entertainment.

SEE FOR YOURSELF: Phil. 4:8

What's the difference between looking at naked people in museums and looking at Playboy?

> "Watch and pray, lest you enter into temptation. The spirit indeed is willing, but the flesh is weak."
> Matt. 26:41

There is one obvious difference. Most of the naked people in the old art in museums are just naked people. They aren't naked people posed specifically to arouse someone sexually. God made us to be aroused sexually but asked us to keep that kind of thing between a man and wife. The women in *Playboy* and other porn are intentionally posing to be sexually enticing. Isn't it hard enough to live with a pure heart without that? Just because art is in a museum doesn't make it OK. Just because a body part is exposed doesn't make it dirty. It's the intent to pull us away from the way God wants us to live that is the bad thing. You've heard that expression, "the spirit indeed is willing, but the flesh is weak"? It's from the Bible and it's true. In our spirits we want to live for God. But our bodies will mess us up every time. Looking at porn will prove that to you.

Is it wrong for them to teach us about sex in school?

No, it's not *wrong* for the schools to have some form of sex education, but it is not the school's responsibility. It's your parents' responsibility to teach you about that, as well as faith and how to live. You might think, *Learn about sex from my parents?* Yes. When Moses was in the process of saying goodbye to the Hebrews he spent a lot of time talking to them about parents teaching kids. He made it clear that it was up to parents to pass down their faith and their roots and their identity as a family. It's up to parents to raise kids and teach them. That doesn't mean everything you ever learn should be from your parents. But what has happened is that parents are sending their kids to church to learn about spiritual stuff and to school to learn about academic stuff, but kids learn their best lessons about life at home.

SEE FOR YOURSELF: Deut. 4:9

Protecting a friend from the worst? Meet Meg.

Brian has this way of looking really hard into a girl's eyes and somehow flirting without being obvious about it. He certainly has charm, there's no question about that. There's just something about him. Even though Meg had no interest in him whatsoever, she had to admit that Brian was very intriguing. She didn't blame Gabrielle for dating him. Since the two girls were so close, Meg ended up spending quite a bit of time with Brian, too. They all went out a lot, so she saw him in action all the time. At first she thought that Brian and Gabrielle were the perfect couple; she was even a little jealous. But she began to have her doubts.

She always knew he was flirty, but it got much worse than just flirtation. One weekend, Meg saw him coming out of his apartment with this girl Monica. She tried to convince herself that it was just innocent, that maybe they were old friends or working on a project together. She didn't fall for it. She knew he was no good. To be honest, she suspected that Monica was clueless. He probably never mentioned that he was dating someone else.

Gabi called that night. She was so excited because Brian had finished working early (yeah right) and was coming over to see her. Inside, Meg burned with anger. How could he do this to her friend? How could she ever break the news to Gabi?

Over the next week, she just kept her ears open for other stories. If she was going to break her best friend's heart, she had to confirm the truth first. She prayed that God would help her either confirm what she had seen or to hear enough to clear his reputation. She got her answer.

One of the guys brought it up. He was concerned about Gabi, too, since he knew a side of Brian that the girls just didn't see. "He's the last person I would ever trust around my girlfriend," he said. Apparently this was not a new pattern for Brian. He always seemed to have a great girl he was dating, and then still managed to spend some time with a few other girls on the side. He was getting around. He didn't like to be tied down at all.

Gabi was such an awesome girl. She didn't deserve this; no girl does. Meg couldn't stand to see her humiliated this way. This whole situation was so awkward, but she knew what she had to do. She talked with her, and as gently as she could, she laid out the truth. She asked her to listen and just trust her and then to find out for herself. At first, Gabi was furious—with Meg for what she was saying but then at him. Deep down she might have suspected it but refused to believe it. What Meg told her confirmed all her fears.

It was so hard for Meg to tell her friend the truth. It was the last thing Gabi wanted to hear. But as both girls discovered, the truth is the only thing that can really set us free.

What is fornication?

Fornication is sex outside of marriage. It means two people have sex without being married. It's mentioned a lot in the New Testament. When it's mentioned it's usually in this way: Don't do it. Don't be a person who does this. Why? Paul probably says it best when he writes the Ephesians, "Be followers of God." Sex is meant for one kind of relationship—marriage. It represents more than a physical act. It represents intimacy and commitment, not to mention the desire to procreate. God put boundaries around it. When we violate those boundaries we aren't imitating God. We are using something He gave us in a way that hurts Him.

> But fornication and all uncleanness or covetousness, let it not even be named among you, as is fitting for saints.
> Eph. 5:1-3

When the Bible says, "Don't let there be a hint of sexual immorality," does that mean "going all the way," or what? Can we do other things?

The real point of that verse is not to rid yourself of every hint of sexuality. That would be impossible. God created us as sexual beings. It is a beautiful thing to Him when done in the boundaries of marriage. That's why we have two genders: male and female. It's the "immorality" part that is the key. God gives us morals and asks us to live by them. There's a line we don't cross if what God thinks matters to us at all. If what you mean by "going all the way" means "having sexual intercourse" then know this: Having sex is a whole process of revving each other's engines up and it concludes in intercourse (instead of starts with intercourse). Just because you stop one step short doesn't mean you aren't involved sexually. In fact, if it's really hard to stop, you may have already gone too far. The Bible says to run away from immorality like it was a raging fire. If you are finding that instead of running away you're trying to see how close you can get without getting too burned, it might be time to reevaluate.

SEE FOR YOURSELF: 1 Cor.6:18

Me and my girlfriend can't stop thinking about sex. My preacher said that, in the Bible, Jesus says that thinking about it is as bad as doing it. I feel guilty all the time. Wouldn't it be better to just do it so we can stop thinking about it?

> But I say to you that whoever looks at a woman to lust for her has already committed adultery with her in his heart.
>
> Matt. 5:28

Jesus did say that looking at a girl with lust is like already having sex with her. It might be as bad as doing it in the sense that you want to disobey God, and you are already thinking about it. But that doesn't mean it's the SAME as doing it. Those are two different statements. Having sex with your girlfriend will change everything. That's a huge decision. It's difficult to hold back. That's why the Bible says it's better to marry than to burn with desire. But somewhere in there, doesn't it matter to you that God has given you guidelines for life? Somewhere, doesn't God's opinion count? We talk about the Bible like it's this book of stuff that gets thrown on us. It's really our access to God's thoughts. He's not sitting up there trying to make things rougher than they already are. It takes work to do the right thing, and when it comes to sex, there's not a much more difficult obedience. But God is right there with you. Can you respect His presence and trust Him that He has good reasons for keeping marriage the place for sex? Your decisions about all this have as much to do with your relationship with God as they do with your relationship with your girlfriend. You can't close a bedroom door in God's face.

So, when is sex OK?

Sex is OK, no, better than OK, when it is reserved for just one person that you have committed your life to with a marriage license in hand. Have you read Song of Songs? The writer of Hebrews says that marriage is great, and the marriage bed is a wonderful accessory, but no fornication or adultery. That means no sex with someone besides your spouse and no sex if you don't have a spouse. That's not a popular perspective in our culture, is it? After all, we've got birth control. This isn't just about birth control, though. It's about committing yourself to life the way God intended it to be. Sex can be exciting, adventurous, and fun, but it's spitting in the face of God outside of marriage.

> Marriage is honorable among all, and the bed unde-filed; but forni-cators and adulterers God will judge.
> Heb. 13:4

Why does God make our bodies ready for sex before we get married?

You know, the customs about the age of marriage have changed so much through the centuries. You're right, though, that it's hard when you feel sexually ready but are far away from marriage age. In Bible days the marrying age was much younger, particularly for women. Our culture makes it even more difficult because sex is a part of so much of our media. We hear about it so much that we feel ready to have sex when we're very young. Put all that together and it's a puzzle to figure out. God didn't plan the whole puberty thing just to make us miserable though. Our bodies develop and our cultural customs change. You're left in the middle of that trying to figure out how to deal with it all. It all comes down to this. Who is the most important decision-maker in all this? Your body tells you one thing. Your culture tells you a whole different set of things. God tells you this, "For your own protection, don't have sex outside of marriage." There are a lot of reasons why that is smart. There are a lot of reasons why it is not easy. It all comes down to Who you are going to listen to.

SEE FOR YOURSELF: 1 Cor. 7:2-3

SIN

Is it possible for me to stop sinning completely?

00. 00. 29   00. 00. 0

Truthfully? Not looking good. We humans are creatures that choose our own way instead of God's. It's our nature. If we could stop on our own, Jesus' death wouldn't have been necessary. If we could stop sinning on our own, He should have just come to earth and said, "Try harder." But He didn't. He came to earth and took our punishment so that we could be forgiven. The real question is, if we can't stop sinning, what do we do about our sin? The prophet Isaiah said we are to wash away our sin, then not sin again. Huh? What bathtub is big enough and why try if we're going to fail? The only way to wash sin away is to go to God and ask forgiveness. He can take it from there. The only reason to try not to sin, even if you're going to anyway, is that God asks us to try. It's the way that we respect our relationship with Him. The best we can do is try to do the good things (Isaiah mentions seeking justice, rebuking the bullies, defending the underdogs) so we don't have time to do the bad. But forgiveness is always waiting.

> Wash yourselves, make yourselves clean; put away the evil of your doings from before My eyes. Cease to do evil, learn to do good; seek justice, rebuke the oppressor; defend the fatherless, plead for the widow.
>
> Isa. 1:16-17

Is painting my tag on a train a sin? It doesn't hurt the train.

No, I guess it doesn't hurt the train. There just seems to be one problem. It's not your train to paint on. Why would it be OK for you to paint on someone else's property? Isn't that disrespecting their boundaries? It has nothing to do with whether you are a great painter or not or how beautiful your tag will be. It only has to do with who gets to make the choice about what happens to that property. When you have your own property, then you'll get to make that choice. Why should you get to make choices about what someone else has worked to own? The Bible doesn't talk about painting tags on trains specifically. But it does say that you can't be trusted with your own stuff until you prove you can take care of stuff in general. Knowing who gets to make what choices about which property is a part of being trustworthy.

SEE FOR YOURSELF: Luke 16:10-12

My Mom reads romance books but won't let me read them because of the dirty parts. If it's dirty and a sin, does it matter how old you are?

And whoever causes one of these little ones who believe in Me to stumble, it would be better for him if a millstone were hung around his neck, and he were thrown into the sea.
Mark 9:42

You're talking about a couple of different categories here. Yes, if something is wrong, it's wrong no matter how old you are. I haven't read your mom's romance novels so I can't answer for that. But, yes, it's also important for your mom to keep some stuff from you until you're old enough to make good choices about it. This reminds me of those disclaimers you see on movies and TV shows that says "For Mature Audiences Only." Now, a lot of times that is a nice way of saying that, really, nobody should be watching the show. The reason they put the warning there is so parents can make the decision whether or not their kids get to see it. They are doing the right thing to provide this protection. Adults need to look out for who gets exposed to violence and sexual content. Some people can't make good decisions about whether or not to mimic the behavior they see. People who are older DO need to think about what they share with people who are younger. Jesus said that it was better for someone to get thrown into the ocean with a heavy rock around his or her neck than to cause someone to stumble in his or her faith. Whether your mom should read her novels is hers to deal with. She's right, though, to be careful with you.

If somebody does something because he's crazy or handicapped, is it still a sin?

This is one of those things where we really have to trust God that He will know what to do better than us. The Bible says that if someone knows to do good, but doesn't do it, THEN it's sin. But, like you're asking, what if they *don't* know to do good? What if their brains aren't working right and they can't tell right from wrong? In our courtrooms there is something called an "insanity plea." That means the judge or jury doesn't hold the person responsible because they didn't know right from wrong in the moment when the crime was committed. Sometimes they call it "temporary" insanity. I'd like to think that if our faltering court system has a plan to deal with this, then God certainly has a better plan.

> Therefore, to him who knows to do good and does not do it, to him it is sin.
>
> **James 4:17**

Is it a worse sin to have an abortion, give an abortion, or kill the doctor who gives abortions?

Everything you described here includes the destruction of a life. How can one be any worse than the other? Sometimes the world gets so far away from where God wanted life to be that it's impossible to sort it out. Your question shows that. You've got people hurting other people. Is one worse than the other because the people are at different ages? Sometimes we get passionate about issues and we forget that God's guidelines apply to us all, even when we are defending His way of life. To get upset (some people call it "righteously indignant"), and hurt some-one because of it, doesn't accomplish God's purposes. It just proves that with our best intentions, we don't walk in God's path.

SEE FOR YOURSELF: Ex. 20:13

If God can't stand sin, but I can't stop sinning, how does that relationship work?

First of all, great question. The answer is that God came as Jesus to die for our sins. The Bible teaches that a price HAS to be paid for sin. It also teaches that we all have sinned. The prophet Isaiah said that we are like sheep who have wandered off the path. We've gone our own way. That's really a good illustration. We can't even keep track of all the choices that get us so far off of our path. So what God did, giving His life instead of ours, covers all those choices. That way we can have a real relationship with Him. He's already got a plan to take care of that sin instead of letting it separate us. It cost Him a lot. We are worth that to Him.

> All we like sheep have gone astray; we have turned, every one, to his own way; and the LORD has laid on Him the iniquity of us all.
> Isa. 53:6

What should I do when I realize that I've sinned?

Hurry up and admit it! The first and only thing to do with sin is take it to God and let Him do His thing—forgive and get rid of it. Too many times we waste our time feeling guilty or not admitting to ourselves what we've done. Worse yet, sometimes we go through this phase of denying our sin or blaming someone else. Big waste. Everybody sins. God knows that better than we do. Our best plan is to go to Him and ask His forgiveness and just start over. People all the way through the Bible did this, individuals as well as groups. It's the only option when it comes to not being bogged down with sin.

SEE FOR YOURSELF: Ezra 9:6

Does everybody sin?

Short answer? Yes. Every single one of us chooses our own way instead of God's way at one point or the other. We actually do it at many points along the way. From the beginning of the Bible when Adam and Eve chose to listen to the serpent instead of God until yesterday when you chose to listen to anyone besides God—we all sin. That doesn't mean everyone around you is a bad person. We don't need God because we are mean. If we did, then the nice people would never become Christians. We need God because we are made in His image but we are cracked and broken. Only He can make us whole. Paul said, "There is none righteous, no, not one." He's right.

> It is written: "There is none righteous, no, not one; there is none who understands; there is none who seeks after God. They have all gone out of the way; they have together become unprofitable; there is none who does good, no, not one."
> **Rom. 3:10-12**

How does my sin make God feel?

God is always ready and willing to forgive you when you admit to Him that you've done something wrong. He's so quick to do that for you that it's easy sometimes to take His forgiveness for granted, to treat it as automatic. After all, He promised He would forgive you, and He does what He promises. But what you need to understand—to feel way down deep in your heart—is how it makes God feel when you decide not to do the right thing. When you sin, it hurts God—just like it hurts you when one of your friends does something that makes you think they don't care about your friendship anymore. It's important for you to realize that when you choose the wrong way, it hurts the Person who gave you everything good that's in your life. That doesn't mean that you should spend a week or two feeling guilty. But being aware of what you've done can help you to truly repent instead of quickly saying "I'm sorry" and then almost as quickly doing it again. Know that your sin hurts God. Be quick to repent. After all, He's the best Friend you've got.

SEE FOR YOURSELF: Is. 63:10; Eph. 4:30; 1 Thess. 5:19

Am I the only one who sins?

Most of us get into trouble by convincing ourselves that we're OK. Basically good people. No major sin happening. No blatant disrespect. Decent grades in school. Things at home are calm. So we're sailing along just fine. But Job says that no human is righteous (innocent) in the sight of God—and that's true—before you get saved. When you become a Christian, God gives you a new heart. What you're dealing with is a sinful *nature,* not a sinful heart. In spite of the fact that you do (and will) sin, the great news is that God is more gracious than you could ever imagine, and you can be more accepted and loved than you ever hoped.

SEE FOR YOURSELF: Rom. 3:23, 24; Gal. 3:22; 1 John 1:8

> Truly I know it is so, but how can a man be righteous before God?
> Job 9:2

Can I be "upright" even if I sin?

God protects the person whose heart is right toward Him. Having your heart right toward Him doesn't have anything to do with being perfect or knocking yourself out trying to do the right thing all the time. A person who has an upright heart knows that he or she isn't perfect. That person realizes that his only hope comes from the fact that Jesus died to make things right for him. Admitting those things takes humility. That's a word that most people don't talk about very often, maybe because their picture of humility is a mealy mouthed person who looks at the floor all the time. But for a real picture of humility, look at Jesus. It's one of the most outstanding parts of His personality. A heart that's humble is the kind of heart God is looking for. That's the kind of person He can use to get the job done. He protects that person in a special way because He knows that person is ready to do what He wants.

SEE FOR YOURSELF: Job 5:19; Ps. 7:10; 121:7-8; 2 Thess. 3:3

How far is too far?
Meet Justin.

Evie and Justin sat facing each other on the couch. They'd been dating for over a year now, so at least they felt comfortable talking about it openly. Honestly, they'd been avoiding the topic for a while, but they had come to a point where they couldn't ignore it. Evie brought it up. She wanted to know what Justin was thinking. After all, they were both virgins, so at least they were coming from the same place. They were in love with each other and had even been talking about their future together and when they could get married. This was no fling. They trusted each other so completely, and now they were facing one of the biggest challenges of their relationship. The question on both of their minds was whether or not they should sleep together. When would it be right?

Evie had always thought she'd wait until she was married, but since she planned to marry Justin anyway, she thought that was good enough. Whether they had sex now or after they were married, it was still just the two of them. She felt so strongly about Justin and felt that she couldn't fully express it. She had always imagined that the first time she had sex would be so special. She knew it would be with Justin.

Justin knew what his parents believed. They had always emphasized that sex was intended for marriage only. But did he believe it as well? If God didn't want them to have sex, then why did he make them so attracted to each other? He didn't see how it could hurt either of them, and they would be smart about it. It seemed like most of their friends had been sexually active for a long time, and everyone thought it was so weird that they weren't, especially since they seemed so perfect for each other.

The conversation went back and forth. They were both struggling with justifying what they wanted with what they believed. And Justin knew that if he said yes, then Evie would, too. He knew that she was waiting to hear what he had to say.

He said no. He knew that if the answer was this hard to decide, then it had to be no. It was so hard when all he could think about was how much he wanted her and loved her, but he knew in his heart what was right. So he said no.

Evie respected that decision immensely. From all of her friends, she knew that very few men would turn down an open invitation. That single decision brought them so much closer together. Sometimes they wondered again, but always they returned to that conclusion.

And when they got married two years later, their wedding night was so unbelievably special that neither of them would have traded it for anything. As Justin held his wife, he knew that they would have given up so much of their joy and trust if they had given in. God blessed them for choosing His way.

Does God see all of my sins or can I hide some from Him?

A woman was being harassed because of the bad things she had done. People yelled and jeered at her because her sin was so ugly. They were going to stone her to death. But Jesus said, "He who is without sin among you, let him throw a stone at her first" (John 8:7). The angry crowd, one by one, dropped their stones and walked away. When each person had looked at his own life, he realized that his sin was just as ugly as hers. As hard as you may try, you aren't sinless. You don't always do the right thing. You're human and you're not perfect. In the pit of sin is where Jesus comes and gently shows you that you can't do it by yourself. You desperately need a Savior. There is no one alive who doesn't. Don't beat yourself up about your sin. Turn to the One who can save you from it.

SEE FOR YOURSELF: Ps. 51; John 8:7; Rom. 3:23; Heb. 12:1

> For there is not a just man on earth who does good and does not sin.
> Eccl. 7:20

Am I really a sinful person, even after Christ has saved me?

Your mom asks you to take out the trash. You get an attitude, moan and complain, and finally take it out after you're both upset. You casually take some cash from your brother's dresser. You need it; he's got it. You're family. So what? Each situation seems kind of harmless—a bad attitude and "borrowing" some money. But God promises to judge all we do. He saw a kid who dishonored his mom and hasn't caught on to the idea of doing "all things without murmuring" (Phil. 2:14). He saw stealing instead of "borrowing." You may choose to whitewash your life and pretend you're an OK guy—not a lot of sin to deal with, no major infractions. But God sees things as they really are. Ask Him to give you His perspective, so that you can begin to clean up the stuff you've been pretending isn't so bad. Then you can walk clean before Him.

SEE FOR YOURSELF: 1 Sam. 2:10; Ps. 9:8; 50:6; Eccl. 12:14; 2 Tim. 4:8

How can I approach God when I have so much sin in my life?

> Therefore thus says the LORD of hosts: "Behold, I will refine them and try them; for how shall I deal with the daughter of My people?"
> Jer. 9:7

Sometimes we get paralyzed in our daily walk with God. We wake up one morning, take a look in the mirror, see our sin and its ugliness, and push God away. We might spend the next weeks or months trying to figure out how to make ourselves more presentable. But you can't refine and purify your own heart. What you can do is stay hooked up to God through prayer, and you can constantly renew your mind by memorizing and meditating on Scripture. God can make the unclean holy and restore beauty to the unlovely. No matter how ugly your heart or how sinful your life has been, God can clean and restore. Ask Him daily to purify your heart. If you're continually allowing God in to remove your sin, your walk with Him stays fresh, and you stay in touch with Him.

SEE FOR YOURSELF: Zech. 13:9; Acts 15:9; Titus 2:14

What would happen to us if we didn't repent of our sin?

The Bible teaches that the payment for sin is death. That means both physical death (like when you have a funeral) and spiritual death (like when you never really connect with God before or after you die). Everyone is going to die physically, sooner or later. If a person never turns away from their sin and toward faith in God's goodness and grace, they will also die spiritually. Jesus taught that very thing. On the other hand, a person who reaches out to God in faith and believes will live forever. When you lay it out like that, it's an easy choice, isn't it?

SEE FOR YOURSELF: Luke 13:3-5

I'm sick of hearing about this sin stuff. Why does the Bible just assume I have sinned?

If we say that we have no sin, we deceive ourselves, and the truth is not in us.
1 John 1:8

The cold hard truth is that we all have sinned. Let's talk definitions. What do you think sin is? Sin isn't just something we do. It is any time we choose our own way over God's way. Another definition of sin is "missing the mark." The mark is perfection. We all miss that mark. It's just reality. We don't have a hope of being perfect. That is one of the things that draws us to God. He came to earth to take our punishment for sin so that we can be perfect in His eyes. That doesn't make us perfect right here and now. We still sin. We still have to work on ourselves to be better and better people. The Bible says that we are believing lies if we say we don't have any sin. The fact that we are all sinful means that we are separate from God. We need His help to connect with Him.

Can I get away with sinning once in awhile?

Wow! God really means business. He intends for us to obey His laws. He gave us laws in order to give us guidance and boundaries. God designed our lives, so He knows better than anyone how they need to operate. Think of Him as the "manufacturer." The manufacturer has set the limits, knowing at what point the whole system will crash and burn. Breaking God's law is sin. God punishes sin for the same reason that a parent fairly punishes a child for disobedience. Sometimes, the consequence of the sin is the punishment. Other times, punishment may come in another form. The promise of punishment is enough to encourage some people to try to stay out of sin. For others, once they've been punished, they know they never want to make the same mistake again. Been there, done that, no thanks.

SEE FOR YOURSELF: Lev. 26:14-18; Ps. 89:32; Lam. 4:22; Hos. 9:9

SOVEREIGNTY OF GOD

> And if the man is poor, you shall not keep his pledge overnight. You shall in any case return the pledge to him again when the sun goes down, that he may sleep in his own garment and bless you; and it shall be righteousness to you before the LORD your God.
>
> Deut. 24:12-13

Can I hide things from God?

We live in a society that notices everything that's wrong. The 6:00 o'clock news, organized protests, flyers on your windshield, newspapers, magazines—everything seems to highlight things that are bad. The world doesn't notice much when something really good happens. Lots of times, kids in school say they act up just to get some attention. You can bet someone will notice when they break the rules, but there are few rewards for kids who do the right thing. We've forgotten that God promises to notice (see Heb. 6:10). He doesn't miss a thing. He isn't sleeping through your sacrifice. He isn't watching the bad kids when you're off doing good. He is pleased to watch you do the right thing. He's faithful to notice every good move you make.

SEE FOR YOURSELF: Ps. 33:13-15; Matt. 13:43; Mark 9:41

With all the violence and unhappiness in the world, is God still in control?

Ever feel like the world is out of control? People are doing the craziest things with the place God has given them. Abusing their bodies with any substance imaginable. Treating one another with total disrespect. Violent attitudes and behavior are rampant. It would be easy to think that God has turned His back and left. He has gotten fed up with the whole mess and just quit. Who would blame Him? We would have quit a long time ago. But not God. He is still in command of the world. His power has not been weakened. His plans have not been changed. He isn't even surprised at how badly we've messed up. He knows that when we choose not to follow Him, we wander around, trying to fix everything ourselves, and finally make things worse. The Commander is still leading. The world still belongs to Him. Will you follow, or will you join the chaos?

SEE FOR YOURSELF: 2 Sam. 23:5; Job 41:11; Is. 9:7; Mark 1:27

Who rules and reigns over the earth?

How many times have you complained to someone, "Hey, that's not fair"? When someone who didn't study half as long as you did for a history test gets a better grade. When you have to be home at eleven but all your friends get to stay out till midnight. When your little sister gets to wear makeup a couple of years before you did.

Life doesn't seem fair, especially when you look at the world around you—murderers who don't go to jail because of legal technicalities, innocent little kids who are hurt by people they trust, people killed by drunk drivers. Sometimes you can think that God doesn't care about justice.

But, of course, He does. It's just that when He looks at these things, He sees a much bigger picture than you do. He sees from the beginning of time to the end of time in one glance. He knows what's in store for people who choose to hurt others and for the innocent people who suffer because of them. And He isn't going to play favorites, either. The only thing that will prevent people from getting exactly what they deserve will be the mercy that Jesus gives. That mercy will only be available to those who have trusted in Him.

SEE FOR YOURSELF: Ps. 7:9; 119:137; Is. 30:18; Zeph. 3:5

> For He is coming to judge the earth. With righteousness He shall judge the world, and the peoples with equity.
> Ps. 98:9

Taking off one's shoes was a sign of respect, a lot like removing one's hat in church. Moses had been told to remove his shoes when God spoke to him from the burning bush.
Josh. 5:15

How is God sovereign?

The most reassuring thing you could know about God is that He is in control. Totally in charge. Doing as He pleases. Our sin has not thrown a wrench in His plans. He is not stressed out by our foolishness. He is not confused about which way to go. He still sits on the throne of heaven. If you think that the world is spinning out of control and that all hope is long gone, then you don't know about the sovereignty of God. He is working in and through what seems like craziness to accomplish His divine purposes. His plans will not be changed. You do not have to be nervous or wonder. God is in charge, both in the world, and in the lives of His believers.

SEE FOR YOURSELF: Ps. 115:3; Jer. 10:13; Rom. 8:28

> Whatever the LORD pleases He does, in heaven and in earth, in the seas and in all deep places.
>
> Ps. 135:6

How can God know what is best for me?

You are like clay in the hands of the potter. The potter decides what shape he wants the clay to become, and then he molds and forms the clay into that shape. If he finds a flaw in the bowl he's making—he starts over. God, in His wisdom, has decided what shape our lives will take. He will mold us until we have become what He has envisioned. Did you know that you are just clay? Think about the job of clay—to rest in the potter's hands and to hold the shape he forms. If you sense that God is molding your life into one that pleases Him, then do the job of clay—rest in His hands and trust Him. The clay cannot argue with the potter. The potter's wisdom is greater, and he ultimately decides on the shapes that please him. Trust God; He will lovingly mold you like a lump of clay. He will work out the flaws, and He may even start over, but the result will be pleasing to His eyes.

SEE FOR YOURSELF: Is. 64:8; Jer. 18:6; Rom. 9:20-21

Does God work in every situation, even coincidences?

You're walking down the hall thinking about the two brand-new five-dollar bills in your wallet, and a guy you owe three bucks to comes around the corner. You're really tempted to cheat on a test, but the smart girl who sits next to you is absent that day. You're thinking about sending a card to a girl who looks like she needs cheering up, and when you find your student directory in the bottom of your locker, it's opened to the page that has her address on it. Coincidences? If you've been hanging out with God for very long, you probably don't think so. He has a way of bringing even these little things together at the right time. It's one of the ways He reminds us that He's got everything under control. That's His way with the big things in life, too. The list that Solomon put together in Ecclesiastes 3:1-8 includes some things that don't sound too good. But everything God allows in your life—even sadness—has a purpose, and He has worked out the timing perfectly. He can do that because He knows you better than you do. And He knows what's coming next, too. If the timing seems lousy to you, trust that God knows something you don't know.

> [God] has made everything beautiful in its time. Also He has put eternity in their hearts, except that no one can find out the work that God does from beginning to end.
> Eccl. 3:11

SEE FOR YOURSELF: Acts 4:28; Rom. 8:28; 2 Tim. 1:9

Why does God let bad things happen to people?

When bad things happen we want to know a reason, don't we? I mean after all, if God controls everything, it seems like there must be a reason behind everything that happens. Jesus' disciples thought so. Once they passed a man who had been blind from birth. They asked Jesus if the man's blindness was caused by his sin or his parents'. Jesus answered, "Neither." When bad things happen, we feel like we can handle it better if we can either find a reason for it or make a reason out of it. The truth is we don't know why God lets life roll on the way it does with good and bad things happening. Probably if we could have stayed in God's ideal world way back at the beginning, the bad things wouldn't have gotten in. But we didn't and they did. God lets people make choices and sometimes we hurt each other. He lets the world sometimes fail us—tragedies happen. All God promises is His presence in all of that. He faces with us whatever life throws our way. We won't know the answer to your question until we see God face-to-face. By then we'll probably understand already.

> Now as Jesus passed by, He saw a man who was blind from birth. And His disciples asked Him, saying, "Rabbi, who sinned, this man or his parents, that he was born blind?"
> John 9:1-2

If God is our Father, who is our mother?

Spiritually, God is our mom and dad. We think in terms of male and female because that's the way reproduction happens on earth. If we all lived forever and didn't need to reproduce for humanity to survive, then the male/female thing wouldn't make so much difference. God is an eternal spirit. He is the perfect balance between the masculine qualities that you see in people and the feminine qualities that you see in people. He is the perfect mom and dad all in one person. When Moses asked God for His name, God said, "I AM." What a strange name. But there is so much truth in that name. He is everything we need when we need it.

SEE FOR YOURSELF: Ex. 3:14

SPIRITUAL MATURITY

00. 00. 29   00. 00. 30

Do I become spiritually mature over time or do I need "practice"?

If your brother, the son of your mother, your son or your daughter, the wife of your bosom, or your friend who is as your own soul, secretly entices you, saying, "Let us go and serve other gods," . . . you shall surely kill him.
Deut. 13:6-9

Most Christians who experiment with other religions (Hinduism, Buddhism, New Age, etc.) lack the maturity needed to learn about other faiths.

00. 08. 62   00. 08. 63   00. 08. 64   00. 08. 65   00. 08. 66

When you're spiritually immature, you can easily get confused and "sucked in" to the deception of other religions. This can be especially true when those other religions claim to be "Christian based" or claim to believe in Jesus. It takes maturity to discern spiritual things. Maturity comes from consistently walking with the Lord, communicating with Him, growing in the knowledge of Him and of His Word, and knowing that areas of your life are different because He is changing you. Some people have fallen into false religions because they weren't mature enough to tell good from "evil in disguise." Satan is the master of trickery. He is more than happy to make other religions look good to you because he wants to pull you away from the truth. Do not experiment with other religions. You may fall into a well-set trap.

SEE FOR YOURSELF: Ex. 20:3; Deut. 6:14; 1 Kin. 9:6-9; Jer. 35:15; John 14:6, 13

When faith is all I have?
Meet Brianna.

I've made some mistakes in my life. I've learned a lot from my past, but I'm still dealing with some stuff. I'm scared of the future and don't know what I should do. I feel very alone.

As I sit here, my hands crossed on my stomach, I think back over the last year and wonder how I came to this. When I first met David, he swept me off my feet. We were so in love, and I believed with all my heart that he was the one. He promised he would propose by next spring, and I had everything planned out in my mind—the wedding, our marriage, and our life together. Everything was perfect.

Until I got pregnant. Somehow that changed everything for him. Maybe David was terrified of being a dad. Maybe he was scared of such a big commitment. Maybe he just changed his mind after all.

Whatever it was, it made him leave, and now I sit here all alone, waiting to feel that movement inside of me that confirms that his child is growing within me.

I moved back home. My parents were really mad, of course, but they will always let me come home. It's just tough now, because they are really recommending that I end my pregnancy, and I feel so alone. I don't know what to do.

If only David would come back. If only he could be excited for our baby and take care of us. If only he would go through this with me.

I know that what's growing inside of me is a baby. That's not the question in my mind. It's that I feel like I'm dying inside right now, and I want my old life back. I will never be the same again. This baby is changing everything. If only I had one person, just one, who was willing to support me and go through this with me. Then I think I could make it.

Will God forgive me? Will God provide for my baby and me if I trust in Him? Will God be enough for me, even though I feel so terribly alone? Do I have enough faith to trust that God can and will do as He promised and bring good even out of a bad situation? Those are the questions that I keep asking.

And I think I know the right answers. I know that He is faithful. I will trust Him on this. I know of a Crisis Pregnancy Center nearby, and I think they might be able to help. I don't see where He's going with everything, but I guess that's what faith is all about.

STRENGTH

What do I do when I'm burnt out?

Everyone goes through times in life when they feel like nothing is happening. Working hard with very few accomplishments. Nothing's new on the horizon. Each day looks the same and feels the same. Goals are just as far away as they've always been. It gets tiring to work so hard, be so committed, and see no fruit. Isaiah says that even young people get tired and weary, so tired that they can stumble and fall. But hope for tired people comes from the Lord. He says that if you trust in Him, He will give you a new strength—not just the ability to survive another day, but new strength that lifts you up and makes you soar. It's the difference between just surviving tomorrow and soaring above the day with the strength and presence of an eagle. You don't have to figure out how to be the eagle. That's God's gift to those who trust in Him and who call on Him on the days when life seems to be going nowhere.

> There is no searching of His understanding. He gives power to the weak, and to those who have no might He increases strength.
> Isa. 40:28-29

SEE FOR YOURSELF: Ps. 65:3, 5; Jer. 15:20; Hab. 3:19

The phrase "right hand" is a way of describing God's strength. Specifically, the phrase is used to describe God's highly visible actions, such as the miracles He performed around the time of the Israelite's Exodus from Egypt.
Ps. 77:10

STRESS

Where is God when I'm stressed out?

00. 00. 29

00. 00. 30

> We are hard pressed on every side, yet not crushed; we are perplexed, but not in despair; persecuted, but not forsaken; struck down, but not destroyed.
>
> 2 Cor. 4:8-9

He's right there beside you, in front of you, inside of you, behind you. He doesn't leave because we get stressed out. But, He doesn't stress out with us. Why? Because He's God. He knows that life will get handled. He's not worried about the little things that sometimes stress us out. Would you want to worship a God who got stressed out with you? God can be a calming presence in the midst of your stress if you'll take a breath and get in touch with Him. Bad things do happen. Life is hard sometimes. But most often being stressed out doesn't make it go any better. In fact, it's usually the opposite. The Bible says we are hard pressed, but not crushed. That's what God knows. He knows our limits. He won't let us be crushed.

Does Jesus care when I'm stressed out?

Seems like everybody is looking for a little peace and quiet these days. There's so much happening so fast in your life and in the world. There's so much to be confused about and you've got a really busy life—school, sports, church, friends, family. Whatever is going on in your life, it can get pretty hectic trying to figure it all out. But stop. It's time for some peace in your life. Jesus is the One who gives you peace. He whispers calmness into your crazy situation. He gives you a break from the frantic worry that sometimes overwhelms you. When you get into His presence, there is peace. When you take your eyes off of your circumstances long enough to turn them toward Him, you immediately find relief. Remember, Jesus refuses to panic. No matter how hurried or confused your life may be, take a second to listen to the Prince of Peace on the throne of your life. Then you won't panic either.

SEE FOR YOURSELF: Is 9:6; John 14:27; Acts 10:36; Col. 3

STRUGGLES

Man is like a breath; his days are like a passing shadow.
Ps. 144:4

How can I appreciate life, even when I'm having a bad day?

Sometimes on a cloudy day, there's a tiny break in the clouds that the sun tries to shine through. Just for a second you can see your shadow—just barely—on the sidewalk. When the clouds shift, your shadow disappears. David said your life is like that shadow—it shows up for just a short moment, and then it's gone. It sure doesn't seem that way right now. Right now, it seems like your life stretches out forever in front of you. In a lot of ways, your life is just beginning. The important thing to do is to make the things you're doing count. The old saying "Time flies when you're having fun" is true. One day you'll wake up and wonder how you got so old. God gives you life one day at a time. When a day or a moment is gone, it's history. Pay attention to your life every day. Don't waste it by wanting to be older or smarter or better-looking. Make it count.

SEE FOR YOURSELF: Job 14:12; Ps. 62:9; Eccl. 6:12

SUCCESS

Is it wrong to pray for success?

> If My people who are called by My name will humble themselves, and pray and seek My face, and turn from their wicked ways, then I will hear from heaven, and will forgive their sin and heal their land.
> 2 Chron. 7:14

It's not wrong. Who doesn't want to win or have good things come their way? The key to any of our requests to God is, what kind of heart are we asking with? There is a wonderful promise in 2 Chronicles that describes how we should ask God. It says we should

1. Humble ourselves (remember who is boss)
2. Pray (listening and talking)
3. Seek His face (really build the relationship, not just when we want something)
4. Turn from our wicked ways (keep working on the sin thing)

If we do those things, God promises to hear and to respond. Praying for success is no different than praying for anything else. It's not as much about the request as the attitude you ask with.

SEE FOR YOURSELF: Deut. 2:7; 15:10; 1 Chr 28:20; Neh. 2:20; Ps. 1:3

Does God measure success by the world's standards?

One of the blessings of obedience is that God will make you successful in your work (see Deut. 28:3-6). But be careful not to confuse God's kind of success with the world's version of success. The world deceives us into believing that we're successful if we wear the right clothes, drive an expensive car, live in a big house, have lots of people working for us, and carry a gold card. God says we have been successful in our work if we have been pleasing to Him (see 2 Cor. 5:9). You've been successful to God today if you've brought glory to Him. It's that simple. Rest easy tonight, knowing that you've been obedient to Him. He'll make you successful in your work. You don't have to worry or wonder what He's going to do to make you look successful. He'll make you successful in His eyes.

SEE FOR YOURSELF: Deut. 28:6.

SUFFERING

My baby brother was born with something wrong with him. How am I supposed to deal with that?

> The LORD also will be a refuge for the oppressed, a refuge in times of trouble.
>
> Ps. 9:9

Wow. That's tough. Sort of changes your life doesn't it?
Sometimes when a little brother or sister has something wrong, it takes all of the family to deal with it. It will probably be easy for you to feel left out. There's a couple of things it might be helpful to remember...

1. It's OK to feel like it's not fair that this has happened to your family. It's OK to go to God with all of your feelings about it. He can handle it.

2. If you start feeling lost in the shuffle, try to remind yourself that it's not that your family loves you any less. Remember that while your brother's problem might be around your whole life, it might not always take as much of everyone's attention as it will at first when it's all new.

3. You can't fix this. You can only care for your family and be as helpful as possible. That's all that you are responsible for.

God can be a hiding place for you in this. He'll always listen, and He is with you. When you're feeling stressed ask Him for help.

TEMPTA-TION

00:00:29

00.00. o

What can I do to not be tempted to sin?

Let's start with the bad news. There's not much you can do to stop the temptation itself. Temptation is a part of life. There's going to be stuff we want to do that we shouldn't. The only good news is figuring out our strategy to face the temptations. Proverbs gives some good advice about that. Proverbs talks a lot about wisdom. Wisdom is different than intelligence. Wisdom is knowing how to deal with life. Wisdom is a near cousin to discretion, the ability to know which way to go in a sticky situation. Proverbs says if you get more of wisdom and discretion then you'll be better able to stand against temptation. So how do you get them? By knowing God enough that you start thinking like Him. That means knowing the Bible and spending time letting God change you. It's a long process, but it's worth the effort.

How can I fight the temptation to cheat or lie?

A false balance is an abomination to the LORD, but a just weight is His delight.
Prov. 11:1

Cheating has to do with integrity. A great way to define integrity is to think of it as "what you do when no one's looking." What do you do when no one is looking? The Lord says that He hates cheating (a false balance). That covers the answers you saw and used from the test next to you, all the homework you copied from your friend before school, the money you secretly "borrowed" from your mom's purse, and the gum you accidentally forgot to pay for but kept anyway. Cheating only brings some small momentary rewards. In the long run, it all catches up to you. God sees the whole thing. Even worse, He sees inside your heart and knows all about your selfish motives. The next time you are tempted to look and think, *It will be only one time* or *It might even help my grade,* listen to the siren that goes off in your head. It's the Holy Spirit saying, "Don't!" You may forfeit some correct answers, but the God who sees everything will not overlook your integrity. His rewards are more valuable than a test grade, and they last for eternity.

SEE FOR YOURSELF: 1 Cor. 13:6; Eph. 4:15, 28

What's wrong with watching too much TV or pigging out on pizza?

Nothing's wrong with doing those things every so often. But you've got to be careful about living in excess all the time. The book of Ecclesiastes has a great verse that says it's good to hold on to one thing while you're holding on to the other. Do you know what that means? It means "balance." Have you ever balanced yourself by holding on to something? It's easier to keep from falling either way by holding on, like the tightrope walker with that big long pole (that he holds with BOTH hands). Going to extremes sometimes is just life. But living in excess all the time, whether it's TV or pizza or any kind of habit, is letting something control your life. That's your job and God's job, not pizza or TVs job.

> Do not be overly wicked, nor be foolish: why should you die before your time? It is good that you grasp this, and also not remove your hand from the other; for he who fears God will escape them all.
>
> Eccl. 7:16-18

How can I resist temptations?

Don't ever let anyone else make decisions about your reputation or your character. So, someone wants you to do something you don't want to do—they plead with you, they promise you the moon, they charm you, they tell you they love you. Your mind is screaming "No!" Your heart is racing. Your gut tells you to run. That's the Holy Spirit speaking to you. Don't miss Him. Do not be deceived! Do not fall into Satan's trap. Protect your integrity. Muster up all your courage and say, "No." Then remove yourself from temptation. Go home. Send (or take) your date home. Get a ride home. Just get away from the pressure to make a bad decision. To have a good name and to be respected is more valuable than silver and gold. You are building your character when you make hard decisions that are right and strong. God sees your faithfulness, and He will bless you.

SEE FOR YOURSELF: Prov. 12:3; 15:21; 22:1; Eph. 6:10-17

THOUGHTS

Does God read my mind even if I don't want Him to?

O God, You know my foolishness; and my sins are not hidden from You.
Ps. 69:5

It's worse than that. God reads our hearts.
He just knows. He knows us. He knows what
we are thinking and feeling even when we don't.
Does that sound like invasion of privacy to you? The truth is,
God made us. He has access to us. We can't hide from Him, not our thoughts, not
our sins, not our actions. Remember the story of Adam and Eve when they first
sinned? They tried to hide from God in the garden. Don't you think that's kind of
a funny picture? Two people in their new fig leaves trying to hide from God. We
do that sometimes though. We think if we don't admit what we are thinking or
feeling, even to ourselves, then no one knows. But God knows. He knows because
He knows us through and through. He knows our tomorrows that we don't even
know yet. There's just no way to hide from Him.

Is God strong enough for this?? Meet Nathan.

They were the best of friends. Over the years, Nathan had a lot of close friends, but really, Grandpop was the one constant person in his life. Most guys don't get to know their grandfathers that well. I guess you could say Nathan was lucky. Grandpop lived only a couple blocks away, and since his parents were such busy people, it seemed like Grandpop was the one person who always had time for him. When he was little, Grandpop had time to watch him till his parents got home from work. He had time to come to all his awards nights and hockey games. He had time to listen to him tell about his day and what he hated about school. He had time to drive Nate anywhere he wanted to go. He had time to talk with him about his faith and to encourage him to rely on God. He knew Nathan better than anyone else did.

When the doctors diagnosed Grandpop with pneumonia, Nate was nervous. He guessed older people were just more susceptible to it, but he knew it was treatable. At least they caught it early.

But it didn't go away. It stayed with him for three months, and he seemed only to get worse, even with all the medicine he was taking. He felt weak a lot, but still, he invited Nathan over all the time and just listened to him talk, asking all the right questions and giving all the right input.

In September, the doctors asked Grandpop to come back to the hospital for some more tests. It seemed like something had to improve soon. This sickness just kept lingering. When a specialist examined him, he found something that took everyone by surprise. Apparently, Grandpop's doctor had misdiagnosed him in the spring. He had all of the symptoms of pneumonia, but really it was a fast-spreading cancer. No wonder he hadn't gotten any better. They said that sometimes these things just happen.

Nathan lost him within a week. He went through an intense grieving period, but it was eclipsed by an anger deeper than he had ever felt before. He raged inside, at that stupid doctor who cost Grandpop his life and at God for allowing it to happen. He who had the power to heal had instead let him die. His heart closed up.

The first month Nathan spent coping—just getting up and going through the day, always conscious that he was now alone. But he couldn't overcome his anger. He turned it all on God; he hated Him.

But God did not give up on him. He never does. Maybe Grandpop kept reminding Him that Nathan was having a tough time. Nate soon discovered that God is tough enough to absorb his anger. He's strong enough to handle his rage. And He kept working on Nathan, slowly but surely, bringing him back to Him.

He had Nathan's attention, all right. And He started to show him what he hadn't been able to see before: that Grandpop was ready to go, that Grandpop wanted to go, and that the one he was really grieving for was himself. Grandpop was better off where he was; Nathan was the one who was miserable without him.

Healing takes time, and it takes effort. God gave Nathan both. Finally, he leaned on God for his strength. Maybe that's what Grandpop had been trying to teach him all along.

TIME

How should I spend my time?

00. 00. 29

Compared to God, who was never born and will never die, your life is like a blade of grass that grows up at dawn and withers by sunset. Our time on earth is short, so the really important question is, "How are you going to spend your life?" Are you going to waste most of it, hoping to make the last few years count, or will you max out your days to the glory of God?

> In the morning they are like grass which grows up; in the morning it flourishes and grows up; in the evening it is cut down and withers.
> **Ps. 90:5-6**

Don't waste any more time. It's time to lock on to the things that you really love to do and pursue them with all your heart. It's time to get serious about your relationship with God. Before you know it, you'll be standing in His presence, giving an account of what you did on earth. It's time to love the people you need to forgive. It's time to plug in to your family. It's time to stop whining and look for the good in your life. The matter is urgent. A blink of the eye and you'll be gone.

SEE FOR YOURSELF: Job 14:2; Eccl. 6:12; Is. 40:6-8

TRUST

> Commit your works to
> the LORD,
> and your thoughts will
> be established.
> Prov. 16:3

How will trusting God make a difference in my life?

There are a lot less worries, for one thing. If you trust God to lead your life, then you know someone who knows a lot more than you is watching out for the details. There's something else, though. In Proverbs it says that if you commit your works to God, your thoughts will be established. This is a pretty huge truth. It really means that when you get your priorities in the right order, when your life is aligned first with God, then your center becomes solid. You know who you are and what you are about. Life can't shake you so easily. We don't trust God for what we'll get out of it. We trust Him because he's God. But it really does make a difference in our lives.

Can I trust God to come through on His promises?

You promise to meet your friend for breakfast a week from Saturday. A family emergency takes you out of town until late Friday night. You remember that you've got a breakfast date, but will your friend remember? You decide to chance it and show up. Pulling into the restaurant parking lot, you see her. She remembered. Wow. No phone calls to say, "We're still on." You were so important to her that she couldn't forget. It made you feel special that she remembered this time with you. You're even more important to God. Trust Him when He promises to remember His promises. He won't lose His calendar or forget your phone number. He will never stand you up. It's a promise.

SEE FOR YOURSELF: Deut. 4:31; Josh. 23:15-16; 2 Sam. 23:5; 1 Kings 8:56; Neh. 1:5

The covenant, or agreement, between God and His people was very similar to a treaty between two political leaders. After a treaty had been established, the two leaders would agree on how it would be written down and where copies of it would be kept.
Deut. 5:2

How do I know God won't break my trust like others have?

> For the word of the LORD is right, and all His work is done in truth. Ps. 33:4

Who do you trust? Most people have a few friends who they think are trustworthy. Most people trust their parents and their brothers and sisters, at least to some extent. Maybe you have a favorite teacher or a coach you feel you can trust. Has someone you trusted ever hurt you? That seems to happen to just about everybody at some point during their lives. Maybe you misjudged your friend and found out that person couldn't be trusted after all.

More often, someone you've trusted for a long time makes a mistake that ends up hurting you. That doesn't mean you should stop trusting that person. It just means you need to accept the fact that that person isn't perfect—and forgive. But trusting God isn't like that. He is perfect. He never lies, never misses the smallest details of any situation, never makes a mistake. You can count on every word He says. Everything He does is meant for something good in your life.

SEE FOR YOURSELF: Is. 49:7; 1 Cor. 1:9; 2 Thess. 3:3

How can I give God everything when I can't even see Him?

Real trust goes a lot deeper than being able to say, "Yeah, sure, I believe in God." James said, "You believe that there is one God. You do well. Even the demons believe—and tremble!" (James 2:19). Real trust means letting go of your life and your heart and giving God control of them. It means obeying Him. James used Abraham as an example: "Do you see that faith was working together with [Abraham's] works, and by works faith was made perfect?" (James 2:22). People who trust God in this way are like Mount Zion. They're immovable, unshakable. The way a mountain stands up against the forces of nature, they are able, by God's Spirit, to stand against all the stuff that life throws at them. But Mount Zion isn't just any mountain. This is the spot in Jerusalem God chose for His temple, the place where He would live among His people. Now that you've put your trust in Him, He makes His home in you.

SEE FOR YOURSELF: Ps. 125:1; Heb. 12:22-29

294

What happens if I trust God instead of others?

If you trust in the Lord with all your heart—not just saying you believe in Him, but really living a godly life—then He promises to do two things. First, He will lead you to the right path. In other words, He will show you what you are supposed to do with your life, what turns to make, when to stop, when to go. He promises to give clear directions to people who are seeking and trusting Him. Second, He will clear the path of obstacles, making it smooth for you. So, not only will He show you the way to walk, but He also promises to go before you and clear away the things that could trip you up. He will fill up the holes you could fall into. He will straighten the road so the walk is easier. He will make the journey more enjoyable for those who trust in Him.

> Trust in the LORD with all your heart, and lean not on your own understanding; in all your ways acknowledge Him, and He shall direct your paths.
> Prov. 3:5, 6

SEE FOR YOURSELF: John 16:13; 2 Cor. 2:14; Rev. 7:17

Can I trust God to help in difficult times?

Remember the story of Shadrach, Meshach, and Abed-Nego (Dan. 3)? The king had them thrown into the fire because they wouldn't bow to him. But the fire didn't burn them up, and when people looked into the flames, they saw four men. Well, the fourth person was Jesus. Because He was with those guys, they didn't burn. In fact, they didn't even smell like smoke when they came out! Well, Jesus is with you in the same way. In Isaiah, He says He is holding your hand. He goes with you through the fire of hard times in your life, preventing the flames from injuring you but letting the heat melt away some of the things about you that are not godly. With your hand in His, He can calm you down when things aren't going so well. If you won't let go of Him, He can lead you to the place He wants you to be.

SEE FOR YOURSELF: Ps. 37:24; Prov. 2:7; Is. 41:13; Hab. 3:19; Rom. 8:26; Heb. 13:6

TRUTH

How can I find truth when everything seems so fake?

> But Joshua said to the people, "You cannot serve the LORD, for He is a holy God. He is a jealous God; He will not forgive your transgressions nor your sins."
> Josh. 24:19

Fake is in. Phony is fashionable: bodies that are beautiful because of plastic surgery; imitation foods that taste sweet—with no sugar. Virtual realities that are only pretend. Somewhere in the world of impostors we've lost our sense of what is true. God can restore the standard. He is not a fake. He is not pretending to be God. He is real, and pure, and holy, and awesome. So if you've been feeling like you can't figure out what's true anymore, get off the stage. Get with God. Some time in the presence of His truth will bring you back to reality.

SEE FOR YOURSELF: Deut. 6:4; John 17:3; Eph. 4:5, 6; 1 Tim. 2

Just because something is true, is it automatically powerful?

If you're talking about faith kinds of things, there definitely is power in the truth. If God says He will do something, there is power in that being true. It's why Jesus said that if you know God's Word and what He is about, the truth will set you free. That means you'll know how life works and you'll be able to face it. You won't have to back down or be confused. When it comes to all life's issues, the truth is very powerful.

SEE FOR YOURSELF: John 8:31-32

VALUES

How do my values affect my decisions?

> Can the Ethiopian change his skin or the leopard its spots? Then may you also do good who are accustomed to do evil.
> Jer. 13:23

Your values are built over a long period of time. By the time you know something is a value of yours (like honesty or hard work), you've lived long enough to know that those things matter to you. Once our values are established, they affect every decision we make. They become our framework. Jeremiah, a prophet in the Old Testament said something very wise about this. "Can the Ethiopian change his skin or the leopard its spots?" He asked this question about doing right and wrong. Can we step out of our values once they become a part of us? It's pretty hard. Think about that poor leopard. All the more reason, then, to examine our lives and make sure our values are pleasing to God.

WAR

If killing is wrong, why do people fight wars about God?

> Reject a divisive man after the first and second admonition, knowing that such a person is warped and sinning, being self condemned.
>
> Titus 3:10-11

Killing is wrong. It was also one of the sins of the first family. One brother killed another brother. Why? Jealousy and resentment. Those have been the same reasons for killing and wars ever since. People might say they are fighting a war about God. They might give religious reasons for the conflict, but look deeper. God did authorize the Hebrews to attack the squatters in their land, but that's the last time we know of that God authorized a battle (until the big one at the end of the world). Since then people have done what people do. They have wanted someone's land or hated someone out of prejudice, and they have started wars because of it. Often they have thrown God's name on the battle, but God has had little to do with it. In fact Paul wrote Titus about this very thing. He wasn't talking about physical battles, but he was addressing conflicts that people claim to be spiritual. Paul said to stay out of it. In fact he said to get rid of anyone who created conflicts of that kind. God is a God of life, not destruction.

WEALTH

Assuredly, I say to you that it is hard for a rich man to enter the kingdom of heaven. . . . it is easier for a camel to go through the eye of a needle than for a rich man to enter the kingdom of God."
Matt. 19:23-24

I read in the Bible where it says it's easier for a camel to go through the eye of a needle than it is for a rich guy to get into heaven. Does God want me to be poor?

I wouldn't say God wants you to be poor. Think about it this way: It's not that the rich man has so much money in his pockets that his hips are too wide to get into heaven's gates. The money isn't the problem. The problem is that in this life it is so easy to trust money to take care of you—if you have a lot of it. If you trust money to take care of you, then it's easier to forget to trust God. That doesn't mean that poor people automatically trust God because they are in need. But they do have more reminders to ask for help. It's the quality of the rich man's faith that makes it hard to enter heaven. Keep in mind too, that in that same passage it says that with God all things are possible. So Jesus wasn't saying that a rich person CAN'T get to heaven by faith. By the way, did you know that there is a rock formation around Israel with a really thin opening that is called the "eye of the needle"? hmmmmm. (And you were thinking that little silver thing that sticks your finger when you try and use it.)

Only big shots wore purple dye made from a shellfish that lived in the Mediterranean Sea. Preparing it was difficult and expensive. Only royalty and other important people could afford it. Purple wasn't the only expensive dye, though. Red and blue dyes were also very valuable.
Ex. 39:24-26

WILL OF GOD

> For whom He foreknew, He also predestined to be conformed to the image of His Son, that He might be the firstborn among many brethren.
>
> Rom. 8:29

What does God want me to be when I grow up?

God gave you a certain set of abilities and skills. He wants you to explore those skills and train them. He wants you to figure out what you can do with them that will support you and will bring you some kind of joy or at least a sense of accomplishment. When you grow up, God wants you to be someone who lives life all the way, someone who is good to the people around him, someone who helps more than hurts, someone who makes a difference in the world for good, even if it's just in your own little corner of the world. If your question is a career question, that probably doesn't answer it. But, truthfully, there might be several things you can do as a career and they would all be fine with God. He is more concerned with who you will be when you grow up than He is with what you will do for a job. God just wants you to be as much like Jesus as you can be.

SEE FOR YOURSELF: Eccl. 3:13

Honoring my parents through obedience?
Meet Dustin.

Dustin's parents just didn't get it. They were kind of older (fifty-three), and most of his friends' parents were like early forties. Other parents were a lot more laid back and cool about stuff. Their parents went for runs with them. Dustin's parents liked to watch old movies. Their parents took them shopping. Dustin's parents tracked their retirement investments on the stock market. Their parents gave them freedom. Dustin's parents gave him rules. If he had been given any choice in the matter, he would have taken their parents over his. Instead he was stuck with curfews, rules, chores, family dinners, family devotions, family traditions, and driving his little sister Missy all over the place. Definitely not his parents of choice.

Sometimes their rules weren't a big deal, like carrying a cell phone and eating fruits and vegetables. Any kid can live with that. But, they also made rules about personal stuff, like who he should and should not be friends with. That was definitely an invasion of his personal space, he thought. Somehow his mom always knew what other kids were like. He didn't know if she had ESP or if she spied on them at school or what. His dad said that she was just a good judge of character. It had to be more than that. Whenever someone stopped by their house, his mom managed to set out some food and get in a conversation with the guy, and by the time he left, she had a strong opinion about whether he'd be a great friend or a bad influence on Dustin. How aggravating! And the worst part was that she was always right about it. No matter how good an act some guy would put on, she could see right through it.

So when Dustin started hanging out with some of the baseball guys, she wasn't happy about it. She had heard things. So they made a deal: Dustin would invite them over, and she would check them out. He resigned himself to it, and he invited the guys over.

As usual, she got right in there with the guys. She had such a sneaky way of doing it. Just by putting out a ton of food and looking busy around the kitchen, she could stay and hear their conversations. And the guys loved her cooking. But Dustin could tell even before they left that his mom wasn't crazy about them. They were nice guys but they came across with bad attitudes. And none of them were Christians.

"Dustin, they're nice guys, but they're definitely not best friend material. You might have a good impact on them, but I wouldn't want you hanging out with them too much."

Dustin just ground his teeth and left the room without a word. He wouldn't speak harshly to his mother, even if he disagreed with her. And he decided to honor her authority, even though he totally did not agree, just because she was his mother.

God honors our good decisions, even if we don't see it at first. Over the next few months, Dustin met another group of really solid guys and started spending a lot of time with them. And the baseball guys? Let's just say Dustin didn't pass up much. It's amazing what happens because of our obedience.

WISDOM

What is the difference between wisdom and knowledge?

> Through wisdom a house is built, and by understanding it is established; by knowledge the rooms are filled with all precious and pleasant riches.
> Prov. 24:3-4

Wisdom is more than knowing facts. It's understanding life. A verse in Proverbs says wisdom builds the house while knowledge fills the rooms. Both are important, but they do different things. A person can be very knowledgeable. You might want them to help you study for finals. But that doesn't make them wise. You wouldn't necessarily want them to advise you on big life decisions. Learning the difference between a wise person and a knowledgeable person saves you a lot of wasted energy in life.

How is God's wisdom different from our wisdom?

God just sees from a whole different perspective than we do. He doesn't look through our sinfulness and our brokenness. He sees from an eternal perspective. In Paul's first letter to the Corinthians, he says that we haven't even thought about what God has in mind for us. He is so far beyond us that we can only understand in bits and pieces. That's why the Holy Spirit is so important. God's Spirit whispers to us as much as we can understand and then helps us to understand more. Without His presence we might not even realize how far above us God's wisdom is or how much we need it.

SEE FOR YOURSELF: 1 Cor. 2:9-10

Grandparents: Are they really full of wisdom?

All those years your grandparents have lived have brought them much wisdom. They have watched several generations go through all the stuff of life, they've seen a lot of people grow up, they've seen people succeed, and they've seen people fail. They may or may not have made wise choices with their lives, but by now they've had lots of time to process the path they chose. They'd be happy to tell you about their successes and the things they would do over again. They'd be so honored that you cared enough to ask. By the time it's too late, and your grandparents are long gone, you'll realize how much they had to offer you. So take some time to get to know them. Ask them lots of questions. Ask about their childhood, their dreams, their disappointments. The smartest people are the ones who can learn from others—you could really learn a lot from your grandparents.

SEE FOR YOURSELF: Prov. 17:6; 20:29 .

Does not the ear test words and the mouth taste its food? Wisdom is with aged men, and with length of days, understanding.

Job 12:11-12

303

WORDS

What's the importance of being careful of what I say?

> Do not let your mouth cause your flesh to sin, nor say before the messenger of God that it was an error. Why should God be angry at your excuse and destroy the work of your hands?
>
> Eccl. 5:6

How many times have you heard it? "Do not let your mouth cause your flesh to sin," or, "Don't let your mouth get you in trouble." How many times have you let it? You were sassy to your mom, and she washed your mouth out with soap. You called your brother a name, and he punched you in the nose. You said something unkind about someone, and it got back to them. Solomon, the writer of Ecclesiastes, is considered one of the wisest men ever. You'd be wise to take his advice. He knew that once you say something to somebody, you can never take it back. If you get angry and scream something you don't really mean, it could still hurt someone. You could say something innocent that gets twisted around and makes you look really bad. Proverbs 18:21 says that "death and life are in the power of the tongue." It's true. Your words are powerful. They can encourage, inspire, comfort, or explain, or they can hurt, bite, sting, or devastate. Choose your words carefully and make them good. Count to ten before you spout off a bunch of insults you'll later regret. Your words can be death or life!

SEE FOR YOURSELF: Prov. 10:14; 18:6, 7, 21; Luke 6:45; Eph. 4:29

WORK

Does it really make a difference if I'm a hard worker?

Forty algebra problems, a paper on the people of Zaire, Spanish vocabulary words—every night another pile of homework. Even though you may get tired of having work to do at home, the sacrifice will be worth it in the end. Verse 24 says that the diligent—those who work hard—become leaders, and the slothful are put on forced labor—become slaves. You may not become a slave in the full sense of the word, but you will become a slave to your lack of knowledge. Without hard work, there won't be success in a career. It will be hard to progress past low-paying jobs, and the lack of discipline will make it hard to hold on to good jobs. If you have goals and if you want to make a difference with your life, then you really need to do your homework. Even when you can't imagine how you will ever use the information, just press on. Know that each little accomplishment is building your character. You will be stronger, wiser, and more disciplined all because you were faithful to do your homework.

SEE FOR YOURSELF: Prov. 24:33-34; Eccl. 9:10; Gal. 6:4

According to the Law of Moses, the last day of the week—the Sabbath day—was to be set aside for rest and worship. The pattern of working six days and resting one was based on God's schedule at creation. For six days He created the universe, and on the seventh He rested.
Neh. 13:15

305

WORRY

I worry a lot. What does the Bible say about that?

Let your requests be made known to God; and the peace of God, which surpasses all understanding, will guard your hearts and minds through Christ Jesus.
Phil. 4:6-7

The Bible actually says a lot about worry. Mostly it say, "DON'T DO IT!" It really doesn't do you any good anyway. It doesn't change the thing you're worried about. Too bad worrying is such a natural human thing to do. Paul wrote to the Philippian church about worrying. He said instead of getting all stressed about what might happen, talk to God about it. He was right. Worrying is a distraction from just going to God and saying, "Help, please." That's the quickest path to peace though. And you know, it's almost impossible to feel peaceful and worried at the same time. So if you can be peaceful, your battle's just about over.

What good is there in worrying?

You control your own destiny. You've heard that before, right? It's true to a certain extent. What you put into your life now will impact what you get out of it later. That's true of how hard you work at school or in your job. It's true of how you treat your parents. It's true of the kind of people you pick to be your friends. But there's a whole lot in life that you can't control. You can't decide whether there's going to be a flood or a drought this year. You can't control how many people get hired for a summer job. You can't control the price of a soda. You can't control what other people do. But all these things can have an effect on you. Does that mean you should get really scared worrying about all the things that could happen without your being able to stop them? That wasn't Jesus' advice. He said not to sweat it. Let God take care of all that stuff that's out of your hands. You just concentrate on doing the things He wants you to do. You'll be a lot less frustrated if you quit worrying about things you can't control.

SEE FOR YOURSELF: Eccl. 8:8; Matt. 6:34; Luke 12:29-31; 1 Pet. 5:7

WORSHIP

Where is God during worship?

00. 00. 29

When we worship God He is there with us. He is our audience. He receives our praise and is thrilled with it. Our worship shows God not only that we believe He exists, but also that we realize His importance. When God called to Moses from the burning bush, he gave Moses some instructions about worship. He told Moses to take off his sandals because the ground was holy. Then He introduced Himself to Moses. Sometimes it can feel like we get together to worship God, but we aren't really sure if God is going to show up. But God promises to be there. Moses didn't wait by the bush until God showed up. God brought him there and walked with him through the process. God leads us through worship as well, teaching to connect with Him.

> Then He said, "Do not draw near this place. Take your sandals off your feet, for the place where you stand is holy ground." Moreover He said, "I am the God of your father—the God of Abraham, the God of Isaac, and the God of Jacob." And Moses hid his face, for he was afraid to look upon God.
>
> Ex.s 3:5-6

What does God get out of our worship?

Keep in mind first of all that God doesn't need anything from us. He is complete on His own. He wants a relationship with us though. In order to have that it's important that we believe that He is and that we understand who He is. When we worship, we give God praise. We tell Him the great things about who He is. We also give Him glory and honor. We recognize that He, and He alone, is the one true God. We offer these gifts of worship to God. So when we truly worship God, what He wants out of it is simple—our wholehearted faith.

SEE FOR YOURSELF: Ps. 29:1-2

Can I worship other gods, too?

There are a lot of other religions out there and a lot of people who worship other gods, but you worship the only true God! You serve the great I Am. You have something that isn't a fairy tale, that isn't phony, that isn't fake. You have the truth that will cause blinders to fall from the eyes of those who don't know God. Why are so many people wrapped up in false religions and worshiping false gods? Because they want to live for a cause. They are searching for power. Because you are living for Jesus, you have the same power living in you that raised Him from the dead (see Rom. 8:11). Now that's power! That's someone and something to live for! Don't settle for boring religion with a bunch of rules and regulations. You can have a radical relationship with Christ! You want to do the right thing because of your relationship with Him. It's a relationship that brings freedom, a relationship that brings life, a relationship that brings power, and a relationship that brings every other good thing. Only Jesus will give you what you're looking for. Embrace the true Christianity you have. You'll have everything you need, and you'll escape the punishment of those who worship false gods.

> You shall not go after other gods, the gods of the peoples who are all around you (for the LORD your God is a jealous God among you), lest the anger of the LORD your God be aroused against you and destroy you from the face of the earth.
> Deut. 6:14-15

SEE FOR YOURSELF: Ex. 3:14; Ezek. 23:49; Matt. 5:16; Rom. 1:19

The inner part of the tabernacle was the worship area. Only gold and silver, the finest and most expensive metals, were good enough to be used as decorations for the holy area. The outer area of the tabernacle was decorated with bronze, a less expensive metal.
Ex. 38:21-31

Can I worship God every day and not just Sunday?

God has revealed Himself in mighty ways because He wants us to worship only Him. He wants us to know that He is all-powerful and supremely wise. There is no one else who can even compare to God. No one else deserves our prayer or our praise. As the One who made us and saved us, only God is worthy of a life completely devoted to Him. He is worshiped when we live our daily lives for His glory. How you spoke to your parents at breakfast, the way you acted at school, what you watch on TV—it all matters when you decide to live a life that worships God. Don't let your friends trick you into believing that what they think counts—what God thinks matters most. Has your life been an act of worship today?

SEE FOR YOURSELF: Ex. 20:5; Josh. 4:24; Ps. 115:12, 13; Joel 2:32

> You shall not fear other gods, nor bow down to them nor serve them nor sacrifice to them; but the LORD, who brought you up from the land of Egypt with great power and an outstretched arm. Him you shall fear, Him you shall worship, and to Him you shall offer sacrifice.
> 2 Kings 17:35-36

Is worship just for fun or does it bring us closer to God?

Worshiping the Lord involves being in His presence, looking with the eyes of your heart at His awesome greatness. Although you can't possibly understand everything about God, piece by piece He'll reveal Himself to you as you keep looking at Him, worshiping Him with your whole heart, living your life in His presence. There is a power in His presence, in continually looking at Him, that changes you way down deep. Paul described it this way: "But we all, with unveiled face," meaning there's no veil blocking our view of Him. "We . . . are being transformed into the same image from glory to glory, just as by the Spirit of the Lord" (2 Cor. 3:18). This is the blessing that He promises to His worshipers—change from the inside out. This blessing allows you to accomplish what God had in mind when He made you—to have a growing friendship with Him and to become like His Son.

SEE FOR YOURSELF: Ezra 8:22, 23; Ps. 103:13; 115:123

309

Check it out!
Get involved!
Make a difference!

Compassion International
God can use you to change the life of a child forever.
www.ci.org

Habitat for Humanity International
A Christian organization and welcomes volunteers from all faiths who are committed to Habitat's goal of eliminating poverty housing.
www.habitat.org

National Right to Life Organization
Taking a stand...making a difference!
www.nrlc.org

National Center for Family Literacy
Promoting family literacy services across the United States.
www.famlit.org

Big Brothers Big Sisters of America
Making a big difference. One child at a time.
www.bbbsa.org

Check out these other groovy products:

Extreme Teen Bible
   —Paperback $19.99
   —Hardcover $24.99
   —Leather $39.99
      Slimey Limey Green
      Lava Orange
      Deep Purple
      Black

Extreme Word
   —Paperback $19.99
   —Hardcover $29.99
      Chromium
      Neutron Blue
   —Leather $39.99
      Pitch Black

Extreme Journey $14.99

Extreme A-Z: Find it in the Bible $19.99

Journal $9.99

Extreme Faith $10.99

30 Days with Jesus $7.99

Extreme Encounters $9.99

Gospel of John $1.50

Extreme for Jesus Promise Book $12.99